BRITAIN'S HI
RAILWAYS

THIRD EDITION

Andy Chard

Published by Platform 5 Publishing Ltd,
52 Broadfield Road, Sheffield, S8 0XJ, England.

Printed in England by The Amadeus Press, Cleckheaton, West Yorkshire.

ISBN 978 1 909431 93 5

▲ The Severn Valley Railway's Class 14 D9551 brings an empty coaching stock working into Highley station during the railway's annual Diesel Gala on 21 May 2022.   **Andy Chard**

Contents

Front Cover Top: During the spring sun on 11 April 2021, on its first visit away from the Didcot Railway Centre, new build GWR Class 2900 4-6-0 2999 "LADY OF LEGEND" heads away from Sterns at Hay Bridge with an afternoon service on the Severn Valley Railway. **Martyn Tattam**

Front Cover Bottom: Visiting the Keighley & Worth Valley Railway for its Summer Diesel Gala, on 10 June 2022, 33202 "Dennis G. Robinson" passes Mytholmes with the 08.55 Keighley–Haworth loop goods train. **Tom McAtee**

Back Cover: On 19 November 2022, BR Standard Class 5MT 73156 heads away from Rothley station with a Loughborough Central to Leicester North service on the Great Central Railway. **Martyn Tattam**

Preface to the Third Edition

Over the last few years Britain's heritage railways have found themselves in something of a battle. It is being fought on several fronts and in some areas more ground has been lost than gained. The battle is their struggle to survive. Using such terms is not overstating the matter because since the previous edition of this book was published, three railways have been lost, another six weren't able to operate any trains during 2022 and others have had to reduce their operational sections because they don't have the funds for essential track repairs, which is the situation that the Weardale, Wensleydale and Northampton & Lamport Railways currently find themselves in. Those that have been lost are the Elsecar Heritage Railway in South Yorkshire, the Tanat Valley Railway in Shropshire and the Dartmoor Railway in Devon, with financial difficulties being the underlying factor in each case. The Llangollen Railway was a near miss too, entering liquidation in 2021 with unsustainable debts, although once the administrators had sold off the rolling stock and assets that were available to them, thankfully the line has been resurrected. Those that remained closed throughout 2022 are the Barry, Beamish, Bowes, Nottingham Heritage and Pallot Railways, plus the National Railway Museum's passenger line and the future of most of these currently looks precarious. A handful of heritage railways have come and gone before, but what makes the last few years different is the number of railways that are closing and struggling simultaneously and that no new lines are opening. It has now been six years since the last new railway opened, which is the longest period there has ever been without a new standard gauge line in the 63-year history of the heritage railway movement. The reasons behind these challenging times are explored in the Introduction and Recent Developments section over the next few pages.

It's not all bad news though. During the last couple of years, several lines have been extended, with the Yorkshire Wolds, Cambrian Heritage and Mid Norfolk Railways now all offering "new track" and the Llangollen Railway is due to start operating regular services to its new Corwen terminus during 2023. Other lines are in the process of being extended, with work currently in progress on the Aln Valley, Churnet Valley, Great Central, Helston, Lincolnshire Wolds, Mid Suffolk, Royal Deeside, Strathspey and Swindon & Cricklade Railways. This counters the contraction taking place elsewhere and brings fresh optimism.

The greatest area of change in this third edition is to the stocklists. Hundreds of updates have been made, with far more sites having had changes to the locomotives and/or multiple units that are present than those where the fleets have remained static. The changes are a big mixture of vehicles moving from one heritage railway to another, movements to and from the main line network and a few scrappings. There have been some notable influxes from the main line network, particularly of High Speed Train (HST) power cars and Pacers. The first preserved HST working took place in April 2022, when 43159 & 43048 carried passengers on the Midland Railway Butterley. For Pacers, so many units have moved to heritage railways recently that it's not been easy keeping track of them all! At the last count, when 143617 arrived at the Tarka Valley Railway at the end of 2022, that took the total number of Pacers at heritage railways to 54 different units.

Every one of the 106 railway listings that follow has been updated. Changes have been made to the railways' histories to reflect recent developments, to the mileage figures where lines have been extended and to the stocklists after many recent movements. In addition, the contact details, opening times and special events have been updated as necessary.

The "use it or lose it" mantra has never been more apt for heritage railways. Every site needs as much support and income as possible and so readers are encouraged to visit these wonderfully varied preserved railways sooner rather than later. Every pound spent on tickets, in gift shops and cafés helps cover their substantial operating costs and represents a step towards securing the future of these living museums which showcase our transport history.

Andy Chard
Spring 2023

Maps used in this book
The maps in this book have been derived from a Creative Commons original and are reproduced by permission of the Creative Commons Attribution-ShareAlike 4.0 International Public License. The original map has been modified by addition of the heritage railways.

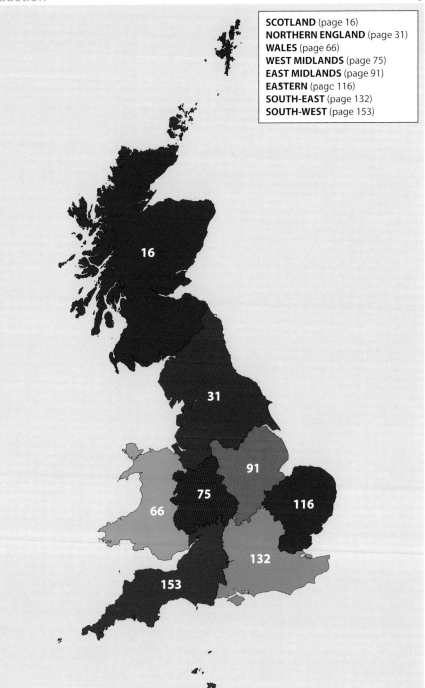

Introduction to Britain's Heritage Railway Movement and Recent Developments

Two monumental changes took place on Britain's railways during the 1950s and 1960s, which triggered the creation of the heritage railway movement and accelerated its growth; the mass withdrawal of steam locomotives and the closure of thousands of miles of railway lines. These roused many to form railway preservation groups. Some worked to save routes, such as the pioneers of the Keighley & Worth Valley Railway, which reopened only a few years after it was closed by British Rail in 1962. Other groups wanted to save steam locomotives from being scrapped and find new homes for them to operate at. These two aims of saving railways and saving locomotives married well and were the objectives of many early heritage railways. Whilst the speed with which BR closed lines, lifted track, demolished stations and sold land for development has been well rued over the years, if BR had not acted so fast, the early preservationists may not have been galvanised to act so quickly either and some of today's well-established heritage railways may not otherwise be with us today.

Heritage railways have been evolving since the early days of preservation. As well as preserving steam locomotives, which remain popular with enthusiasts and the public alike, diversification and innovation have brought new sights and sounds. During the early years of the 1960s, heritage railways didn't look much different to the main line network. That began to change once British Rail eradicated steam locomotives and banned them from working on the main line in 1968. As the national operator gradually modernised its stations, trains and infrastructure through the 1960s, 1970s and 1980s, the distinction between the main line network and heritage railways began to become more apparent. The next generation of enthusiasts then saw some of their favourite types eliminated sooner than expected and in response, groups formed to save diesel-hydraulic locomotives during the 1970s and types such as the Class 55 "Deltics" and Class 40 "Whistlers" during the 1980s. These then began to arrive at heritage railways, increasing the variety of traction in operation.

▲ In addition to the trains, the preserved architecture adds to the appeal of Britain's heritage railways. Quorn and Woodhouse station was built in 1899 and has been preserved in 1940s condition, as it was under the ownership of the London & North Eastern Railway. This authentic period scene was captured on 30 April 2022.   **Ian Beardsley**

The adaptation and progress continued, such that standard gauge heritage railways now have slightly more diesel locomotives than steam, with around 870 and 850 respectively at the end of 2022. This represents a decline of a few dozen of each since the previous edition of this book was published in early 2021. Diesel multiple unit (DMU) vehicles are fast catching up; there are now several hundred of these alongside the locomotives, and railcar-themed events are a regular fixture at an increasing number of railways. Some sites have no steam locomotives and others have lines built at locations with no railway history, neither of which undermine their viability. There are enterprising groups which have restored coaching stock, steam or diesel locomotives to main line standards, so that they can be hired to commercial operators, generating invaluable income to plough back into the heritage scene. In some cases, the members' expertise has been utilised to create specialist subsidiaries or businesses, such as South Devon Railway Engineering at its namesake home, or the Scottish Railway Preservation Society at the Bo'ness & Kinneil Railway, which operates main line charter trains and hires its coaching stock to other operators.

After Britain's railways were privatised in the 1990s, the rate of change on the national network accelerated and wholesale replacement of trains left very few locomotive-hauled services. Passenger numbers grew to unprecedented highs, which required the network to be further modernised, so it could be run as efficiently as possible. Network Rail carries out massive infrastructure upgrades every year, which involve the demolition of signal boxes and the removal of many semaphore signals. Major stations such as Birmingham New Street, Derby, Liverpool Lime Street and Reading have been completely rebuilt in recent years. Together, these changes mean that what the public have now become accustomed to when travelling by train is completely different to what they find at a heritage railway. Practises such as exchanging tokens, pulling leavers to move signals and punching holes in Edmondson tickets were the norm little more than a generation ago, as they had been since Victorian times. Nowadays though, they are almost exclusively confined to heritage railways. Consequently, the importance of these living and moving museums has increased. They not only preserve heritage trains, but the Victorian architecture and practises that put them in context. Heritage railways give a unique view of some of Britain's historical achievements, which at one point were the latest technology, while allowing visitors to enjoy some beautiful scenery from the comfort of their seats.

Recent Pressures

As mentioned in the preface, over the last few years, after more than half a century of steady growth, the heritage railway movement has begun to creak under the strain of some new pressures. As the table below shows, the number of new railways opening has been in steady decline since the turn of the century. This could be due to the sector reaching maturity, or it could be because it is becoming increasingly difficult to get new projects off the ground. Railways now have to contend with a rising regulatory and legislative burden, at a time when financial and volunteer resources are in shorter supply.

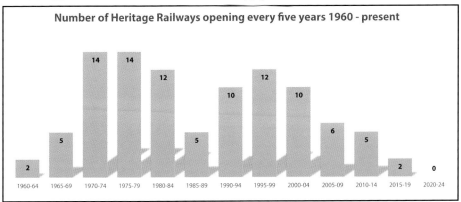

Number of Heritage Railways opening every five years 1960 - present

1960-64	1965-69	1970-74	1975-79	1980-84	1985-89	1990-94	1995-99	2000-04	2005-09	2010-14	2015-19	2020-24
2	5	14	14	12	5	10	12	10	6	2	5	0

The graph makes it clear that the number of new heritage railways is declining. Only two new lines have opened in the last decade – the Aln Valley Railway in 2013 and the Llanelli & Mynydd Mawr Railway in 2017. No other ten-year period has seen such a small number of new projects; even the movement's first decade, the 1960s, saw the much higher number of seven new heritage railways opening.

▲ Several new build steam and diesel locomotive projects are taking shape across a variety of heritage railways. One of these is Class 3MT 2-6-2T 82045 which is seen among a mixture of other locomotives at the Severn Valley Railway's Bridgnorth terminus on 21 May 2022.   **Robert Pritchard**

▼ Another ambitious new build project is the Ivatt Diesel Re-creation Society's scheme to rebuild the prototype diesel-electric LMS locomotive 10000. This will use the chassis of 58022, the remains of which are seen at the Ecclesbourne Valley Railway's Wirksworth Yard on 29 May 2022.

Steve Donald

So what is behind the bleak picture that is emerging in the 2020s, where existing railways are struggling and closing, and new lines aren't opening? Cracks had begun to appear before the pandemic. When the Office of Rail and Road (ORR) inspected the West Somerset Railway in 2018, several deficiencies were found and the line had to close for a lengthy period in 2019 to remedy these. Similarly, the Aln Valley Railway closed between 2020 and 2021 after an ORR inspection identified a number of improvements that needed to be made. Both railways have since addressed the issues raised, but this illustrates how heritage railways are now subject to much higher standards of scrutiny, legislation and safety. Compliance is good and necessary, but it comes at a cost, especially for organisations that rely heavily on volunteers, the vast majority of whom prefer to work with trains and people than with risk assessments and control measures!

Rising and ultimately unmanageable debts have already brought about the closures of four railways during the 2020s, leading to four very different outcomes. The Elsecar Railway's trustees had to surrender the lease to the council in 2020 and more than two years on, it looks unlikely to reopen. The Weardale and Dartmoor Railways were a casualty of their shared parent company entering administration. The former was then acquired by a local organisation, enabling it to remain a heritage railway. The latter was purchased by Network Rail so that the line to Okehampton could re-join the national network, however that was at the expense of the heritage line to Meldon. Finally, in the case of the Llangollen Railway, administrators were appointed in 2021 and after parts of it were pruned and sold off, it has since reopened.

Other railways have had to close in recent years while costly unbudgeted repairs were carried out after episodes of extreme weather. When the River Churnet flooded in 2019, it washed away a section of the Churnet Valley Railway, which had to be rebuilt. Multiple landslips damaged the Bo'ness & Kinneil Railway in 2020, requiring repairs that cost over £100,000. Subsidence damage to the Bristol Harbour Railway forced it to reduce its running length and whilst repairs have begun, these are not yet complete.

To add insult to injury, heritage railways are increasingly suffering malicious attacks. During 2019 over £80,000 worth of damage was caused at the Nottingham Heritage Railway when 112 carriage windows were smashed, and the East Kent Railway also incurred significant damage during an arson attack that year. In 2020 the Border Union Railway was damaged by vandals, tens of thousands of pounds worth of signalling equipment was stolen from the Churnet Valley Railway and the Derwent Valley Railway had three break-ins and thefts in as many months. More recently in 2022, three attacks in one week caused £25,000 worth of damage at the Foxfield Railway, when 24 panes of glass were smashed on a Pacer. Also in 2022, the Bo'ness & Kinneil Railway suffered a similar attack and in more ways than one had to pick up the pieces. These attacks are costly to remedy and require finances that the railways either don't have or that are earmarked for other projects. They also have a less visible effect, eroding staff and volunteer morale, although some generous responses from the public and funding bodies have greatly helped.

During 2020 and 2021, the pandemic and lockdown restrictions decimated the incomes of all heritage railways while their fixed costs still had to be paid. Practically every site launched an emergency appeal and the results were extremely positive. It has been estimated that the public generously donated more than £6m, but it soon became clear that that wasn't enough, and in what might just have saved the heritage railway sector from collapse, a series of government grant schemes were quickly created. Between the National Lottery Heritage Emergency Fund and the government's Culture Recovery Fund, a further £10m worth of grants were distributed to Britain's heritage railways. The size of the sums involved illustrates how much it costs to run preserved railways and perhaps what good value their ticket prices represent.

As the railways staggered through the effects of covid, they were dealt another heavy blow. Steam locomotives require washed bituminous lump coal and the last domestic mine to produce this closed in 2020. Two new mines, either of which could have secured the necessary coal supply for Britain's heritage railways, were planned for north-eastern England; one at Highthorn in Northumberland and another at Dewley Hill near Newcastle. Despite lobbying in favour of these from the Heritage Railway Association and other organisations, in 2020 the government refused permission for the Highthorn mine to open and Newcastle City Council refused planning permission for the Dewley Hill mine. The decisions were motivated by the political pressures around being seen to be reducing carbon emissions, but bizarrely these decisions only served to increase emissions. With no British mine, coal now has to be imported from another continent, which not only vastly inflates the costs that heritage railways incur (and those of the British steelmaking industry which also requires coal), but it also increases carbon emissions. Transporting coal thousands of miles from locations such as the USA, Australia and

South America generates between five and six times more carbon dioxide than the movement of domestically sourced coal does. This has created the ridiculous situation where heritage railways have to pay significantly more for coal than they did a few years ago and the emissions produced from transporting it so far are also significantly higher. There was a sign that the political wind has changed direction slightly in December 2022, when the government approved the first new coal mine for 30 years at Woodhouse in Cumbria, after considerable lobbying in favour of it from residents and local government, although the coal to be extracted from this is for steelmaking and isn't suitable for steam trains.

The overall effect of the significantly higher prices that heritage railways now have to pay for coal is that a shift has begun over the last two years, with railways reluctantly beginning to scale down the operation of steam trains, which are the main attraction for most visitors. For example, after taking a strong steam-only stance for decades, during 2022 the Bluebell Railway introduced a regular diesel diagram for the first time in its 62-year history. Similarly, Peak Rail has reduced the number of steam-hauled trains that operate and ended top & tail working on most services, running with a single locomotive to reduce operating costs. An unfortunate consequence of this is that Peak Rail's trains have been cut back to Matlock Riverside, as run rounds can't take place at Matlock (Network Rail) station. Also in 2022, the East Lancashire and Llangollen railways announced they were scaling back steam trains due to the increased price of coal.

Some sites have now begun to look into alternatives, such as the Keighley & Worth Valley Railway which trialled bio-coal in 2022, as this is partly comprised of biomass. Also in 2022, the Kent & East Sussex Railway began trialling an ovid coal substitute known as Heritage Wildfire, in an effort to try and find a replacement for the ever more costly coal which it now has to purchase from Columbia.

▲ Heritage railways are not able to return all the locomotives, multiple units, coaches and wagons in their possession to operational condition, or maintain them as such. Hunslet 0-6-0ST 1953 "JACKS GREEN" last worked in 1987 and has since become a static exhibit, as seen at the Nene Valley Railway's Wansford base on 15 November 2021.   **Alisdair Anderson**

▲ During its 2022 Diesel Gala, the East Lancashire Railway provided a new attraction; for an additional charge passengers could travel in the brake van of a demonstration goods train. On 30 June 2022, Class 42 D832 "ONSLAUGHT" passes Burrs Country Park with one of these, the 13.40 Bury–Ramsbottom. **Tom McAtee**

During 2022, just as visitor numbers started heading back towards pre-covid levels, another crisis began to emerge – energy prices. To compound the difficulties caused by coal prices, the cost of diesel shot up, which is the other fuel that heritage railways are heavily reliant upon. The cost of electricity, which powers everything from lighting and security systems to contactless card machines, also rose sharply. These further rises added more pressure on the budgets of these small and already squeezed charities. For example, in late 2022 the Embsay & Bolton Abbey Steam Railway said that it anticipates its annual energy costs, excluding coal and diesel, to increase from £30,000 to £90,000. It responded with an innovative plan, installing more than a thousand solar panels on the roof of its engine shed, which will mitigate the price rises.

Heritage railways manage to strike a good balance of preserving the past and moving with the times. Plenty of sites have recently begun offering new attractions to appeal to more visitors, such as the winter lights trains that have been introduced on various railways to complement their popular Santa Specials. Pacer and HST running days look set to become a regular fixture, as they attract new segments of the enthusiast community and in the case of Pacers, they offer the added benefit of reduced running costs. Another creative new attraction was introduced at the East Lancashire Railway's 2022 Diesel Gala. A series of full-length freight trains ran and for an additional charge, visitors could travel in the brake vans of these. This new experience proved to be very popular and will no doubt be repeated in future years.

Heritage railways continue to make a significant contribution to Britain's leisure activities, tourism and culture. According to the Heritage Railway Association, they attract millions of annual visitors and contribute more than £600m to Britain's economy each year. They provide 4,000 jobs nationally and bring together more than 22,000 volunteers. There are over 100 sites operating standard gauge trains and substantially more when narrow gauge railways and tramways are included.

These railways are comprised of people, as much as they are of infrastructure and rolling stock. Committed and tenacious pioneers fundraised and negotiated the purchase of railway trackbeds, locomotives and carriages from BR and its successors. They restored, and in many cases rebuilt, the rolling stock, depots and station buildings, before any trains could run. The backbone of what has been achieved to date is a legion of volunteers, who now form the vast majority of the workforce on today's heritage railways. This brings valuable social benefits that aren't obvious to visitors or easy to quantify; the volunteers form communities where friendships are made, and where engineering and customer facing skills are developed. New volunteers are continually sought and the railways will be delighted to hear from any readers who may want to help!

This book lists the heritage railways and museums within Great Britain and the Channel Islands, where trains carry passengers on a standard gauge line (4 foot 8½ inches). It introduces some fascinating corners of Great Britain, with quintessential rural branch lines and attractions that bring Britain's industrial or military history to life, such as the Northampton Ironstone, Appleby Frodingham and Chatham Dockyard Railways. Some sites don't fit into any obvious category and are better seen than described; Bressingham and Fawley Hill for example. There is a diverse geographical spread, with routes which traverse the Scottish Highlands (Strathspey, Keith & Dufftown), the rugged North of England (Wensleydale, Eden Valley, Stainmore, Lakeside & Haverthwaite), rural Wales (Llangollen and others), urban areas (Bristol Harbour, Ribble and Epping Ongar) and offer dramatic coastal views (North Norfolk, Dartmouth and West Somerset). Each site has its own merit and therefore reasons to be visited.

▲ Some railways have extensive depot facilities, which offer interesting and varied views to visitors, enthusiasts and photographers alike. On 16 July 2022, this varied collection of locomotives could be seen at the Mid Hants Railway's Ropley shed, with from left to right 33111, 50027 (with 33025 & 33029 just visible behind), 08032, 506 and 30925. **Tony Christie**

Layout of Information

The heritage railway listings have been split into nine regions. The first eight are arranged in geographical order from north to south and the final section lists heritage railways which are nearing the point of operating passenger trains. Within each region, the railways are in alphabetical order and each listing follows the same format.

1. Introduction and History

The history of each site is summarised, including key dates and landmark events from the time the railway was created, through its evolution to heritage status today. Many sites make the journey of ascension, decline and restoration; however, some have taken a different route or become a heritage railway after an entirely different history. The focus on how the site came to be a heritage railway briefly gives credit to many years of hard work and persistence by its founders. As heritage railways are a fluid and developing movement, future extension plans have been researched and are included. Some are long-term aspirations and for others, track is being laid as this book is being read.

2. Contact Details

Contact details follow the same format and if necessary the railway's website can be consulted for the latest timetable information, locomotive rosters or special event details.

3. Transport Links

Where there is a main line rail connection, this is stated, otherwise the nearest main line railway station and its distance from the site is given, as it may be possible to walk or travel by taxi. Car parking facilities are listed, with postcodes for map and satnav applications and where there is no charge for parking, this is mentioned. If a railway can be reached by another mode of transport, details are given. For example, several railway lines share their route with cycle paths or walkways and some of these have cycle hire facilities adjacent to stations. Others can be reached by boat, including the Battlefield Line (by canal) or the Swanage, Lakeside & Haverthwaite and Dartmouth Railways which all have connecting waterborne services.

4. Opening Times

The dates and times on which the railway operates are summarised. These vary greatly across sites, with some operating almost every day of the year, through to those which do so on a select few dates. Most railways have a set pattern of running dates and times, however, these can be subject to change and opening times may differ from those stated. Readers may therefore wish to check railways' websites or social media outlets for the latest information before travelling.

5. Line Mileage and Journey Time

The line mileage figures provide information on the length of each railway and the distance between stations and termini. Mileages are given to the nearest quarter of a mile, in line with those in national rail network timetables. Where the operational section is short (generally less than one mile) or there is only one station or boarding point, mileage figures are not always shown in list format. The journey times are the minimum needed to make a round trip and can vary depending on the starting point. Further time should be allowed where journeys are broken to explore the attractions and facilities along the route.

6. Stock List

All standard or broad gauge main line locomotives, industrial locomotives and multiple units based at each site are listed. The lists do not include coaches, wagons, London Underground and narrow gauge vehicles. Steam locomotives are shown first, followed by diesel and electric locomotives and then multiple units. The lists are arranged in approximate increasing size order, within each type. See 6.1 for details of types. The stocklists show the vehicles currently located at the railways, although some may not be present on a given date, such as when a locomotive visits another heritage railway, is on short-term hire to a main line operator or is elsewhere for repairs. Further technical information and details of the names and former numbers carried by main line locomotives and multiple units can be found in Platform 5 Publishing's "Preserved Locomotives of British Railways" and "Diesel and Electric Loco Register".

6.1 Rolling Stock Type

The vast majority of rolling stock listed is comprised of steam locomotives, diesel locomotives and multiple units, with a small number of more unusual vehicles. Each item listed falls into one of the following categories.

Steam: Steam locomotives, with all main line and industrial examples at each railway listed.
Diesel: Locomotives with diesel engines. All main line, shunting and industrial examples are given.
Electric: Locomotives powered by electricity, supplied by AC overhead, DC overhead or DC third rail systems.
Electro-Diesel: Locomotives with diesel engines, which are also capable of drawing electric power.
Battery: Battery-powered locomotives.
Gas Turbine: Locomotives powered by gas turbines (only two are listed).
Petrol: Locomotives powered by a petrol engine (only two are listed).
Steam Railcar: Steam powered single car (only two are listed).
DMU: Diesel Multiple Units; single or multiple carriages powered by self-contained diesel engines.
DEMU: Electric Multiple Units fitted with a diesel engine, enabling power from either source.
EMU: Electric Multiple Units; self-contained carriages powered by overhead or third rail electric power supplies.
Battery EMU: Battery-powered multiple units (only one is listed).

6.2 Number

This lists the number carried, or in some cases the name, by which the vehicle can be identified. Industrial locomotives which have not been given a number or name are listed by their works number, which was assigned by the locomotive builder. Where a locomotive's name is visible and the identifying number is not, for clarity both the name and number are given. Where the number is a low and commonly held value, such as a one or two-digit number, the works number is also shown in brackets if this is known. In some cases, a second previously carried number has been added in brackets, where this may be helpful in identifying or distinguishing the vehicle from another. The number currently carried is listed, irrespective of whether that was the most recently carried number in main line service, which in some cases means that locomotives of the same class are listed with very different numbers. For example, steam locomotive 21C123 at the Bluebell Railway (BR number 34023) carries its Southern Railway number, whereas classmate 34059 at the same location carries its BR number (its previous Southern Railway number was 21C159). For first generation multiple units, individual vehicle numbers are given, as the partners to which they are attached can be changed. As Pacer set formations rarely change, the individual vehicle numbers and the set numbers to which they are more commonly referred are both given.

6.3 Builder

The builder that constructed the locomotive or multiple unit is shown. These are a combination of commercial builders, railway companies including British Rail/Railways and modern organisations that have constructed replica or new-build locomotives. Some of the builders have been abbreviated and a complete list, including their full names, is given in Appendix I.

6.4 Details

For all steam locomotives and some smaller diesel locomotives with driving wheels connected by coupling rods, the Whyte notation is used. The three numbers separated by dashes consist of the leading (non-driving) wheels, followed by the number of driving wheels and then the number of trailing (non-driving) wheels. Many steam locomotives have one of the following suffixes: T – side tank, PT – pannier tank, ST – saddle tank, WT – well tank, CT – crane tank, F – fireless, G – geared, VBT – vertical boiler tank, VBGT – vertical boiler geared tank. For example, 2-4-0ST would be a saddle tank locomotive with 2 leading wheels, 4 driving wheels and no trailing wheels. For locomotives where driving wheels are connected by means other than coupling rods, w is used to indicate powered axles. For example, 4w indicates a four-wheeled bogie with all four wheels powered. The suffixes DE, DM and DH denote diesel-electric, diesel-mechanical and diesel-hydraulic respectively. For some main line diesel and electric locomotives, the number of driven axles is represented by a letter (A = 1, B = 2, C = 3), followed by a number which states the number of non-powered axles. When the letter o is used, this indicates that each axle is individually powered. The majority of multiple units and diesel and electric locomotives are listed by their TOPS class. This is a system introduced by British Railways in 1968 which classified locomotives by a two digit class number and multiple units by a three digit class number.

7. Attractions

This lists attractions at the site, particularly those which are railway related, such as museums, restored signal boxes and miniature railways, as well as any other facilities or services which may be of interest. Some of the more well-known attractions in the surrounding area are also given, including nearby heritage railways, to give ideas for combined visits.

8. Special Events

Heritage railways hold a rich variety of events every year, including beer festivals, live music, transport themed events, family activities and Santa Specials. Many of these attract thousands of visitors and can be a good opportunity to explore something new, inspire children, or something to avoid depending on one's priorities! The information on special events has either been provided by the railways or is based on previous years' calendars of activities. Readers are advised to check the latest information before travelling for particular events.

9. Appendices

Appendix I gives the abbreviations and full names of all the locomotive and multiple unit builders found in the individual railway listings.

Appendix II lists the general abbreviations used in this book.

Appendix III lists all the heritage railways in alphabetical order, with their region and the page number on which they can be found. This acts as a useful index to find the entry for each railway in this book.

Updates and Contact Details

Every effort has been made to ensure the information given is correct, with each of the railways and a large variety of reference sources having been consulted. The content has been updated to early 2023 and the author would be pleased to hear from any reader with information about any inaccuracies or suggestions for enhancements to future editions. Please send any comments to the publisher's address on the title page of this book, or by email to: updates@platform5.com. The author and publisher cannot take responsibility for any errors, changes or cancellations that may take place.

▲ Photo charters are an example of the creative ways heritage railways are finding to attract new visitors and generate additional income. This evocative image was taken during a photo charter in the yard at the Great Central Railway's Quorn and Woodhouse station on 12 August 2021. It captures so much more than the train, which is headed by BR Standard 5MT "Black 5" 45305. Clearly a lot of thought and planning have gone into details such as the type and positioning of the motor vehicles, the goods they are carrying and how the staff are dressed to create this authentic mid-20th century scene.   **Martyn Tattam**

SCOTLAND

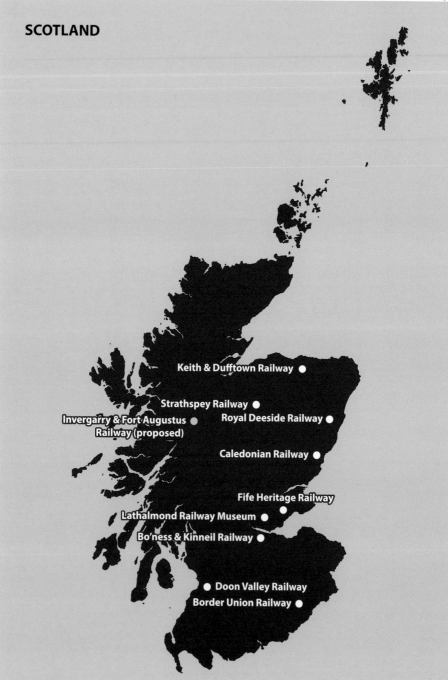

Keith & Dufftown Railway ●

Strathspey Railway ●

Invergarry & Fort Augustus ●   Royal Deeside Railway ●
Railway (proposed)

Caledonian Railway ●

Fife Heritage Railway
Lathalmond Railway Museum ● ●
Bo'ness & Kinneil Railway ●

● Doon Valley Railway
Border Union Railway ●

Region 1 – Scotland

Bo'ness & Kinneil Railway

Introduction and History

The branch line from Manuel to Bo'ness Harbour on the Firth of Forth opened in 1848 and was initially only used for carrying minerals and other freight. Passenger services did not commence until 1856 and were withdrawn a century later in 1956, when Bo'ness station was closed. The branch line continued to be used for carrying freight; however, the station was demolished and its original site is now a car park. The Scottish Railway Preservation Society (SRPS) formed in 1961 and started a collection of steam locomotives, which was initially housed at a base in Falkirk, until 1979 when the society acquired the Bo'ness site. The first preserved trains ran in 1981 after a new station was constructed at Bo'ness on the site of former sidings, near where the original station stood. All the buildings at Bo'ness have been brought from other stations or railway sites. The running line was extended to Kinneil Halt in 1987, Birkhill in 1989 and it reached Manuel in 2010, although the station at Manuel was not opened until 2013. The railway museum at the Bo'ness site opened in 1995, was extended in 2002 and a new engineering facility to house the locomotive collection was built in 2022.

Contact Details

Website: www.bkrailway.co.uk
Tel: 01506 825855
Email: enquiries.railway@srps.org.uk
Address: Bo'ness & Kinneil Railway, Bo'ness Station, Union Street, Bo'ness, EH51 9AQ.

Transport Links

By Rail: The nearest railway station is Linlithgow, which is four miles away.
By Road: Free car parking is available at Bo'ness (EH51 9AQ).

Opening Times

The railway operates on Saturdays, Sundays and Tuesdays and selected other weekdays from April until October and for special events during December. Trains run between approximately 10.45–16.30, depending on which timetable is in operation. The Museum of Scottish Railways at Bo'ness is open every day from April to October.

Line Mileage and Journey Time

0.00	Bo'ness
1.00	Kinneil Halt
3.50	Birkhill
4.75	Manuel

A return journey takes about one hour.

Stock List

Type	Number	Builder	Details
Steam	6 (2127)	Andrew Barclay	0-4-0CT
Steam	3 (1937)	Andrew Barclay	0-4-0ST
Steam	6 (2043)	Andrew Barclay	0-4-0ST
Steam	CITY OF ABERDEEN (912)	Black Hawthorn	0-4-0ST
Steam	3640	Hawthorn Leslie	0-4-0ST
Steam	13 (2203)	Neilson Reid	0-4-0ST
Steam	68095	North British	0-4-0ST
Steam	419	Caledonian Railway	0-4-4T
Steam	65243	Neilson & Co	0-6-0
Steam	LORD ASHFIELD (1989)	Andrew Barclay	0-6-0F
Steam	3 LADY VICTORIA	Andrew Barclay	0-6-0ST
Steam	68007	Bagnall	0-6-0ST
Steam	19 (3818)	Hunslet	0-6-0ST
Steam	5 (3837)	Hunslet	0-6-0ST
Steam	20 (2068)	Andrew Barclay	0-6-0T
Steam	24 (2335)	Andrew Barclay	0-6-0T

Steam	1 (5710)	Neilson & Co	0-6-0T
Steam	61994	LNER	2-6-0
Steam	80105	British Railways	2-6-4T
Steam	45170	North British	2-8-0
Steam	246 (62712)	LNER	4-4-0
Steam	49 (62277)	North British	4-4-0
Steam	9561	Sentinel	4wVBT
Steam	9627	Sentinel	4wVBT
Steam	9631	Sentinel	4wVBT
Electric	1131	Fairfield Shipbuilding & Engine Co.	0-4-0
Diesel	FGF (552)	Andrew Barclay	0-4-0DH
Diesel	D2767	North British	0-4-0
Diesel	Tiger (27415)	North British	0-4-0
Diesel	262998	Ruston & Hornsby	0-4-0
Diesel	321733	Ruston & Hornsby	0-4-0
Diesel	7 (275883)	Ruston & Hornsby	0-4-0
Diesel	P6687	Ruston & Hornsby	0-4-0
Diesel	521(457299)	Ruston & Hornsby	0-4-0
Diesel	1 (343)	Andrew Barclay	0-6-0
Diesel	D3558	British Railways	Class 08
Diesel	19001 (82119)	British Rail	Class 19
Diesel	20020	English Electric	Class 20
Diesel	25235	British Railways	Class 25
Diesel	26024	BRCW	Class 26
Diesel	26038	BRCW	Class 26
Diesel	27001	BRCW	Class 27
Diesel	27005	BRCW	Class 27
Diesel	37025	English Electric	Class 37
Diesel	37214	English Electric	Class 37
Diesel	37261	English Electric	Class 37
Diesel	37403	English Electric	Class 37
Diesel	47643	British Railways	Class 47
DMU	51017, 51043, 59404 & 79443	British Railways	Class 126
EMU	61503, 75597 & 75632	Pressed Steel	Class 303

Attractions

The Museum of Scottish Railways at Bo'ness is Scotland's second largest railway museum. There is also a Brass Rubbing Trail, an 'O' gauge model railway and a picnic area at Bo'ness. Steam and diesel footplate experiences are available on the railway. Other attractions in the area include the Kinneil Estate and Museum, Kinneil Nature Reserve, Bo'ness Motor Museum, the Linlithgow Museum, Linlithgow Palace and the city of Edinburgh.

Special Events

Events that usually take place on the railway include:

Easter Egg Specials.
Day Out with Thomas.
Father's Day Event in June.
Afternoon Tea and Evening Fish & Chip Specials.
1950s themed events.
Steam and Diesel Galas.
Santa Specials, Winter Diesel Day and Hogmanay trains during December.

Border Union Railway

Introduction and History
The Border Union Railway, which was marketed as the Waverley Route, ran from Edinburgh to Carlisle via Hawick. It opened in 1862, providing an alternative route from Scotland to England across tough terrain, which required many curves and steep gradients. It was earmarked for closure in Dr Beeching's 1963 report and, despite fierce opposition, was closed in 1969. Between 2012 and 2015, the northern section of the railway was relaid between Edinburgh and Tweedbank and now forms the well-used Borders Railway. In 2002 the Waverley Route Heritage Association obtained a lease for a section of trackbed south of Whitrope Tunnel and its base at Whitrope Heritage Centre is on this. The centre formally opened in 2012 and has an operational section of running track. The railway hopes to extend south by a further two miles in the future, taking it to Riccarton Junction.

Contact Details
Website: www.wrha.org.uk
Telephone: 07366 260584
Email: info@wrha.org.uk
Address: Border Union Railway, Whitrope, Hawick, Roxburghshire, TD9 9TY.

Transport Links
By Rail: The site is in a remote location and the nearest stations are Tweedbank (29 miles) and Carlisle (34 miles).
By Road: Car parking is available at Whitrope Heritage Centre (TD9 9TY), which is on the B6399, immediately south of Whitrope Tunnel.

Opening Times
The usual operating times are 10.00 to 16.00 on the first Saturday of the month from April to October, plus during occasional special events and some bank holiday weekends. In addition, bookings can be made in advance for the railway to operate on other dates, providing volunteers are available to accommodate this.

Line Mileage and Journey Time
0.00   Whitrope Tunnel
0.25   Whitrope Halt
0.50   Golden Bridge

A round trip takes about 30 minutes.

Stock List

Type	Number	Builder	Details
Diesel	3777	Hibberd	4wDM
Diesel	411319	Ruston & Hornsby	4wDM
Diesel	D5340	BRCW	Class 26
DMU	RB004	BREL/Leyland	Prototype Railbus
DMU	142019 (55560 & 55610)	BREL/Leyland	Class 142
DMU	142020 (55561 & 55611)	BREL/Leyland	Class 142
EMU	69316	BREL	Class 422

Attractions
The railway has a collection of second generation diesel multiple units, with a Class 141 prototype railbus and two Class 142 Pacers. These, along with the diesel shunter and restored brake van, are used to carry passengers and Class 26 D5340 provides demonstration runs on some occasions. There is an exhibition showing the history and operations of the railway, which includes a signalling experience and various artefacts. The buffet coach provides refreshments and contains further railway exhibits. Other attractions in the region include Hermitage Castle to the south, the village of Newcastleton with a Stane from the Seven Stanes Walk and a nearby golf course. To the north, Hawick is the home of cashmere, with textile outlets, a whisky distillery and the annual common riding.

Caledonian Railway

Introduction and History

The railway between Brechin and Bridge of Dun opened in 1848 and later became part of the original Caledonian Railway. The line closed to passenger services in 1952 but continued to be used for freight traffic for almost 30 years until this ended in 1981. Two groups formed in 1979, the Caledonian Railway (Brechin) and the Brechin Railway Preservation Society, to preserve the line. The first locomotive arrived in 1979; however, it wasn't until 1993 when a Light Railway Order was obtained, that passenger services could begin between Brechin and Bridge of Dun. Initially there were aspirations to extend the railway a further three and a half miles from Bridge of Dun to Dubton where the trackbed has been built upon, but this is no longer being pursued.

Contact Details

Website: www.caledonianrailway.com
Tel: 01356 622992
Email: enquiries@caledonianrailway.com
Address: Caledonian Railway, The Station, Park Road, Brechin, DD9 7AF.

Transport Links

By Rail: The nearest railway station is Montrose, which is four miles from Bridge of Dun station.
By Road: Free car parking is available at both Brechin (DD9 7AF) and Bridge of Dun (DD10 9LH).

Opening Times

The railway operates on Sundays from June and on Saturdays & Sundays from July to early September, plus on selected other running dates for special events. The Whistle Stop Coffee Shop at Brechin station opens from 10.00 on Wednesdays to Saturdays.

Line Mileage and Journey Time

0.00   Brechin
4.00   Bridge of Dun

A return journey takes about one hour.

Stock List

Type	Number	Builder	Details
Steam	1863	Andrew Barclay	0-4-0ST
Steam	1376 BAC No. 1	Peckett	0-4-0ST
Steam	16 (2759)	Bagnall	0-6-0ST
Steam	6 (2749)	Bagnall	0-6-0ST
Steam	2879	Hunslet	0-6-0ST
Steam	2153	Peckett	0-6-0ST
Steam	1889 MENELAUS	Peckett	0-6-0ST
Steam	2107 HARLAXTON	Andrew Barclay	0-6-0T
Diesel	3747	Hibberd	0-4-0
Diesel	421700	Ruston & Hornsby	0-4-0
Diesel	458957 DEWAR HIGHLANDER	Ruston & Hornsby	0-4-0
Diesel	211	Yorkshire Engine Co.	0-4-0
Diesel	212 MAVIS (2684)	Yorkshire Engine Co.	0-4-0
Diesel	2654	Yorkshire Engine Co.	0-4-0
Diesel	D3059	British Railways	Class 08
Diesel	12052	British Railways	Class 11
Diesel	12093	British Railways	Class 11
Diesel	D9553	British Railways	Class 14
Diesel	20016	English Electric	Class 20
Diesel	20081	English Electric	Class 20
Diesel	20088	English Electric	Class 20
Diesel	20166	English Electric	Class 20
Diesel	25072	British Railways	Class 25
Diesel	25083	British Railways	Class 25
Diesel	26035	BRCW	Class 26
Diesel	D5301	BRCW	Class 26
Diesel	D5314	BRCW	Class 26

Diesel	D5353	BRCW	Class 27
Diesel	D5370	BRCW	Class 27
Diesel	37097	English Electric	Class 37
DEMU	60146, 60150, 60673, 60677, 60827 & 60831	British Railways	Class 205

Attractions

The railway has a large collection of steam and diesel locomotives comparative to its size; the original railway station and railway yard can be seen at Brechin. Nearby attractions include Brechin Castle and Gardens (open on selected dates), Lunan Bay, Montrose Basin Nature Reserve and the coastal town of Montrose.

Special Events

Events that usually take place on the railway include:

Easter Eggspress event.
A music event is due to take place during June 2023.
Food and drink themed events including "Take the Sloe Train" and "Whisky Whistler".
Days Out With Thomas.
Murder on the Brechin Express.
Diesel Weekends.
Polar Express Trains during December.

▲ The Caledonian Railway's D5314 (26014) arrives at Brechin with the 14.00 from Bridge of Dun on 14 August 2022.   **Andy Chard**

Doon Valley Railway

Introduction and History

The railway between Ayr and Dalmellington opened in 1856, carrying passengers and freight from the iron and coal pits at Dalmellington. Passenger services were withdrawn in 1964 and regular freight traffic continued to use the branch until 1978, when many of the collieries closed. The Ayrshire Railway Preservation Group (ARPG) formed in 1974, with the aim of preserving the area's railway heritage. The group were initially based at the former Minnivey Colliery in Ayrshire from 1980 and moved to the current site at Dunaskin, on the former Dalmellington branch, in 2002. To better reflect the primary purpose of operating heritage trains, the organisation's name was changed from the Scottish Industrial Railway Centre to the Doon Valley Railway in 2019. The railway has a collection of industrial steam and diesel locomotives, many of which were built by Andrew Barclay & Sons at nearby Kilmarnock. In February 2023 it transpired that the owners of the land and buildings which the railway use are to sell these and the railway has until July 2023 to raise the £250k needed to purchase them. Please see the DVR website for the latest information and details on how to donate.

Contact Details

Website: www.doonvalleyrailway.co.uk
Tel: 01292 269260
Email: info@doonvalleyrailway.co.uk
Address: Doon Valley Railway, Dunaskin Bridge, Waterside, Ayr, KA6 7JH.

Transport Links

By Rail: The nearest stations to the Dunaskin site are Maybole (11 miles) and Ayr (12 miles).
By Road: Free parking is available at Dunaskin.

Opening Times

The usual opening times are 10.30–16.00 on Sundays between April and the end of September. Trains operate during these times and are usually steam-hauled.

Line Mileage and Journey Time

0.0   Dunaskin
1.00   Laight Level Crossing
2.50   Minnivey

Trains currently run to Laight Level Cross and a return journey takes about 25 minutes.

Stock List

Type	Number	Builder	Details
Steam	8 (1952)	Andrew Barclay	0-4-0F
Steam	1 (2368)	Andrew Barclay	0-4-0ST
Steam	10 (2244)	Andrew Barclay	0-4-0ST
Steam	16 (1116)	Andrew Barclay	0-4-0ST
Steam	19 (1614)	Andrew Barclay	0-4-0ST
Steam	23 (2260)	Andrew Barclay	0-4-0ST
Steam	25 (2358)	Andrew Barclay	0-6-0ST
Diesel	7	Andrew Barclay	0-4-0
Diesel	AC118 M3571	Andrew Barclay	0-4-0
Diesel	Powfoot No. 1	Andrew Barclay	0-4-0
Diesel	Lily of the Valley	Fowler	0-4-0
Diesel	107	Hunslet	0-4-0
Diesel	27644 (ARMY 409)	North British	0-4-0
Diesel	421697	Ruston & Hornsby	0-4-0
Diesel	324 Blinkin Bees (284239)	Ruston & Hornsby	0-4-0
Diesel	417890 Johnnie Walker	Ruston & Hornsby	0-4-0
Diesel	BE116 DY322	Ruston & Hornsby	0-4-0
Diesel	10012	Sentinel	0-4-0

Attractions

Steam or diesel locomotives give brake van rides on the former industrial railway line which runs east from the Dunaskin site. A museum is located within the engineering workshop which dates back to 1847. There are a variety of steam and diesel locomotives to see, with both standard and narrow gauge exhibits, plus a model railway and photographic archives to explore. Nearby attractions include the Galloway Forest Park, the Scottish Dark Sky Observatory, the village of Straiton and the coast and beaches on the southern Firth of Clyde.

Special Events
Events that usually take place on the railway include:

Classic Vehicle Show.
Teddy Bears Day Out.
Halloween Trains during October.
Santa Trains during December.

Fife Heritage Railway

Introduction and History
The Lochty Private Railway ran on a former mineral railway in Fife from 1967 until it closed in 1992. The Kingdom of Fife Railway Preservation Society then formed in 1992 to find a new home for the remaining railway stock, which was initially moved to the now-closed railway at Methil Power Station. In 2001 the society acquired the nearby former marshalling yard at Kirkland, near Leven, and in 2003 after laying track and landscaping the site, the rolling stock was moved there. It opened to the public in 2008; the first steam train ran in 2016 and the railway now has half a mile of track, an engine shed and several sidings. The heritage railway previously hoped to use the disused Leven branch and run trains on this towards Cameron Bridge, however this will no longer be possible as the Leven branch is being reinstated as part of the main line network. Work to revive the Leven branch has recently begun and despite there initially being plans to the contrary, this is now unlikely to include a connection to the Fife Heritage Railway.

Contact Details
Website: www.fifeheritagerailway.co.uk
Email: enquiries@fifeheritagerailway.com
Address: Fife Heritage Railway, Kirkland Sidings, Leven, Fife, KY8 4RB.

Transport Links
By Rail: The nearest railway station is Markinch, which is six miles from the railway.
By Road: On-site parking is available (KY8 4RB).

Opening Times
Trains operate on the last Sunday of the month from April to October and during December for Santa Express services.

Line Mileage and Journey Time
The railway currently runs for half a mile and the journey time is relatively short.

Stock List

Type	Number	Builder	Details
Steam	17	Andrew Barclay	0-4-0ST
Steam	10 FORTH	Andrew Barclay	0-4-0ST
Steam	3 (2046)	Andrew Barclay	0-4-0ST
Diesel	400 RIVER EDEN	North British	0-4-0DH
Diesel	1 Largo Law (449753)	Ruston & Hornsby	0-4-0DE
Diesel	7 (313390)	Ruston & Hornsby	0-4-0DM
Diesel	2 The Garvie Flyer	Ruston & Hornsby	0-4-0DE
Diesel	4	Ruston & Hornsby	0-4-0
Diesel	10	North British	0-6-0
DMU	52029	British Railways	Class 107

Attractions
The café is open on railway operating days. Other nearby attractions include Methil Heritage Centre, Leven Beach and Riverside Park in Glenrothes. The Lathalmond Railway Museum is 23 miles away and the Bo'ness & Kinneil Railway is 35 miles away.

Special Events

Events that usually take place on the railway include:

Easter Bunny event.
Steam and diesel Galas.
Halloween event in October
Santa Express during December.

Keith & Dufftown Railway

Introduction and History

The three railway lines that converge at Keith were constructed in stages. The route from Aberdeen reached Keith in 1856 and the line from Inverness arrived in 1858, creating a through route. The branch from Keith to Dufftown opened in 1862 and this was extended from Dufftown to Nethy Bridge in 1863 and forward to Boat of Garten in 1866, allowing through running to Aviemore. The line had rail connections at many of the distilleries along the route, allowing whisky to be transported by rail. Through passenger services from Keith to Aviemore via Dufftown ceased in 1965, followed by freight in 1968. Whisky trains ran from Aberlour to Keith until 1971 and from Dufftown until 1985. Occasional charter services continued to visit Dufftown until the last of these ran in 1991. The Keith and Dufftown Railway acquired the line in 1998 and the first trains in preservation ran in 2000. The railway is no longer connected to the national network, as a short section of track in Keith has been lifted; however, it is hoped that this can be reinstated in the future.

Contact Details

Website: www.keith-dufftown-railway.co.uk
Tel: 01340 821181
Email: info@keith-dufftown-railway.co.uk
Address: Keith Town Station, Keith, Banffshire, AB55 5BR.

Transport Links

By Rail: The nearest station is Keith, which is less than one mile from Keith Town station.
By Road: Free parking is available at Dufftown (AB55 4BA) and Keith Town station (AB55 5BR).

Opening Times

Trains operate every Saturday and Sunday from mid-April to early October, on most Fridays within this period and on selected other dates.

Line Mileage and Journey Time

0.00	Dufftown
4.50	Drummuir
10.25	Keith Town

A return journey takes about 1 hour 40 minutes from Dufftown (longer if starting from Keith).

Stock List

Type	Number	Builder	Details
Diesel	415	Andrew Barclay	0-4-0
Diesel	The Wee Mac	Clayton	0-4-0
Diesel	Spirit O Fife	English Electric	0-6-0
DMU	50628, 51568, 52053, 56224 & 56491	British Railways	Class 108
DMU	140001 (55500 & 55501)	BREL/Leyland	Class 140
DMU	144022 (55822, 55858 & 55845)	Alexander/BREL	Class 144

Attractions

Keith Town station has a shop, which includes various railway books and model railway items. The railway offers a diesel shunter driving experience, which is unusual among heritage railways, as driving experiences tend to use main line steam or diesel locomotives. At Dufftown visitors can look around the locomotive shed and heritage centre by arrangement, plus the shop and Sidings Café which are housed inside converted carriages. The station is less than one mile from the centre of historic Dufftown, which is known as the whisky capital of the world and has seven working distilleries. Other attractions in the region include the 13th Century Balvenie Castle and the Speyside Way, which is a traffic-free path along much of the railway trackbed to Grantown-on-Spey near the Strathspey Railway, which is approximately 33 miles away.

Special Events

Events that usually take place on the railway include.

Children's Easter event during April.
Food and drink related events include the Spirit of Speyside Whisky Festival, Pie & Pint Specials and Fish & Chip specials.
1940s Weekend.
Teddy Bears' Weekend.
Halloween Ghost Train.
Santa Specials during December.

Lathalmond Railway Museum

Introduction and History

This region of Fife was home to a number of railways and narrow gauge tramways built to carry minerals, the first of which opened in 1864. During the Second World War, the Royal Navy built a stores and transit depot on the Lathalmond site, for the nearby Rosyth Dockyard and this facility used the extensive railway network until 1971. The Royal Navy site closed in 1993 and in 1995 part of the grounds were acquired by the Scottish Vintage Bus Museum to house its exhibits. In 1997 the Shed 47 Railway Restoration Group was formed, taking its name from that of the Royal Navy's former locomotive shed (Shed 47). Since then the group have returned to use a section of the vast standard gauge railway network that occupied the site and the running line is adjacent to the bus museum.

Contact Details

Website: www.shed47.org
Tel: 07775 121156
Email: mail@shed47.org
Address: Shed47 Railway Restoration Group at SVBM, M90 Commerce Park, Lathalmond, KY12 OSJ.

Transport Links

By Rail: The nearest station is Dunfermline Town, which is three miles away.
By Road: Car parking is available on site (KY12 OSJ).

Opening Times

The railway museum opens 12.30–16.30 every Sunday from the first Sunday in April to the first Sunday in October, plus on selected other dates. Standard gauge trains run on selected Sundays.

Line Mileage and Journey Time

The standard gauge railway line is 400 metres long and the journey time is relatively short.

Stock List

Type	Number	Builder	Details
Steam	17	Andrew Barclay	0-4-0ST
Steam	29	Andrew Barclay	0-4-0ST
Diesel	DS48 (265617)	Ruston & Hornsby	4wDM
Diesel	236 (372)	Andrew Barclay	0-4-0DM
Diesel	385	Andrew Barclay	0-4-0DM
Diesel	4210140	Fowler	0-4-0
Diesel	D2650	Hunslet	0-4-0
Diesel	251	Hunslet	0-4-0

Attractions

The site is shared with the Scottish Vintage Bus Museum, which opens simultaneously. It is the home of the 1942-built locomotive shed, a working weighbridge and a 2-foot gauge railway, which runs for 300 metres. The Knockhill Racing Circuit is nearby; to the east is the Fife Heritage Railway and to the south is the Forth Bridge, across which is the Bo'ness & Kinniel Railway and the city of Edinburgh.

Special Events

2 July 2023: Lathalmond Wartime.

The vintage bus museum has special events on particular dates. These are subject to a charge by the bus museum and standard and narrow gauge trains usually run on these dates from 11.00. Other events may be added during 2023 – please check the website.

▲ Vehicles 50628 & 56224, which form one of the Keith & Dufftown Railway's Class 108 DMUs, head away from Keith Town station with the 14.30 to Dufftown on 14 August 2022.   **Andy Chard**

Royal Deeside Railway

Introduction and History

When the railway from Aberdeen to Banchory was completed in 1853, Crathes Castle station on the route opened as a private station for the Laird of Crathes. The line was extended to Aboyne in 1859 and to its final terminus Ballater in 1866. In 1863 Crathes Castle became a public railway station, being renamed Crathes and until the route's closure in 1966, it was regularly used by the Royal Family to reach Balmoral Castle. The Royal Deeside Railway Preservation Society formed in 2003 and began restoring the line in 2003. A base was established at Crathes and as the previous station had become a private residence, the new Milton of Crathes station was built at a more accessible location. The railway currently runs for one mile and is in the process of being extended westwards along the original trackbed. Once a new bridge to carry the Deeside Way footpath over the Burn of Bennie has been installed, the railway can be reinstated on the original bridge, allowing the line to continue west. The long-term aim is to reach Banchory, which will give the line a running length of over 2 miles.

Contact Details

Website: www.deeside-railway.co.uk
Tel: 01330 844416
Email: opsdir@deeside-railway.co.uk
Address: The Royal Deeside Railway, Milton of Crathes, Banchory, Aberdeenshire, AB31 5QH.

Transport Links

By Rail: The nearest railway stations are Portlethen (14 miles) and Aberdeen (16 miles).
By Road: Parking for the railway is available at the Milton of Crathes art & craft village (AB31 5QH).

Opening Times

Trains depart on the hour between 11.00 and 16.00 on selected Sundays from April to September, every Sunday during July and August and on selected other dates including Santa Specials during December. The trains are usually hauled by a steam locomotive, however they can be worked by a Class 03 diesel.

Line Mileage and Journey Time

From Milton of Crathes the railway operates for one mile. A return journey takes about 20 minutes.

Stock List

Type	Number	Builder	Details
Steam	BON ACCORD	Andrew Barclay	0-4-0ST
Steam	6 (2110)	Peckett	0-4-0ST
Steam	SALMON	Andrew Barclay	0-6-0ST
Diesel	D2037	British Railways	Class 03
Diesel	D2094	British Railways	Class 03
Diesel	D2134	British Railways	Class 03
Battery EMU	79998 & 79999	British Railways	Derby Lightweight

Attractions

The railway is situated within the Milton of Crathes complex which includes craft shops, galleries, a children's play area and a restaurant. There is a Victorian station, a railway carriage tearoom, a shop and great views of the surrounding hills as the line follows the River Dee. Steam driving experiences and charter trains can be arranged. The region is home to Crathes Castle garden and estate, the city of Aberdeen, Balmoral Castle, Craigievar Castle and Grampian Transport Museum.

Special Events

Events that usually take place on the railway include:

Mother's Day event with Cream Teas.
End of Season Gala.
Santa Specials and Mince Pie Specials during December.

Strathspey Railway

Introduction and History

The railway from Aviemore to Forres, which includes the route of today's Strathspey Railway, opened in 1863. The route from Dufftown to Nethy Bridge (see Keith & Dufftown Railway) also opened in 1863 and was extended south to Boat of Garten in 1866. The Aviemore to Forres via Boat of Garten route was the original Highland Main Line, until the direct route from Aviemore to Inverness was completed in 1898. This led to the line via Boat of Garten becoming a secondary route and passenger services eventually ceased in 1965. Freight traffic, which mainly consisted of locally produced whisky, ended in 1968 when the line was closed. The first preservation group formed in 1971, buying the trackbed from British Rail and the first trains ran from a site north of Aviemore to Boat of Garten in 1978. The railway was extended into the main line station at Aviemore in 1998, providing a convenient connection to the national network. A northern extension to Broomhill opened in 2002 and the line has recently been further extended to the disused bridge over the River Dulnain. The next step will be to reinstate the line over the Dulnain, however realignment work will then be required where the railway meets the A95. The long-term aim is to extend to Grantown-on-Spey, which is just over two miles from the railway's current northern limit.

Contact Details

Website: www.strathspeyrailway.co.uk
Tel: 01479 810725
Email: Written enquiries can be made via the website.
Address: Strathspey Railway, Aviemore Station, Dalfaber Road, Aviemore, PH22 1PY.

Transport Links

By Rail: Main line rail connection at Aviemore; just cross the footbridge to Platform 3.
By Road: Car parking is available at Aviemore (PH22 1PD – use the main line station postcode), Boat of Garten (PH24 3BH) and Broomhill (PH26 3LX).

Opening Times

The annual running season usually begins in February and the railway then operates on almost every weekend until the end of the year, plus on selected weekdays and on most days during the summer.

Line Mileage and Journey Time

0.00	Aviemore
5.25	Boat of Garten
9.25	Broomhill
10.25	Current line end / River Dulnain (not in regular use)

A return journey takes about 1 hour 45 minutes.

Stock List

Type	Number	Builder	Details
Steam	2 (2020)	Andrew Barclay	0-4-0ST
Steam	BIRKENHEAD (7386)	Robert Stephenson & Hawthorns	0-4-0ST
Steam	828	Caledonian Railway	0-6-0
Steam	9	Robert Stephenson & Hawthorns	0-6-0ST
Steam	WPR17 (2017)	Andrew Barclay	0-6-0T
Steam	46512	British Railways	2-6-0
Steam	46464	British Railways	2-6-0
Steam	45025	Vulcan Foundry	4-6-0
Diesel	517	Andrew Barclay	0-4-0
Diesel	27549	North British	0-4-0
Diesel	260756	Ruston & Hornsby	0-4-0
Diesel	265618	Ruston & Hornsby	0-4-0
Diesel	277V	Thomas Hill	4wDH
Diesel	D2774	North British	D2/10
Diesel	D3605	British Railways	Class 08
Diesel	D5302	BRCW	Class 26
Diesel	D5325	BRCW	Class 26

Diesel	D5394	BRCW	Class 27
Diesel	D5862	Brush Traction	Class 31
Diesel	37674	English Electric	Class 37
DMU	51990, 52008 & 52030	British Railways	Class 107
DMU	56047	British Railways	Class 114
DMU	51367, 51402 & 59511	Pressed Steel	Class 117

Attractions

The railway has a variety of heritage rolling stock and travels through the spectacular Scottish highland scenery. The shops at the railway's three stations include a selection of second-hand railway books and magazines. Aviemore is in the Monadhliath and Cairngorm mountain region and Boat of Garten has a golf and tennis club. The RSPB observation hide at the Osprey Centre is 1.5 miles from the station. There are many walks and cycle routes in the area, most notably the Speyside Way which follows much of the former railway line and the Keith & Dufftown Railway is at the northern end of this, approximately 33 miles away.

Special Events

Events that usually take place on the railway include:

Afternoon tea, traditional lunch and evening dining trains.
Summer Event during July.
Halloween Event.
Santa Express and Mince Pie Specials during December.

▲ Only a few months after it had moved to the Strathspey Railway, 37674 rests on the rear of the 09.15 Aviemore–Dulnain Bridge, with 31327 just visible on the front of the train. **Andy Chard**

▲ On 12 March 2022, LMS Class 2MT 2-6-0 46512 passes Lower Lackgie with a train bound for Aviemore on the Strathspey Railway.   **Gordon Edgar**

▼ Crewe Heritage Centre is the home of the preserved electric Advanced Passenger Train (APT) 370003, which is seen on display there on 16 July 2022.   **Steve Donald**

NORTHERN ENGLAND

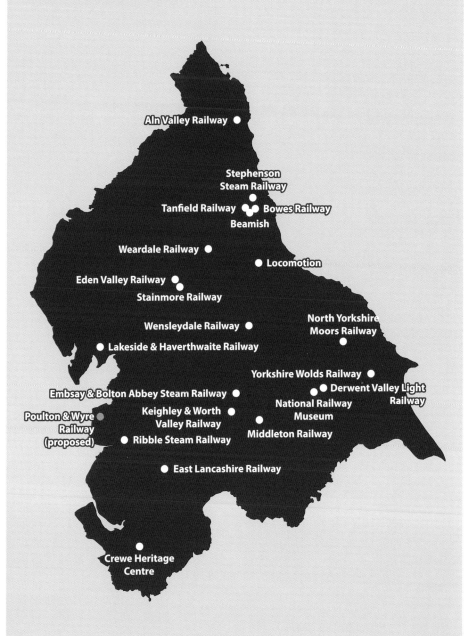

Aln Valley Railway

Stephenson Steam Railway

Tanfield Railway Bowes Railway

Beamish

Weardale Railway

Locomotion

Eden Valley Railway

Stainmore Railway

Wensleydale Railway

North Yorkshire Moors Railway

Lakeside & Haverthwaite Railway

Yorkshire Wolds Railway

Embsay & Bolton Abbey Steam Railway

Derwent Valley Light Railway

National Railway Museum

Poulton & Wyre Railway (proposed)

Keighley & Worth Valley Railway

Ribble Steam Railway

Middleton Railway

East Lancashire Railway

Crewe Heritage Centre

Region 2 – Northern England

Aln Valley Railway

Introduction and History

The 2.75-mile branch line from Alnmouth to Alnwick opened in 1850 and remained in use for well over a century, until it closed to both passenger and freight traffic in 1968. The Aln Valley Railway was established during the 1990s and built a new station and base at the Lionheart site. This is on the outskirts of Alnwick, as the trackbed nearer the town centre has been built upon. The first passenger trains operated on a short stretch of track in 2013, which was then increased to a length of three quarters of a mile. In 2019 it was further extended by another half mile to a new eastern terminus, Greenrigg Halt, although the coronavirus pandemic delayed its opening until 2021. More than half of the branch has now been reinstated and works to extend it further are ongoing.

Contact Details

Website: www.alnvalleyrailway.co.uk
Tel: 0300 030 3311
Email: getintouch@alnvalleyrailway.co.uk
Address: Lionheart Railway Station, Lionheart Enterprise Park, Alnwick, NE66 2EZ.

Transport Links

By Rail: Alnmouth Railway Station is four and a half miles from Lionheart by road.
By Road: Ample parking is available at the Lionheart site (NE66 2HT), which is close to the A1 and Alnwick town centre. Parking is free, although a voluntary contribution may be requested during special events.
By Bike: There is a cycle route from the centre of Alnwick to the nearby Lionheart Enterprise Park.

Opening Times

The railway usually operates on Saturdays, Sundays and Bank Holidays from April to September, with occasional exceptions, plus on selected other dates, including during December.

Line Mileage and Journey Time

0.00   Alnwick Lionheart
1.25   Greenrigg Halt

A round trip on the line takes about half an hour.

Stock List

Type	Number	Builder	Details
Steam	3799 PENICUIK	Hawthorn Leslie	0-4-0ST
Steam	MERLIN (1967)	Peckett	0-4-0ST
Steam	48 (WD 75015)	Hunslet	0-6-0ST
Steam	60 (3686)	Hunslet	0-6-0ST
Steam	9 RICHBORO	Hudswell Clarke	0-6-0T
Steam	20 (1731)	Hudswell Clarke	0-6-0T
Diesel	20/110/711 (615)	Andrew Barclay	0-6-0
Diesel	8199	Drewry	0-6-0
Diesel	12088	British Railways	Class 11
DMU	144004 (55804 & 55827)	Alexander/BREL	Class 144
DMU	144016 (55816, 55852 & 55839)	Alexander/BREL	Class 144

Attractions

The 7¼ inch- gauge Go Loco Miniature Railway at Alnwick Lionheart opened in 2022. The Alnwick site also has a museum with photographs and artefacts from the branch line's history, a café, shop, children's playground, model railway and some restored vintage carriages. Driving Experiences are available using diesel locomotives. Alnwick has a number of attractions including Alnwick Castle and other nearby destinations include Holy Island, Dunstanburgh Castle and Craster, home of the kipper.

Special Events
Events that usually take place on the railway include:

Easter Steam Weekend and Easter Bunny Hunt.
Music Festival during May.
Classic & Vintage Vehicles Weekend during June.
1940s Weekend during July.
Teddy Bears' Picnic during August.
Model Rail Exhibition during September.
Halloween Ghost Trains.
Santa Specials and Mince Pie Specials during December.

Beamish: The Living Museum of the North

Introduction and History
Beamish is a 350-acre site with a large variety of interactive displays of industrial life through Georgian, Victorian, Edwardian and 20th century England. The museum opened on its current site in 1972 and has a variety of original and replica buildings, a working tramway and standard and narrow gauge railways. The standard gauge line has a railway station, which was relocated from Rowley, County Durham and this was reopened by poet Sir John Betjeman in 1976. After more than four decades of operation, renewal works are being carried out and the NER branch line (as the standard gauge line is known) is not expected to open during 2023. There are however, several other rail-related attractions, including the Pockerley Wagonway, a narrow gauge railway and a colliery railway.

Contact Details
Website: www.beamish.org.uk
Tel: 0191 370 4000
Email: museum@beamish.org.uk
Address: Beamish Museum, Regional Resource Centre, Beamish, County Durham, DH9 0RG.

Transport Links
By Rail: Chester-le-Street is the nearest railway station and is five miles away.
By Road: Ample car parking is available at the museum.

Opening Times
The Museum usually opens 10.00–16.00 every day except Christmas Day and Boxing Day. The wagonway, narrow gauge line and colliery railway operate on selected days – please check the website or the transport blog at www.beamishtransportonline.co.uk for the latest information.

Line Mileage and Journey Time
The standard gauge railway from Rowley station is approximately one sixth of a mile and the journey time is relatively short.

Stock List

Type	Number	Builder	Details
Steam	"Puffing Billy" (replica)	Alan Keef	0-4-0G
Steam	7006 "Roker"	Robert Stephenson & Hawthorns	0-4-0CT
Steam	1370	Peckett	0-4-0ST
Steam	South Durham Malleable No. 5	South Durham Steel & Iron	0-4-0ST
Steam	18	Stephen Lewin	0-4-0ST
Steam	1	Head Wrightson	0-4-0VBGT
Steam	17	Head Wrightson	0-4-0VBT
Steam	"Steam Elephant" (replica)	Alan Keef	0-6-0
Steam	1532 NEWCASTLE	Manning Wardle	0-6-0ST
Steam	1	Black Hawthorn	2-4-0CT

Attractions
The museum recently opened the first phase of its 1950s town, complete with a period chip shop, Italian café, artist's house and a hairdresser; this will be enlarged with more features to be added in 2024. A new trolleybus route is also planned, although no date has been set for its

opening. The site also includes an 1820s landscape, a 1900s town, a pit village, colliery and a 1940s farm. There is a 1.5-mile working tramway and the railway has an 1850 goods shed, an 1896 signal box, a wrought iron footbridge and a coal drop. At certain times, themed visitor experiences are available for an additional charge and these include the Tram Driving Experience. A bus service operates around the site and this includes an adapted bus for wheelchair users. Nearby heritage railways include the Tanfield Railway (3 miles away), Bowes Railway (8 miles) and Stephenson Steam Railway (16 miles). The cities of Newcastle and Sunderland are 10 and 14 miles from Beamish respectively.

Special Events
1–2 April 2023: Spring Steam Gala

Seasonal events take place at Easter, Halloween and Christmas.

Bowes Railway

Introduction and History
The first incarnation of what became Bowes Railway was a wooden horse-drawn wagonway built during the 1720s to carry coal from the Durham Coalfield to the River Wear. When the standard gauge railway opened in 1826, it was one of the world's first railways. It was 15 miles long and carried coal to the River Tyne at Jarrow. Trains were locomotive-hauled at each end of the railway and the six-mile middle section was rope-worked, as this included some very steep gradients. Most of the line was closed between 1968 and 1974 and the final 3.5-mile section was operated by the National Coal Board until 1974. The original part of the railway which dates from 1826 was acquired for preservation in 1976. In 2002 Bowes Railway was granted museum status and the site is now registered with Historic England as a Scheduled Ancient Monument. Two other parts of the original Bowes Railway have been preserved; Springwell Bankfoot Loco Shed, which is the home of North East Bus Preservation Society and Marley Hill Shed and Yard, which are part of nearby Tanfield Railway. Bowes Railway is now the only remaining standard gauge rope hauled railway in the world.

Contact Details
Website: www.bowesrailway.uk
Tel: 0191 416 1847
Email: Written enquiries can be made from the website.
Address: Bowes Railway, Springwell Road, Gateshead, NE9 7QJ.

Transport Links
By Rail: Bowes Railway is 2.5 miles from Heworth Metro station and 4 miles from Newcastle Central.
By Road: Car parking is available at Bowes Railway (NE9 7QJ).

Opening Times
The opening times are 10.00–16.00 on Thursdays and 11.00–1600 on Fridays and Saturdays. Guided tours are available on request for no additional charge.

Line Mileage and Journey Time
0.00   Springwell Halt
1.00   Wrekenton

The Springwell to Wrekenton section can carry passengers and a return journey takes about 30 minutes. The railway line also continues north to the start of Springwell Incline and south to the rope hauling house at Blackham's Hill. Passenger and goods demonstration trains are not currently operating, however it is hoped that they will return soon.

Stock List

Type	Number	Builder	Details
Steam	22	Andrew Barclay	0-4-0ST
Steam	WST	Andrew Barclay	0-4-0ST
Diesel	PINKY	Ruston & Hornsby	0-4-0DH
Diesel	PERKY	Ruston & Hornsby	0-4-0DH
Diesel	101	Hibberd	0-4-0DM
Diesel	6263	Hunslet	0-4-0
Diesel	476140	Ruston & Hornsby	0-4-0

Attractions

The standard gauge rope-hauled railway is unique. It has some well-preserved early features designed by George Stephenson, including the "Kip and Dish" and the brake cabin at the top of Springwell Bank. The colliery yard has a varied collection of more than 40 railway wagons built between the 1880s and 1960s, including the restored wagon in which the Queen Mother travelled in 1976. The restored colliery workshops, which have been in use since 1826, house a museum with many exhibits, including narrow gauge mining locomotives, historic machines including an operational Fairbairn Naylor MacPherson & Co wheel lathe and an operational blacksmith's workshop. The Bowes Model Railway Club operate the model railway on selected dates and there is a tea room and gift shop. Nearby transport-themed attractions include the Tanfield Railway, Beamish and the North-East Land, Sea & Air Museum. Newcastle, Sunderland and the coast are all only a few miles away.

Special Events

Events that usually take place on the railway include:

1950s & 1960s lunch.
Children's school summer holiday event.
Fireworks event in November.
Christmas themed event in December.

▲ 08528 carries out a shunting demonstration at the Derwent Valley Light Railway's Murton Park base on 27 June 2021.   **Andy Chard**

Crewe Heritage Centre

Introduction and History

Crewe Heritage Centre opened in 1987 on the site of the railway yard immediately north of Crewe station, at the point where the Chester line and West Coast Main Line split. The site includes Crewe North Junction signal box, which was preserved after it was decommissioned in 1985, complete with a viewing balcony which is ideal for watching passing trains. A main line rail connection allows visiting steam and diesel locomotives and some of the home-based locomotives to travel to other sites.

Contact Details

Website: www.crewehc.org
Tel: 01270 212130
Email: Written enquiries can be made via the website.
Address: The Crewe Heritage Centre Trust Ltd, Vernon Way, Crewe, Cheshire, CW1 2DB.

Transport Links

By Rail: The Heritage Centre is less than a mile from Crewe railway station.
By Road: Car parking is available on site (CW1 2DB).

Opening Times

The Centre opens 10.00–16.30 (last admission 15.30) on Saturdays, Sundays and Bank Holidays from April to October inclusive.

Line Mileage and Journey Time

There are a variety of standard gauge lines within the centre and part of one of these is sometimes used for giving diesel-hauled brake van rides.

Stock List

Type	Number	Builder	Details
Electric	86622	English Electric	Class 86
Electric	87035	BREL	Class 87
Electric	91120	BREL	Class 91
Diesel	10007	Sentinel	0-4-0
Diesel	132C	Thomas Hill	0-4-0DH
Diesel	03073	British Railways	Class 03
Diesel	37108	English Electric	Class 37
Diesel	43018	British Railways	Class 43
Diesel	43081	British Railways	Class 43
DMU	56356	Metropolitan Cammell	Class 101
EMU	48103, 48106, 48404, 48602, 48603, 49002, 49006	BREL	Class 370

Attractions

Several new exhibits have recently arrived including two HST power cars, a Class 37, a Class 86 and a Class 91 which is on long-term loan. The centre is also home to one of the two remaining Advanced Passenger Trains (APT). There are three complete signal boxes, with information on how they were used and the viewing platform gives direct views of trains travelling through Crewe. There is also a 7¼ inch gauge miniature railway which visitors can ride on. The region is also home to Crewe's Lyceum Theatre, Crewe Hall, Nantwich, Tatton Park and Jodrell Bank.

Special Events

Rail-themed activities and events are held at the centre and in addition, third party organised events take place, such as toy & train collectors fairs, beer festivals and music themed events.

Derwent Valley Light Railway

Introduction and History

Tho railway from York Layerthorpe to Cliff Common near Selby opened in 1913 as a light railway, with lower speed limits and weight limits from its beginning. Regular passenger services were withdrawn as early as 1926, although passenger specials continued to use the route occasionally. The line carried a variety of local goods, some via the railway connection to the Rowntree factory in York. The DVLR was one of the few lines to remain in private ownership both after the 1923 Grouping and the formation of British Railways in 1948. The southern section between Wheldrake and Cliff Common closed in 1964, after the main line connection near Selby had been lost and levels of traffic were declining. Seasonal passenger steam trains returned to the northern section between 1977 and 1979, but after a further decline in use, the remainder of the railway closed in 1981 and the track was later lifted. In 1982 the Yorkshire Farming Museum acquired the Murton Park site, which included part of the railway. In the following years, the DVLR Society relaid a section of track and built the new Murton Park station. The first trains in preservation ran in 1992.

Contact Details

Website: www.dvlr.org.uk
Tel: 01904 489966
Email: info@dvlr.org.uk
Address: Derwent Valley Light Railway, Murton Park, Murton Lane, Murton, York, YO19 5UF.

Transport Links

By Rail: Thc nearest station is York, which is four miles away.
By Road: Free parking is available at Murton Park (YO19 5UF), chargeable only during occasional special events.

Opening Times

Trains operate from Murton Park station on Sundays and Bank Holidays from April until October, as well as on selected other dates and during December for Santa Specials. Entry to the railway is with a ticket to the Murton Park complex, which comprises of the Derwent Valley Light Railway and Yorkshire Museum of Farming.

Line Mileage and Journey Time

0.00   Murton Park
0.40   Line end

A return journey takes approximately 20 minutes.

Stock List

Type	Number	Builder	Details
Steam	E B WILSON (1795)	Manning Wardle	0-4-0ST
Diesel	2 (421419)	Ruston & Hornsby	4wDM
Diesel	3 KEN COOKE (441934)	Ruston & Hornsby	4wDM
Diesel	JIM (417892)	Ruston & Hornsby	4wDM
Diesel	OCTAVIUS ATKINSON (466630)	Ruston & Hornsby	4wDM
Diesel	BRITISH SUGAR YORK (327964)	Ruston & Hornsby	0-4-0DM
Diesel	16	Drewry	0-4-0DM
Diesel	70037	Drewry	0-4-0DM
Diesel	4100005 CHURCHILL	Fowler	0-4-0
Diesel	D2245	Robert Stephenson & Hawthorns	Class 04
Diesel	08528	British Railways	Class 08

Attractions

The operational signal box at Murton Park was transferred from Muston near Filey and the station building was transferred from Wheldrake and rebuilt at Murton Park. There is a museum and shop at the Murton Park base. Railway themed attractions include pump trolley experiences, driving experiences and a signal box experience. The adjacent Yorkshire Museum of Farming has a variety of animals, exhibits, a nature trail and a reconstructed Viking village. The Roman city of York is four miles from Murton Park and has many attractions including the National Railway Museum, the City Walls, The Shambles and York Minster.

Special Events

A variety of events are held at the Murton Park site through the year, with seasonal Easter and Christmas-themed events, plus a variety of historical and family orientated activities.

East Lancashire Railway

Introduction and History

The railway between Heywood and Bury opened in 1841. The line between Clifton Junction, Bury and Rawtenstall then opened in 1846 and was extended north to Bacup in 1852. The line north of Rawtenstall to Bacup closed in 1966; passenger services between Heywood and Bury were withdrawn in 1970 and between Bury and Rawtenstall in 1972. Freight trains from Bury to Rawtenstall continued until 1980, when British Rail closed Bury Bolton Street station and relocated the terminus of the line from Manchester to Bury Interchange. The route from Manchester to Bury used third rail electric multiple units until 1992, when these were superseded by Metrolink trams. In 1972 the ELR Preservation Society took possession of the former Castlecroft Goods Shed immediately north of Bolton Street station. After the main line electric services to Manchester Victoria moved to Bury Interchange in 1980, Bolton Street station became the railway's base. Heritage trains to Ramsbottom began in 1987, were extended to Rawtenstall in 1991 and to Heywood in 2003, after a steeply graded line was built across the Metrolink line to Bury. The railway remains connected to the main line network between Heywood and Castleton and the ELR plans to extend to a new station at Castleton, which would increase its length by a further 1.5 miles.

▲ Class 105 vehicles 56121 & 51485 pause at Ramsbottom with the 16.50 Rawtenstall–Bury on 12 November 2022.   **Tom McAtee**

Contact Details

Website: www.eastlancsrailway.org.uk
Tel: 0333 320 2830 or 0161 764 7790.
Email: enquiries@eastlancsrailway.org.uk
Address: East Lancashire Railway, Bolton Street Station, Bury, Lancashire, BL9 0EY.

Transport Links

By Rail: Bury Interchange (Metrolink) is less than half a mile away from Bolton Street station. Heywood station is three miles from Castleton railway station by road.
By Road: Parking is available at all stations, however this is subject to charges at Bury (BL9 0EY) and is limited at Ramsbottom (BL0 9AL) and Rawtenstall (BB4 6AG). There is ample free parking at Heywood (OL10 1NH).

Opening Times

Trains operate on Saturdays and Sundays all year round, plus on a large number of weekdays between April and September and during selected weekdays in winter.

Line Mileage and Journey Time

0.00	Heywood
4.00	Bury Bolton Street
5.25	Burrs Country Park
6.50	Summerseat
8.00	Ramsbottom
10.00	Irwell Vale
12.00	Rawtenstall

A return journey takes up to 2 hours 40 minutes, depending on the starting point.

Stock List

Type	Number	Builder	Details
Steam	7164 (7232)	Sentinel	4wVBGT
Steam	1 (1927)	Andrew Barclay	0-4-0ST
Steam	52322	Lancashire & Yorkshire	0-6-0
Steam	752	Beyer Peacock	0-6-0ST
Steam	2890	Hunslet	0-6-0ST
Steam	32 (680)	Hudswell Clarke	0-6-0T
Steam	47298	Hunslet	0-6-0T
Steam	47324	North British	0-6-0T
Steam	5643	GWR	0-6-2T
Steam	42859	LMS	2-6-0
Steam	46428	British Railways	2-6-0
Steam	13065	LMS	2-6-0
Steam	80097	British Railways	2-6-4T
Steam	3855	GWR	2-8-0
Steam	7229	GWR	2-8-2T
Steam	45212	Armstrong Whitworth	4-6-0
Steam	45337	Armstrong Whitworth	4-6-0
Steam	45407	Armstrong Whitworth	4-6-0
Steam	44871	LMS	4-6-0
Steam	34092	British Railways	4-6-2
Diesel	3438	Hibberd	4wDM
Diesel	9009	Simplex	4wDM
Diesel	400 Bardon	Andrew Barclay	0-4-0DM
Diesel	4002	Hudswell Clarke	0-6-0
Diesel	D2956	Andrew Barclay	Class 01
Diesel	D2062	British Railways	Class 03
Diesel	07013	Ruston & Hornsby	Class 07
Diesel	08164	British Railways	Class 08
Diesel	08479	British Railways	Class 08
Diesel	08944	British Railways	Class 08
Diesel	09024	British Railways	Class 09
Diesel	D9502	British Railways	Class 14
Diesel	D9531	British Railways	Class 14

Diesel	D8233	British Thomson-Houston	Class 15
Diesel	D5054	British Railways	Class 24
Diesel	D7629	Beyer Peacock	Class 25
Diesel	D5705	Metropolitan Vickers	Class 28
Diesel	6536	BRCW	Class 33
Diesel	33046	BRCW	Class 33
Diesel	33109	BRCW	Class 33
Diesel	D7076	Beyer Peacock	Class 35
Diesel	37109	English Electric	Class 37
Diesel	40135	English Electric	Class 40
Diesel	D832	British Railways	Class 42
Diesel	45108	British Railways	Class 45
Diesel	45135	British Railways	Class 45
Diesel	47765	British Railways	Class 47
Diesel	50015	English Electric	Class 50
Diesel	D1041	British Railways	Class 52
Diesel	56006	Electroputere	Class 56
DMU	50437, 50455, 50494, 50517, 59137 & 59228	BRCW	Class 104
DMU	51485 & 56121	Cravens	Class 105
DMU	51813, 51842 & 59701	BRCW	Class 110
DMU	144009 (55809 & 55832)	Alexander/BREL	Class 144
DMU	144010 (55810 & 55833)	Alexander/BREL	Class 144
DMU	56289	Pressed Steel	Class 121
DMU	55001	GRCW	Class 122
EMU	70549	British Railways	Class 411
EMU	65451 & 77172	British Railways	Class 504

Attractions

The ELR has one of the largest and most varied collections of rolling stock at a heritage railway. Bury Transport Museum is adjacent to Bolton Street station. The railway offers Real Ale Trail guided tours, with information on the history of the area; platform 2 at Bolton Street is home to The Trackside real ale pub and Buffer Stops Bar is part of Rawtenstall station. Photography, steam and diesel driving experiences are available. Attractions in the area include Bury Art Museum, Bury's Fusilier Museum, Helmshore Mills Textile Museum, Irwell Sculpture Trail, Greater Manchester Museum of Transport, The Whitaker Museum & Art Gallery and Ski Rossendale.

Special Events

Events take place on the railway all year round and these include:

1940s Weekend (usually in May).
A variety of steam, diesel and DMU galas.
Halloween Ghost Trains.
Santa Specials and Mince Pie specials during December.
In addition, there are a large variety of on-board events including dining experiences, wine & gin tasting services and murder mystery trains.

Eden Valley Railway

Introduction and History
The railway between Clifton near Penrith and Kirkby Stephen via Warcop opened in 1862, forming a through route across the Pennines to Bishop Auckland and Darlington. Closure was proposed in 1959 and following a battle resisting this, passenger traffic ended in 1962, when the Appleby to Clifton section closed. The line south of Warcop closed in 1974 when quarry traffic ended and after Ministry of Defence trains ceased in 1989, the line south to Warcop fell into disuse. The Eden Valley Railway Society formed in 1995; the first brake van rides were provided in 2003 and regular services began in 2006. The railway's operational line has gradually been extended north from its Warcop base and there are plans to extend it a further three miles to Appleby, giving a northern terminus near to Appleby's main line station.

Contact Details
Website: www.evr-cumbria.org.uk
Tel: 01768 342309
Email: enquiries@evr-cumbria.org.uk
Address: Eden Valley Railway, Warcop Station, Warcop, Appleby, Cumbria, CA16 6PR.

Transport Links
By Rail: Appleby is the nearest railway station and is six miles from the Warcop site.
By Road: Free parking is available at Warcop (CA16 6PR), which is the only site with public access.

Opening Times
Trains operate 11.00–16.00 on Sundays and most Bank Holidays between April and October, plus on selected weekdays (predominantly Tuesdays & Wednesdays) during June, July and August.

Line Mileage and Journey Time
0.00   Warcop
2.25   Operational line end

A return journey takes approximately 25 minutes.

There is also a separate line which runs south from Warcop for one third of a mile. This can only be travelled on as part of a Driver for a Fiver experience (see below).

Stock List

Type	Number	Builder	Details
Diesel	2181	Drewry	0-4-0
Diesel	21	Fowler	0-4-0
Diesel	ND3815 (2389)	Hunslet	0-4-0
Diesel	130c	Thomas Hill	0-4-0
Diesel	8343	Robert Stephenson & Hawthorns	0-6-0
Diesel	37042	English Electric	Class 37
Diesel	47799	British Railways	Class 47
DEMU	60108, 60658 & 60808	British Railways	Class 205
EMU	61798, 61799, 70229 & 70354	British Railways	Class 411
EMU	61804, 61805, 70539 & 70607	British Railways	Class 411
EMU	68003, 68005 & 68010	British Railways	Class 419
EMU	69335	BREL	Class 420

Attractions
The railway has a varied collection of operational rolling stock, including electric vehicles, main line diesel and shunting locomotives. "Driver for a Fiver" experiences using a diesel shunter (usually number 21) are available on Sundays during the operating season (subject to staff availability, so please check before travelling for this). There is a second-hand book shop with railway books, tickets and many non-railway books. There are two model railways of different gauges (N and O) and a small museum within the signal box, which has many artefacts from the railway's past. Hot drinks and light snacks are also available. The Stainmore Railway at Kirkby Stephen is eight miles away, making a combined visit possible on a day when both sites are open. The railway is located between the Yorkshire Dales National Park, the Lake District and the North Pennines (an Area of Outstanding Natural Beauty), giving many opportunities to explore the landscape of northern England.

Embsay & Bolton Abbey Steam Railway

Introduction and History

The railway between Skipton and Ilkley opened in 1888 and after declining use, it was closed by British Rail in 1965. The first preservation group formed in 1968, initially hoping to preserve the line from Skipton to Grassington, which deviated from the line to Bolton Abbey and Ilkley at Embsay Junction. The majority of the Grassington branch has survived and continues to be used today by freight trains to Rylstone and the group instead acquired Embsay station during the early 1970s. The first section of railway from Embsay opened to the public in 1981 and this was extended to Holywell Halt in 1987 and to Bolton Abbey in 1997. There are long-term aims to extend the railway further east to Addingham and to reconnect to the main line network at Embsay Junction, which would allow through running between Bolton Abbey and Skipton.

Contact Details

Website: www.embsayboltonabbeyrailway.org.uk
Tel: 01756 710614
Email: office@ebar.org.uk
Address: Bolton Abbey Station, Skipton, North Yorkshire, BD23 6AF.

Transport Links

By Rail: The nearest station is Skipton, which is two miles from Embsay.
By Road: There is ample parking at Bolton Abbey (BD23 6AF) and Embsay (BD23 6QX) stations.

Opening Times

Trains operate on most Saturdays, Sundays and Bank Holidays through the year, plus Tuesdays and selected other weekdays between April and October and every day during August.

Line Mileage and Journey Time

0.00   Bolton Abbey
2.25   Holywell Halt
3.50   Embsay
4.00   Embsay Junction line end (not regularly used)

A return journey takes about one hour.

Stock List

Type	Number	Builder	Details
Steam	22 (2320)	Andrew Barclay	0-4-0ST
Steam	YORK No.1 (2474)	Yorkshire Engine Co.	0-4-0ST
Steam	7661	Robert Stephenson & Hawthorns	0-4-0ST
Steam	1821	Hudswell Clarke	0-6-0ST
Steam	SLOUGH ESTATES No. 5	Hudswell Clarke	0-6-0ST
Steam	1440	Hunslet	0-6-0ST
Steam	2414	Hunslet	0-6-0ST
Steam	3788	Hunslet	0-6-0ST
Steam	WD194 (3794)	Hunslet	0-6-0ST
Steam	7 BEATRICE	Hunslet	0-6-0ST
Steam	8 (3776)	Hunslet	0-6-0ST
Steam	PRIMROSE No.2	Hunslet	0-6-0ST
Steam	S134 WHELDALE	Hunslet	0-6-0ST
Steam	7086	Robert Stephenson & Hawthorns	0-6-0ST
Diesel	1 (440)	Andrew Barclay	0-4-0
Diesel	The Bug/Clockwork Orange	Baguley	0-4-0
Diesel	4200003	Fowler	0-4-0
Diesel	H.W. Robinson (4100003)	Fowler	0-4-0
Diesel	887	Ruston & Hornsby	0-4-0
Diesel	36 (D1037)	Hudswell Clarke	0-6-0
Diesel	D2078	British Railways	Class 03
Diesel	D2203	Vulcan Foundry	Class 04
Diesel	08054	British Railways	Class 08
Diesel	08773	British Railways	Class 08
Diesel	38	British Railways	Class 14

Diesel	D8110	English Electric	Class 20
Diesel	31119	Brush Traction	Class 31
Diesel	D5600	Brush Traction	Class 31
Diesel	37294	English Electric	Class 37
Diesel	D1524	Brush Traction	Class 47
DMU	3170	NER	Autocar
DMU	142094 (55744 & 55790)	BREL/Leyland	Class 142

Attractions

The North Eastern Railway Autocar operates on the railway; after being restored, this unique vehicle returned to service during 2019 and is now almost 120 years old. Trains with a variety of food and drink related themes operate (see events below), some of which feature Queen Victoria's Golden Jubilee Saloon and the LNWR Director's saloon. Bolton Abbey station is home to the Hambleton Valley Miniature Railway, a signal box display which can be accessed when staff are present, and a wetland area. Embsay station has a gift shop, a well-stocked railway bookshop, a coffee shop and picnic area. The site of Bolton Abbey, the priory and River Wharfe are about one and a half miles from Bolton Abbey station. The market town of Skipton is nearby, where Skipton Castle, canal boat trips and Craven Museum and Gallery can be found. The Keighley & Worth Valley Railway (see below) is relatively close and the area is on the edge of the Yorkshire Dales National Park.

Special Events

11 March 2023: The Great Gatsby Murder Mystery.
10 & 11 June and 23 & 24 September 2023: A Taste of Faulty Towers.
15 July 2023: The Sherlock Holmes Whodunit
7 October 2023: Pirate Murder Mystery

Further events that usually take place on the railway include:

A large variety of dining trains.
Mother & Father's Day events.
Diesel Days.
Wizard Express trains during October.
Santa Trains during December.

▲ This atmospheric view captures Hudswell Clarke 0-6-0ST "ILLINGWORTH" heading towards Embsay on the Embsay & Bolton Abbey Railway on 15 February 2022. **Tom Marshall**

Keighley & Worth Valley Railway

Introduction and History
The steeply graded branch line from Keighley to Oxenhope, which follows the course of the River Worth, opened in 1867. Passenger services ceased in 1961 and freight ended in 1962. Shortly after this, a group of local people and rail enthusiasts formed a preservation society and purchased the line from British Railways, with the cost being paid in instalments over a 25-year period. The line reopened to passengers in 1968, making it one of the pioneers of railway preservation. The 1970 film The Railway Children and the 2022 sequel were both filmed on the railway, with Oakworth station being used as a film set. The first film greatly raised the profile and popularity of the line, which at the time was one of a very small number of operational heritage railways. The K&WVR remains connected to the national network at Keighley, where the station has two main line and two K&WVR platforms. Occasional main line charter trains travel through to Oxenhope, such as when the railway celebrated its 50th anniversary in 2018.

Contact Details
Website: www.kwvr.co.uk
Tel: 01535 645214
Email: admin@kwvr.co.uk
Address: Keighley & Worth Valley Railway, The Railway Station, Haworth, West Yorkshire, BD22 8NJ.

Transport Links
By Rail: Main line connection at Keighley; just walk over the footbridge.
By Road: Parking is available at all stations except Damems, which it is not recommended to drive to, as the access road is unmade. All car parks are free, except Haworth (BD22 8NJ) which is pay and display. Keighley station car park (BD21 4HP) can be very busy Monday–Saturday as it is shared with the main line station. Ingrow West (BD21 5AX) and Oxenhope (BD22 9LB) have large free car parks.

Opening Times
Trains operate during weekends all year round, on selected weekdays throughout the year and daily from June to August and during school holidays.

Line Mileage and Journey Time
0.00	Keighley
1.25	Ingrow West
2.00	Damems
2.25	Oakworth
3.50	Haworth
4.75	Oxenhope

A return journey takes about 1 hour 15 minutes.

Stock List
Type	Number	Builder	Details
Steam	7069	Robert Stephenson & Hawthorns	0-4-0CT
Steam	TINY (2258)	Andrew Barclay	0-4-0ST
Steam	LORD MAYOR	Hudswell Clarke	0-4-0ST
Steam	51218	Lancashire & Yorkshire	0-4-0ST
Steam	957	Beyer Peacock	0-6-0
Steam	43924	Midland Railway	0-6-0
Steam	5775	GWR	0-6-0PT
Steam	118	Hudswell Clarke	0-6-0ST
Steam	1704	Hudswell Clarke	0-6-0ST
Steam	31	Hudswell Clarke	0-6-0T
Steam	47279	Vulcan Foundry	0-6-0T
Steam	1054	LNWR	0-6-2T
Steam	85	Neilson Reid	0-6-2T
Steam	78022	British Railways	2-6-0
Steam	41241	British Railways	2-6-2T
Steam	80002	British Railways	2-6-4T

▲ English Electric "Thumper" 205009 stands at the Eden Valley Railway's Warcop station on 31 July 2022. **Alisdair Anderson**

▼ On 19 March 2022, the 123-year-old Neilson Reid 0-6-2T No. 85 hauls a train over Mytholmes Viaduct on the Keighley & Worth Valley Railway. **Tom Marshall / K&WVR**

Steam	48431	GWR	2-8-0
Steam	5820	Lima Locomotive Co.	2-8-0
Steam	90733	Vulcan Foundry	2-8-0
Steam	75078	British Railways	4-6-0
Steam	45596	North British	4-6-0
Diesel	431763	Ruston & Hornsby	0-4-0
Diesel	23 MERLIN	Hudswell Clarke	0-6-0
Diesel	D2511	Hudswell Clarke	0-6-0
Diesel	32 HUSKISSON	Hunslet	0-6-0
Diesel	08266	British Railways	Class 08
Diesel	08993	British Railways	Class 08
Diesel	20031	English Electric	Class 20
Diesel	25059	British Railways	Class 25
Diesel	37075	English Electric	Class 37
Diesel	D0226 VULCAN	English Electric	Experimental 0-6-0
DMU	51189 & 51803	Metropolitan Cammell	Class 101
DMU	50928 & 51565	British Railways	Class 108
DMU	143625 (55666 & 55691)	Alexander/Barclay	Class 143
DMU	144011 (55811 & 55834)	Alexander/BREL	Class 144
DMU	79962 & 79964	Waggon und Maschinenbau	Railbus

Attractions

The K&WVR has some of the best preserved Victorian station buildings on a British heritage railway. Railstory at Ingrow contains two accredited museums, The Vintage Carriages Trust's Carriage Works and the Bahamas Locomotive Society's "Engine Shed", each showcasing different areas of railway interest. Haworth is the railway's hub, with the main locomotive shed and workshop, a model railway and a gift shop at the station. The Exhibition Shed at Oxenhope allows visitors to see a variety of locomotives. Within reach from the railway are the Bronte Parsonage in Haworth, Saltaire, Bingley Five Rise Locks, the city of Bradford and the Embsay & Bolton Abbey Steam Railway.

Special Events

May 2023: Flying Scotsman Centenary.
June 2023: Diesel Gala.
June & July 2023: Vintage Trains
October 2023: Beer & Music Festival

Additional events that usually take place on the railway include:

Steam and Diesel Galas.
Pullman Dining Experience trains.
Carol Service, Elf Express and Mince Pie Specials during December.

Lakeside & Haverthwaite Railway

Introduction and History

The eight-mile branch from Ulverston to Lakeside on the banks of Lake Windermere opened in 1869. Initially it predominantly carried freight, including iron ore, sulphur and coal to power the steam vessels that worked on the lake. Freight traffic declined through the 20th century and instead, the line was increasingly used by holidaymakers travelling to the Lake District. During the 1930s and 1940s passenger services were suspended for a number of long periods. The railway closed to passengers in 1965 and the final freight and enthusiast specials ran in 1967. In the same year, a group of enthusiasts formed The Lakeside Railway Society and began negotiations with British Rail to acquire the line. The trackbed was purchased in 1970; however, improvements to the A590 meant that the southern section could not be saved and its track was lifted in 1971. The line reopened as heritage railway in 1973 and trains continue to connect with cruises on Lake Windermere, as they first did in 1869.

Contact Details

Website: www.lakesiderailway.co.uk
Tel: 01539 531594
Email: info@lakesiderailway.co.uk
Address: Haverthwaite Railway Station, Near Ulverston, Cumbria, LA12 8AL.

Transport Links
By Rail: Ulverston and Cark railway stations are both six miles from Haverthwaite.
By Road: Car parking is available at Haverthwaite station (LA12 8AL).
By Boat: Windermere Lake Cruises operate on most days and some services connect with L&HR trains. Please check the timetable before travelling.

Opening Times
Trains operate from the beginning of April to the end of October and on selected dates during December. Haverthwaite Station Tea Room opens 10.00–16.00 Monday to Fridays through the year.

Line Mileage and Journey Time
0.00   Haverthwaite
2.00   Newby Bridge
3.00   Lakeside

A return journey takes at least half an hour.

Stock List

Type	Number	Builder	Details
Steam	2333 DAVID	Andrew Barclay	0-4-0ST
Steam	2682	Bagnall	0-6-0ST
Steam	2996 VICTOR	Bagnall	0-6-0ST
Steam	3698 REPULSE	Hunslet	0-6-0ST
Steam	No. 14 (1245)	Andrew Barclay	0-6-0T
Steam	46441	British Railways	2-6-0
Steam	42073	British Railways	2-6-4T
Steam	42085	British Railways	2-6-4T
Diesel	7120	LMS	0-6-0
Diesel	D2072	British Railways	Class 03
Diesel	D2117	British Railways	Class 03
Diesel	20214	English Electric	Class 20
DMU	52071 & 52077	BRCW	Class 110

Attractions
Visitors can look around the engine shed in Haverthwaite and see a selection of steam and diesel locomotives. The station has a picnic area, woodland adventure playground, gift shop and tea room. The Lakeland Motor Museum is a short walk from Haverthwaite station. At Lakeside, the station is adjacent to the Lakes Aquarium and the pier on Lake Windermere, where cruises to Bowness and Ambleside leave. On the opposite shore of Lake Windermere is Fell Foot National Trust Park, with views of Windermere and the fells. The railway is within the Lake District National Park, which has many other attractions and spectacular scenery.

Special Events
Events that usually take place on the railway include:

Easter Egg Weekend.
Local Pensioner Days on selected dates.
Witches & Wizards Week during October.
Tinsel Trains during December.

Locomotion, Shildon

Introduction and History
The railway from Stockton and Darlington arrived at Shildon in 1825, when the line opened to carry coal from the area's collieries. When "Locomotion" No. 1 made its inaugural run on the route in September 1825, it was the world's first steam-hauled passenger train. After this opening day event, the railway carried passengers in horse-drawn coaches, until the horses had been replaced with locomotives by 1833. Locomotion is a railway museum with a short demonstration line that operates on part of the original Stockton and Darlington Railway. The museum opened in 2004 as a satellite site of the National Railway Museum in York and is adjacent to Shildon station, which is served by trains on the branch line between Darlington and Bishop Auckland. In 2022, planning permission was granted for a new exhibition building that will be known as "The New Hall" and when this is complete it will house the largest undercover collection of heritage railway vehicles in the world.

Contact Details
Website: www.locomotion.org.uk
Tel: 0330 058 0058
Email: info@sciencemuseumgroup.ac.uk
Address: Locomotion, Dale Road Industrial Estate, Dale Road, Shildon, DL4 2RE.

Transport Links
By Rail: The nearest station is Shildon, which is a three-minute walk from the museum.
By Road: There is plenty of free parking at the site (DL4 2RE).

Opening Times
The Museum opens 11.00–16.00 (to 17.00 in the summer) on Wednesdays to Sundays. Train rides operate on selected dates through the year (for a small charge), check the website for the dates.

Line Mileage and Journey Time
The railway at Locomotion runs for half a mile and the journey time is relatively short.

Stock List

Type	Number	Builder	Details
Steam	Hetton Lyon	George Stephenson	0-4-0
Steam	LOCOMOTION	George Stephenson	0-4-0
Steam	SANS PAREIL (Replica)	BREL	0-4-0
Steam	SANS PAREIL	Timothy Hackworth	0-4-0
Steam	IMPERIAL No.1	Andrew Barclay	0-4-0F
Steam	JUNO (3850)	Hunslet	0-6-0ST
Steam	44 CONWAY	Kitson	0-6-0ST
Steam	77 (7412)	Robert Stephenson & Hawthorns	0-6-0ST
Steam	49395	LNWR	0-8-0
Steam	790	LNWR	2-4-0
Steam	1621	NER	4-4-0
Steam	5000	LMS	4-6-0
Steam	34051	Southern Railway	4-6-2
Steam	390	Sharp Stewart	4-8-0
Gas Turbine	PC1, PC2, TC1 & TC2	BREL	APT-E
Diesel	D2090	British Railways	Class 03
Diesel	08064	British Railways	Class 08
Diesel	08911	British Railways	Class 08
Diesel	41001	BREL	Class 43 Prototype
Diesel	43102	British Railways	Class 43
Diesel	DELTIC	English Electric	Co-Co
Electric	755	Siemens	Bo
Electric	1 (26500)	Brush Traction	Bo-Bo
Electric	E5001	British Railways	Class 71
DMU	142001 (55542 & 55592)	BREL/Leyland	Class 142
EMU	10656 & 12123	Southern Railway	2 Bil
EMU	11179	Southern Railway	4 Cor

EMU	65617	BRCW	Class 306
EMU	65217 & 65417	Metropolitan Cammell	Class 306
EMU	61275 & 75395	British Railways	Class 414
Battery	1	North Staffordshire Railway	2-A

Attractions

The museum houses a number of unique exhibits from the National Collection, including the prototype gas turbine Advanced Passenger Train, the sole surviving prototype High Speed Train power car and the prototype DELTIC locomotive. Some exhibits periodically move to and from the National Railway Museum's main site in York and other heritage railway sites. There is a shop with a large number of railway related books, gifts and model railway items. The Weardale Railway is only four miles from Locomotion and the Wensleydale Railway is 26 miles away. Other attractions in the area include the National Trust's Moulton Hall, the market town of Darlington and the city of Durham.

▲ With Leeds city centre providing the backdrop, on 14 September 2021, Manning Wardle 0-6-0ST 1601 "MATTHEW MURRAY" ascends the gradient on the Middleton Railway. **Tom Marshall**

Middleton Railway

Introduction and History
The Middleton Railway operates from a site to the south of Leeds city centre with a rich industrial railway history and boasts several world firsts. It was initially a horse-drawn wagonway used to carry coal on wooden tracks and in 1759 it became the first railway to be authorised by an Act of Parliament. It has operated trains every year since, making it the oldest continuously operating railway in the world. It was the site where Matthew Murray's "Salamanca" became the first commercially-operated steam locomotive in 1812, and in June 1960 it became the first standard gauge preserved railway, two months before the Bluebell Railway began operating. To mark the heritage railway's 60th anniversary in 2020, Hunslet diesel 7401 repeated the landmark journey it made exactly six decades earlier, when it departed Moor Road at 16.45. Sadly, this was not open to the public due to coronavirus pandemic restrictions. The line remains connected to the national network at Leeds Midland Road, on the route between Leeds and Woodlesford. There are plans to extend the railway further south into Middleton Park when resources allow.

Contact Details
Website: www.middletonrailway.org.uk
Tel: 07376 744 799 (between 10.00 & 16.00)
Email: info@middletonrailway.org.uk
Address: The Middleton Railway, The Station, Moor Road, Hunslet, Leeds, LS10 2JQ.

Transport Links
By Rail: The nearest railway station is Leeds, which is under two miles away.
By Road: Free car parking is available at Moor Road station (LS10 2JQ).

Opening Times
Trains operate on Saturdays, Sundays & Bank Holiday Mondays from April to September, on Sundays during October and on the weekends before Christmas during December. They also run on the Wednesdays during school holidays between April and October, with services between 10.30 and 16.00 on most days.

Line Mileage and Journey Time
0.00   Moor Road
1.00   Middleton Park

In addition, the branch to the main line network runs for one third of a mile but this is not used to carry passengers. A return journey takes about 25 minutes.

Stock List

Type	Number	Builder	Details
Steam	6	Hawthorn Leslie	0-4-0ST
Steam	HENRY DE LACY II	Hudswell Clarke	0-4-0ST
Steam	Mirvale	Hudswell Clarke	0-4-0ST
Steam	SLOUGH ESTATES No. 3	Hudswell Clarke	0-4-0ST
Steam	No. 11	Hunslet	0-4-0ST
Steam	2103	Peckett	0-4-0ST
Steam	1684	Hunslet	0-4-0T
Steam	1310	NER	0-4-0T
Steam	385	Hartmann	0-4-0WT
Steam	BROOKES No. 1	Hunslet	0-6-0ST
Steam	MATTHEW MURRAY	Manning Wardle	0-6-0ST
Steam	SIR BERKELEY	Manning Wardle	0-6-0ST
Steam	M.S.C No. 67	Hudswell Clarke	0-6-0T
Steam	1540	Hunslet	2-6-2T
Steam	68153	Sentinel	4wT
Diesel	D2999	Beyer Peacock	0-4-0
Diesel	3900002	Fowler	0-4-0
Diesel	HARRY	Fowler	0-4-0
Diesel	CARROLL	Hudswell Clarke	0-4-0
Diesel	MARY	Hudswell Clarke	0-4-0
Diesel	1786	Hunslet	0-4-0

Diesel	6981	Hunslet	0-4-0
Diesel	AUSTINS No. 1	Peckett	0-4-0
Diesel	MD&HB 45	Hudswell Clarke	0-6-0
Diesel	7051	Hunslet	0-6-0
DMU	RDB998901	Drewry	Railcar

Attractions

The Engine House and museum have many historical and hands-on exhibits from the railway's long history and there is a shop, small café and conference facility at the Moor Road site. The new mezzanine floor has recently been completed and is used during special events; this will eventually become part of the museum and feature the work and Legacy of Blenkinsop and Murray. Middleton Park is accessible from its namesake railway station, with an ancient woodland, grassland, boating lake and visitor centre to explore. Nearby attractions in Leeds include the Royal Armouries, the Tetley and Leeds City Museum.

Special Events

Events that are planned for 2023 include:

1 April: Community Day.
8–10 April: Easter Weekend.
15 April: Victorian Weekend featuring the launch of SIR BERKELEY.
10–11 June: 90+ Years of the Diesel event.
9–10 July: Model Railway Exhibition.
23–24 September: Autumn Steam Festival.

Santa Specials during December.

▲ On 25 September 2022, LNER Class A4 60007 "SIR NIGEL GRESLEY" hauls the North Yorkshire Moors Railway's wood-panelled Teak Set through the region's rugged scenery. **Tom Marshall**

National Railway Museum, York

Introduction and History

The National Railway Museum (NRM) is adjacent to York railway station and the East Coast Main Line. It opened in 1975 on the site of the former York North depot and incorporates a turntable from this. The NRM was the amalgamation of two previous railway museums, both of which closed in 1973; British Railways' Transport Museum in Clapham and York Railway Museum which was established by the London & North Eastern Railway in 1928. The NRM holds the National Collection of historically important locomotives and rolling stock and a vast number of railway artefacts. Many of the artefacts and rolling stock are on display, although at any one time some are in storage and others are at the museum's sister site at Shildon (see above), or on loan to other museums or heritage railways. Some parts of the museum are being redeveloped, with "Wonderlab: The Bramall Gallery" due to open in 2023. This interactive gallery aims to inspire children aged 7–14 to think like engineers and become the next generation of railway engineers.

Contact Details

Website: www.railwaymuseum.org.uk
Tel: 0330 058 0058
Email: info@ScienceMuseumGroup.ac.uk
Address: National Railway Museum, Leeman Road, York, YO26 4XJ.

Transport Links

By Rail: The NRM is less than half a mile from York railway station.
By Road: The museum's car park on Leeman Road costs £10 per day.

Opening Times

The NRM opens 10.00–17.00 on Wednesdays to Sundays during term time and daily during school holidays.

Line Mileage and Journey Time

There is a demonstration railway line in South Yard, a 200-metre section of which is used for giving passenger rides as far as the Network Rail boundary (trains used to run much further until a few years ago). The line is not currently in use due to the redevelopment work that it taking place and it is not known when passenger trains will return.

Stock List

Type	Number	Builder	Details
Steam	ROCKET	Robert Stephenson & Co.	0-2-2
Steam	ROCKET (replica)	Locomotion Enterprises	0-2-2
Steam	ROCKET (replica)	Robert Stephenson & Co	0-2-2
Steam	BAUXITE No. 2	Black Hawthorn	0-4-0
Steam	3 "Coppernob"	Bury Curtis & Kennedy	0-4-0
Steam	Agenoria	Foster Rastrick	0-4-0
Steam	214 GLADSTONE	LBSCR	0-4-2
Steam	245	LSWR	0-4-4T
Steam	1275	Dübs & Company	0-6-0
Steam	C1 (33001)	Southern Railway	0-6-0
Steam	1247	Sharp Stewart	0-6-0ST
Steam	82 BOXHILL	LBSCR	0-6-0T
Steam	92220	British Railways	2-10-0
Steam	30587	LSWR	2-4-0WT
Steam	66	Kitson	2-2-4T
Steam	1008	Lancashire & Yorkshire	2-4-2T
Steam	13000	LMS	2-6-0
Steam	2500	LMS	2-6-4T
Steam	1	GNR	4-2-2
Steam	673	Midland Railway	4-2-2
Steam	737	SECR	4-4-0
Steam	990	GNR	4-4-2
Steam	4003	GWR	4-6-0
Steam	6229	LMS	4-6-2

Steam	4468	LNER	4-6-2
Steam	60103	LNER	4-6-2
Steam	35029	Southern Railway	4-6-2
Steam	KF7	Vulcan Foundry	4-8-4
Diesel	7050	English Electric	0-4-0
Diesel	D2860	Yorkshire Engine Co.	Class 02
Diesel	09017	British Railways	Class 09
Diesel	D8000	English Electric	Class 20
Diesel	31018	Brush Traction	Class 31
Diesel	D200	English Electric	Class 40
Diesel	43002	British Railways	Class 43
Diesel	47798	British Railways	Class 47
Diesel	D9002	English Electric	Class 55
DMU	51562 & 51922	British Railways	Class 108
DMU	4	Park Royal	Railcar
EMU	8143	Southern Railway	3 Sub
EMU	3308	GEC-Alsthom	Class 373
EMU	28249	Metropolitan Cammell	LNWR
EMU	22-141	Hitachi	O Series
Electric	26020	British Railways	Class 76
Electric	84001	North British	Class 84
Electric	87001	BREL	Class 87

Attractions

The large site has a large and varied collection of locomotives and coaches including "Mallard", the world's fastest steam locomotive, Queen Victoria's royal train carriages, examples of the Japanese Bullet Train, Eurostar and historically important diesel locomotives, including the first-built High Speed Train power car. Many locomotive nameplates are mounted on the wall of the Great Hall. Hands-on activities and regular talks include signalling demonstrations, how a steam engine works and turntable demonstrations. There is a miniature railway and a viewing balcony adjacent to the East Coast Main Line. York city centre is within walking distance, where York Minster, The Shambles, City Walls and many other attractions can be found. The Derwent Valley Light Railway is four miles away.

Special Events

Until 17 June 2023: Flying Scotsman Watercolours Exhibition.
Until June 2024: Innovation Platform Exhibition.

Other exhibitions take place; please check the NRM website for the latest information.

North Yorkshire Moors Railway

Introduction and History

The railway from Whitby to Grosmont opened in 1835 and was extended south to Pickering in 1836. It was extended further south from Pickering to Rillington in 1845, where it joined the present day York to Scarborough line. The route between Grosmont and Levisham was realigned in 1865, when today's station at Goathland opened. Passenger services between Whitby and Malton via Pickering ceased in 1965 and freight services ended in 1966. The NYMR began in 1967, when a group of local people formed the North Yorkshire Moors Railway Preservation Society, with the aim of reopening the line. After several open days, the line between Grosmont and Pickering reopened in 1973. Since 2007 the NYMR has operated trains on Network Rail's Esk Valley route to Whitby, with less frequent services continuing to Battersby too. This required the NYMR to become a registered Train Operating Company and gives it more than 40 miles of railway over which it can operate trains. As 2023 will see the heritage railway's 50th anniversary, a series of events will be held to mark this.

Contact Details

Website: www.nymr.co.uk
Tel: 01751 472508
Email: info@nymr.co.uk
Address: North Yorkshire Moors Railway, 12 Park Street, Pickering, North Yorkshire, YO18 7AJ.

Transport Links

By Rail: The NYMR connects with main line services at Grosmont and Whitby.
By Road: There are car parks at Pickering (YO18 7AJ), Levisham (YO18 7NN), Goathland (YO22 5NF), Grosmont (YO22 5QE) and Whitby (YO21 1YN). Charges apply at each of these.

Opening Times

Trains operate every day from late March to early November and during December for Santa Specials.

Line Mileage and Journey Time

0.00	Whitby	0.00	Grosmont
6.25	Grosmont	3.25	Glaisdale
9.75	Goathland	17.75	Battersby (Grosmont to Battersby during special events only)
15.00	Newtondale Halt		
18.25	Levisham		
24.25	Pickering		

A return journey from Whitby to Pickering (or vice versa) takes about four hours, or two hours 40 minutes between Grosmont and Pickering.

Stock List

Type	Number	Builder	Details
Steam	2702	Bagnall	0-4-0ST
Steam	"Lucie " (1625)	Cockerill	0-4-0VBT
Steam	65894	LNER	0-6-0
Steam	29 (4263)	Robert Stephenson & Hawthorns	0-6-2T
Steam	5 (3377)	Robert Stephenson & Hawthorns	0-6-2T
Steam	63395	NER	0-8-0
Steam	92134	British Railways	2-10-0
Steam	3672	North British	2-10-0
Steam	76079	British Railways	2-6-0
Steam	62005	North British	2-6-0
Steam	80135	British Railways	2-6-4T
Steam	80136	British Railways	2-6-4T
Steam	926	Southern Railway	4-4-0
Steam	45428	Armstrong Whitworth	4-6-0
Steam	75029	British Railways	4-6-0
Steam	44806	LMS	4-6-0
Steam	825	Southern Railway	4-6-0
Steam	30830	Southern Railway	4-6-0
Steam	34101	British Railways	4-6-2
Steam	60007	LNER	4-6-2
Diesel	12139	English Electric	0-6-0
Diesel	D2207	Vulcan Foundry	Class 04
Diesel	08495	British Railways	Class 08
Diesel	08556	British Railways	Class 08
Diesel	08850	British Railways	Class 08
Diesel	D5032	British Railways	Class 24
Diesel	D5061	British Railways	Class 24
Diesel	D7628	Beyer Peacock	Class 25
Diesel	37264	English Electric	Class 37
Diesel	47077	British Railways	Class 47
DMU	50160, 50164, 50204, 51511 & 59539	Metropolitan Cammell	Class 101

Attractions

The railway offers digital photography workshops, steam and diesel footplate experiences and engine shed tours. These are available on selected dates and should be booked in advance. There are several tea rooms along the route, a railway bookshop at Pickering and a 1950s railway memorabilia shop at Grosmont. Between Whitby, Pickering and the North Yorkshire Moors National Park through which the line travels, there are many attractions, natural features and scenery to explore.

Special Events
Events that usually take place on the railway include:

1960s Festival.
Steam and Diesel Galas.
Railway in Wartime event (usually during October).
October half term Light Spectacular Trains.
Santa Specials during December.

Ribble Steam Railway

Introduction and History
The steeply graded branch line, which leaves the West Coast Main Line immediately south of Preston station, was opened as far as Victoria Quay in 1846. The first one third of a mile of this involves a 1 in 29 descent, a cutting and a tunnel, before it levels off beside the River Ribble. The railway was extended to Preston Docks in 1882, where a network of lines developed and this had more than 25 miles of track at its peak. As larger container-based ports grew during the 1970s and 1980s, traffic levels to the docks declined, however the Preston Docks branch remains in commercial use today. Regular oil trains travel to the site of the Ribble Steam Railway, where the tanks are shunted into the nearby bitumen works. When Southport Railway Museum closed in 1999, many of its exhibits were transferred to the Preston site. Since 2005, the Ribble Steam Railway has been operating heritage passenger trains on a 1.5-mile section of the branch, which it continues to share with main line freight services. The heritage site has a large museum containing many locomotives and the railway runs adjacent to the River Ribble and through Preston Marina.

Contact Details
Website: www.ribblesteam.org.uk
Tel: 01772 728800
Email: enquiries@ribblesteam.co.uk
Address: Ribble Steam Railway, Chain Caul Road, Preston, Lancashire, PR2 2PD.

Transport Links
By Rail: The nearest railway station is Preston, which is two and a half miles away.
By Road: Free car parking is available (PR2 2PD).

Opening Times
Trains operate on Saturdays and Sundays from April to September, with hourly departures which are usually steam-hauled, except on diesel gala days.

Line Mileage and Journey Time
0.00   Museum station
1.50   Line end / Network Rail boundary

A return journey takes about 20 minutes.

Stock List

Type	Number	Builder	Details
Steam	20	Sharp Stewart	0-4-0
Steam	Glenfield 1	Andrew Barclay	0-4-0CT
Steam	Heysham No. 2 (1950)	Andrew Barclay	0-4-0F
Steam	1865	Andrew Barclay	0-4-0ST
Steam	BRITISH GYPSUM No. 4	Andrew Barclay	0-4-0ST
Steam	EFFICIENT	Andrew Barclay	0-4-0ST
Steam	JN DERBYSHIRE	Andrew Barclay	0-4-0ST
Steam	JOHN HOWE	Andrew Barclay	0-4-0ST
Steam	272	Grant Richie	0-4-0ST
Steam	19	Lancashire & Yorkshire	0-4-0ST
Steam	1439	LNWR	0-4-0ST
Steam	1935 HORNET	Peckett	0-4-0ST
Steam	737 DAPHNE	Peckett	0-4-0ST

Steam	1999	Peckett	0-4-0ST
Steam	1925 CALIBAN	Peckett	0-4-0ST
Steam	2003 JOHN BLENKINSON	Peckett	0-4-0ST
Steam	7485 AGECROFT No. 2	Robert Stephenson & Hawthorns	0-4-0ST
Steam	17	Sharp Stewart	0-4-0ST
Steam	THE KING (48)	Borrows	0-4-0WT
Steam	WINDLE (53)	Borrows	0-4-0WT
Steam	NIDDRIE 7	Andrew Barclay	0-6-0ST
Steam	EARL FITZWILLIAM	Avonside	0-6-0ST
Steam	1568	Avonside	0-6-0ST
Steam	1883	Avonside	0-6-0ST
Steam	MDHB 26	Avonside	0-6-0ST
Steam	COURAGEOUS	Bagnall	0-6-0ST
Steam	13 (3732)	Hawthorn Leslie	0-4-0ST
Steam	21 (3931)	Hawthorn Leslie	0-6-0ST
Steam	1450	Hudswell Clarke	0-6-0ST
Steam	3155 WALKDEN	Hunslet	0-6-0ST
Steam	3696 RESPITE	Hunslet	0-6-0ST
Steam	3793 SHROPSHIRE	Hunslet	0-6-0ST
Steam	GLASSHOUGHTON No. 4	Hunslet	0-6-0ST
Steam	1954	Hunslet	0-6-0ST
Steam	1636 FONMON	Peckett	0-6-0ST
Steam	30072	Vulcan Iron Works	0-6-0T
Steam	4979	GWR	4-6-0
Steam	8024	Sentinel	4wVBT
Steam	9373	Sentinel	4wVBT
Petrol	965 HOTTO	Howard	Petrol Loco
Diesel	21999 FLUFF	Fowler	0-4-0
Diesel	4160001 PERCIL	Fowler	0-4-0
Diesel	1031	Hudswell Clarke	0-4-0
Diesel	D628 MIGHTY ATON	Hudswell Clarke	0-4-0
Diesel	D629 SPARKY	Hudswell Clarke	0-4-0
Diesel	27653 BICC	North British	0-4-0
Diesel	10226 ENERGY	Sentinel	0-4-0
Diesel	10282 ENTERPRISE	Sentinel	0-4-0
Diesel	10283 PROGRESS	Sentinel	0-4-0
Diesel	STANLOW No. 4	Thomas Hill	0-4-0
Diesel	D2870	Yorkshire Engine Co.	0-4-0
Diesel	663	English Electric	0-6-0
Diesel	671	English Electric	0-6-0
Diesel	03189	British Railways	Class 03
Diesel	D2148	British Railways	Class 03
Diesel	D2595	Hunslet	Class 05
Diesel	D9539	British Railways	Class 14
DMU	79960	Waggon und Maschinenbau	Railbus
Battery	EE788	English Electric	Battery Loco
Battery	2000	Greenwood & Batley	Battery Loco

Attractions

The railway has the largest collection of industrial locomotives in the country. Admission includes unlimited travel for the day and access to exhibits in the museum and workshop. The line follows an interesting route, passing Preston Marina and crossing a swing bridge which it shares with a road. There is a café, a miniature railway and a children's playground at the site. Preston town centre is nearby, as are the Ribble Estuary National Nature Reserve, Fylde coast and Lytham St Annes.

Special Events

Events that usually take place on the railway include:

Mother's Day Cream Tea.
Steam and Diesel Galas.
Children and family oriented events.
Spooky Trains during October.
Santa Special Steam Experiences during December.

Stainmore Railway

Introduction and History

The railway between Barnard Castle and Tebay via Kirkby Stephen East opened in 1861, with the northern spur to Clifton and Penrith via Appleby opening in 1862 (see the Eden Valley Railway). Passenger services were withdrawn on the Kirkby Stephen East to Tebay route in 1952, although summer Saturday holiday trains continued to use it until 1961. The line to Clifton closed to passengers in 1962 and to freight in 1974 when traffic to Hartley Quarry ceased. The first preservation group formed in 1997 and subsequently acquired the Kirkby Stephen East site. Since then, Kirkby Stephen East station building has been restored and just over one quarter of a mile of railway track has been re-laid. Heritage trains began operating in 2011 and there are long-term plans to extend the line north towards the Eden Valley Railway.

Contact Details

Website: www.kirkbystepheneast.co.uk
Tel: 01768 371700
Email: suelizjones@hotmail.com
Address: Stainmore Railway Company, Kirkby Stephen East Station, South Road, Kirkby Stephen, Cumbria, CA17 4LA.

Transport Links

By Rail: Kirkby Stephen railway station is just under one mile away.
By Road: Free car parking is available at Kirkby Stephen East (CA17 4LA).

Opening Times

Kirkby Stephen East station opens on Sundays from April until October and on selected weekdays during July and August. Steam or diesel-hauled trains are usually in operation. Please check the website or contact the railway for the latest information.

▲ The 1863-built Sharp Stewart No. 20 leads Hawthorn Leslie No. 21 on the Ribble Steam Railway during the afternoon of 26 March 2022. **Gordon Edgar**

Line Mileage and Journey Time
The railway is just over a quarter of a mile long and the journey takes about 10 minutes.

Stock List

Type	Number	Builder	Details
Steam	LYTHAM ST. ANNES (2111)	Peckett	0-4-0ST
Steam	2084 FC TINGEY	Peckett	0-4-0ST
Steam	65033	NER	0-6-0
Steam	68009	Hunslet	0-6-0ST
Steam	910	NER	2-4-0
Diesel	3958 ELIZABETH	Hibberd	0-4-0
Diesel	305	Yorkshire Engine Co.	0-4-0DH
Diesel	STANTON No. 50	Yorkshire Engine Co.	0-6-0

Attractions
Kirkby Stephen East station includes a number of restored rooms with original features, including the Booking Hall, Booking Office, Foreman's Office, Station Master's Office and Waiting Room which houses a small museum. There is a shop, children's play area and a wide range of rolling stock, including 1875-built 2-4-0 number 910 which belongs to the National Collection. The 2019-built carriage shed houses several historically important coaches, including the sole remaining 1902-built NER Stores Van 5523. Driving experiences are available, with a choice of steam or diesel locomotive and the railway can be booked for a bespoke private event on a Saturday when it isn't open to the public. The Pennine market town of Kirkby Stephen is nearby and the Temperance Hall Museum of Costume is less than a mile away from the site. Brough Castle is five miles away and there are plenty of walking and cycling routes in the area, some of which are along the trackbed of the former Stainmore Line. The Eden Valley Railway at Appleby is only eight miles away, making a combined visit possible on a day when both sites are open.

Special Events
Events that usually take place on the railway include:

Easter event during April.
Model Railway Show at Kirkby Stephen East station (usually in June).
Heritage Open Days.
Christmas event during December.

Stephenson Steam Railway

Introduction and History
The railway and museum are located on the site of former wagonways in an area rich in industrial and railway history. After the coal trains ceased, during the 1970s the site of the museum and current railway were used as a testing centre by the Tyne and Wear Metro before its services began in 1980. In the early 1980s North Tyneside Council acquired the test sheds and a partnership was made with Tyne & Wear Archives & Museums to create a facility with a steam-hauled passenger railway. A single track line was relaid from the museum to Percy Main, being completed in 1989 and the first passenger trains ran on this in 1991. The museum showcases the railway pioneers George Stephenson and his son Robert.

Contact Details
Website: www.stephensonsteamrailway.org.uk
Tel: 0191 277 7135
Email: info@stephensonsteamrailway.org.uk
Address: Stephenson Steam Railway, Middle Engine Lane, North Shields, Tyne & Wear, NE29 8DX.

Transport Links
By Rail: The museum is two miles from Percy Main on the Tyne and Wear Metro, Yellow Route.
By Road: There is free parking at the museum (NE29 8DX).

Opening Times

The museum opens 11.00–16.00 on Saturdays, Sundays from April until October, plus on selected weekdays during school holidays. Trains operate on Sundays and they may also run on other dates during school holidays. The museum can be telephoned on the day to confirm and can provide details of which locomotive is working.

Line Mileage and Journey Time

0.00   Middle Engine Lane
1.75   Percy Main

A return journey takes around half an hour.

Stock List

Type	Number	Builder	Details
Steam	Billy	George Stephenson	0-4-0
Steam	401 SIR THOMAS BURT	Bagnall	0-6-0ST
Steam	NIGHTINGDALE/ SEACOLE (ILLINGWORTH)	Hudswell Clarke	0-6-0ST
Steam	3785	Hunslet	0-6-0ST
Steam	5 JACKIE MILBURN	Peckett	0-6-0ST
Steam	5	Kitson	0-6-0T
Steam	1 TED GARRET JP MP	Robert Stephenson & Hawthorns	0-6-0T
Electric	E4	Siemans Harton	Electric E4
Electric	3267	Metropolitan Cammell	Motor Parcel Van
Diesel	10	Consett	0-6-0
Diesel	03079	British Railways	Class 03
Diesel	08915	British Railways	Class 08

Attractions

The Museum has a range of exhibits including George Stephenson's 1816 locomotive "Billy", which is the world's third oldest surviving steam locomotive and a forerunner to the famous "Rocket". Display panels tell the story of railway pioneers George and Robert Stephenson and the worldwide impact of their inventions. Steam or diesel locomotives carry passengers in vintage carriages on the railway line. Heritage railways within the area include the Bowes Railway (ten miles away), Tanfield Railway (12 miles) and Beamish museum (17 miles). The city of Newcastle upon Tyne, Whitley Bay and the coast are all near to the location of the museum.

Special Events

Events that usually take place on the railway include:

Drive a Diesel Locomotive.
Elf Express and Winter Warmers during December.

Tanfield Railway

Introduction and History

The Tanfield Railway is known as the oldest railway in the world, as the first line was built to carry coal from Causey to Dunston Staithes on the River Tyne in 1725. During the 1830s it was converted from a horse-drawn wagonway to a railway. East Tanfield was the final colliery to use the line and after this closed in 1964, the railway closed and the track was lifted. Nearby Marley Hill engine shed, however, continued to be used by the National Coal Board until 1970. A group formed during the 1960s aiming to preserve the steam railway heritage of the North-East. After Marley Hill engine shed closed in 1970, it was initially used by the nearby Beamish Museum as a storage site and Beamish gave the group access, so they could restore steam locomotives and railway items belonging to both organisations. Beamish moved its rolling stock to its new railway when this opened in 1976. A connecting curve was then built from Marley Hill to the Tanfield branch. The first preserved passenger trains ran for half a mile from Marley Hill in 1977 and the railway was extended north to Sunniside in 1982. It was further extended south along the former trackbed and reached Causey in 1992 and the site of East Tanfield Colliery in 1993. There are long term aspirations to extend the railway west from Marley Hill to Byermoor, although these are not currently being pursued.

Contact Details
Website: www.tanfield-railway.co.uk
Tel: 07508 092365
Email: info@tanfield-railway.co.uk
Address: Tanfield Railway, Old Marley Hill, Gateshead, Tyne and Wear, NE16 5ET.

Transport Links
By Rail: The nearest station is Dunston (four miles), Newcastle is six miles away.
By Road: There is free parking at Marley Hill (NE16 5ET) and East Tanfield (DH9 9UY).
By Bike: The Tanfield Railway Path runs from Gateshead to Sunniside and Marley Hill. The Bowes Railway Path arrives at Marley Hill from the east.

Opening Times
Trains operate on Sundays from Spring until October and on selected weekdays, Saturdays and Bank Holidays. The weekends before Christmas feature North Pole Express trains and these need to be booked in advance.

Line Mileage and Journey Time
0.00	Sunniside
0.75	Andrews House
1.75	Causey Arch
2.50	East Tanfield

A return journey takes about one hour.

Stock List

Type	Number	Builder	Details
Steam	7007	Robert Stephenson & Hawthorns	0-4-0CT
Steam	266 WELLINGTON	Black Hawthorn	0-4-0ST
Steam	2711	Hawthorn Leslie	0-4-0ST
Steam	2 (2859)	Hawthorn Leslie	0-4-0ST
Steam	L&HC14	Hawthorn Leslie	0-4-0ST
Steam	1672 IRWELL	Hudswell Clarke	0-4-0ST
Steam	3 (2009)	R & W Hawthorn	0-4-0ST
Steam	21 (7796)	Robert Stephenson & Hawthorns	0-4-0ST
Steam	7409 Sir CECIL. A. COCHRANE	Robert Stephenson & Hawthorns	0-4-0ST
Steam	6	Andrew Barclay	0-4-2ST
Steam	3746	Hawthorn Leslie	0-6-0F
Steam	1015	Andrew Barclay	0-6-0ST
Steam	20 (2779)	Bagnall	0-6-0ST
Steam	STAGSHAW	Hawthorn Leslie	0-6-0ST
Steam	3575	Hawthorn Leslie	0-6-0ST
Steam	RENISHAW IRONWORKS No.6	Hudswell Clarke	0-6-0ST
Steam	16 (7944)	Robert Stephenson & Hawthorns	0-6-0ST
Steam	38 (7763)	Robert Stephenson & Hawthorns	0-6-0ST
Steam	44 (7760)	Robert Stephenson & Hawthorns	0-6-0ST
Steam	47 (7800)	Robert Stephenson & Hawthorns	0-6-0ST
Steam	49 (7098)	Robert Stephenson & Hawthorns	0-6-0ST
Steam	62 (7035)	Robert Stephenson & Hawthorns	0-6-0ST
Steam	38 (1823)	Hudswell Clarke	0-6-0T
Steam	3 TWIZELL	Robert Stephenson & Co	0-6-0T
Steam	4 (9559)	Sentinel	4wVBT
Electric	E10 (862)	Siemens	4w
Electric	E9 (1565)	AEG, Berlin	Bo-Bo
Electric	7078	Robert Stephenson & Hawthorns	Bo-Bo
Diesel	14 (D21)	Armstrong Whitworth	0-4-0DE
Diesel	2 (D22)	Armstrong Whitworth	0-4-0DE
Diesel	3716	Hibberd	0-4-0
Diesel	758206	Hunslet	4wDM
Diesel	54781	Lister Blackstone	4wDM
Diesel	6980	Robert Stephenson & Hawthorns	0-4-0
Diesel	7697	Robert Stephenson & Hawthorns	0-4-0
Diesel	7901	Robert Stephenson & Hawthorns	0-4-0

Diesel	1 HUSKY	Robert Stephenson & Hawthorns	0-4-0
Diesel	35	Ruston & Hornsby	0-4-0
Diesel	4240010	Fowler	0-6-0
Diesel	501	Hunslet	0-6-0
Diesel	7746	Robert Stephenson & Hawthorns	0-6-0
Diesel	3565	Baguley	2w-2
Battery	3872 DEREK SHEPHERD	Hawthorn Leslie	Bo-Bo

Attractions

The railway has a particularly large collection of industrial locomotives, including steam, diesel and electric examples. The Marley Hill site, with its 1854-built engine shed, houses many of these, along with several restored vintage carriages. Engine shed tours and afternoon tea "Director Class" travel are usually available on Sundays between April and September. Causey Arch, which was built in 1727 and is a Grade 1 Listed structure, is the world's oldest railway bridge and is adjacent to Causey Arch station. There are several walking paths in the area, including the Tanfield Railway Path, which continues north on the trackbed from Sunniside and the Bowes Railway Path, which runs east from Marley Hill. Other attractions in the area include the North-East Land, Sea & Air Museum, Newcastle, Sunderland and the East coast. Nearby heritage railways include Beamish (three miles away), Bowes Railway (six miles), North Tyneside Steam Railway (12 miles) and Weardale Railway (20 miles).

Special Events

Events that usually take place on the railway include:

Mothering Sunday event.
Easter Eggstravaganza trains.
Heritage Open Days.
1940s Weekend.
Tanfield Ghost Train.
North Pole Express and Mince Pie Specials during December.

▲ Class 122 "Bubblecar" 55012 makes its way alongside the River Wear and passes Parson Byers with a Weardale Railway service on 13 August 2022.   **Gordon Edgar**

Weardale Railway

Introduction and History

The railway first reached Bishop Auckland in 1843 when the line from Shildon to Crook was built. The Wear Valley line from Bishop Auckland to Stanhope opened in 1862 and was extended to Wearhead in 1895. Bishop Auckland became a major junction and at its height, seven routes converged at the station. Passenger services on the Weardale route were withdrawn in 1953, after which the line was cut back from Wearhead to the cement works at Eastgate. The heritage and tourist value of the railway was recognised as early as 1983 when intermittent charter trains ran to Stanhope and these became timetabled summer weekend services between 1988 and 1992. In 1993 rail traffic to the cement works ended and British Rail announced its intention to close the line. A preservation group formed in 1993 and trains from Wolsingham to Stanhope returned in 2004. The main line connection at Bishop Auckland was reinstated in 2009 and from 2010 the railway extended to a new station at Bishop Auckland. From 2008, the railway was owned by the American railway company Iowa Pacific Holdings (IPH), using the subsidiary British American Railway Services (BARS). IPH entered insolvency in 2019 and in 2020 the railway was purchased by a local charity, The Auckland Project. The new owner hopes to reinstate services to Darlington by partnering with a train operating company and there are long-term aims for services to run on the disused line to Eastgate. During 2022 however, the line east of Wolsingham was taken out of use, reducing the operational section to the 5.25-miles between Stanhope and Wolsingham.

Contact Details

Website: www.weardale-railway.org.uk
Tel: 07719 757755
Email: info@weardale-railway.org.uk
Address: Weardale Railway, Stanhope Station, Station Road, Stanhope, DL13 2YS.

Transport Links

By Rail: Bishop Auckland West station is a short walk from Bishop Auckland main line station.
By Road: Free parking is available at Stanhope (DL13 2YS). There is also limited parking at Frosterley (DL13 2SL) and Wolsingham (DL13 3BL).

Opening Times

Trains usually operate on Saturdays from late May to the end of October and on selected Wednesdays during those months.

Line Mileage and Journey Time

0.00	Bishop Auckland West
4.25	Witton-le-Wear
10.75	Wolsingham
12.25	Kingfisher Halt
14.00	Frosterley
16.00	Stanhope
19.25	Eastgate (the line is disused beyond Stanhope)

A journey along the length of the line takes between one and two hours, depending on the starting point.

Stock List

Type	Number	Builder	Details
Steam	40	Robert Stephenson & Hawthorns	0-6-0T
Diesel	H050	English Electric	0-6-0DE
Diesel	3994	English Electric	0-6-0DH
Diesel	6294	Hunslet	0-6-0DH
Diesel	7541	Hunslet	0-6-0DH
Diesel	10187	Sentinel	0-6-0DH
Diesel	10232	Sentinel	4wDH
Diesel	08874	British Railways	Class 08
Diesel	31285	Brush Traction	Class 31
Diesel	31459	Brush Traction	Class 31
Diesel	31465	Brush Traction	Class 31
DMU	50980 & 52054	British Railways	Class 108

| DMU | 55012 | GRCW | Class 122 |
| DMU | 142078 (55728 & 55774) | BREL/Leyland | Class 142 |

Attractions
The railway travels through Weardale in the North Pennines, which is an Area of Outstanding Natural Beauty. Many footpaths and bridleways are within reach from the railway's stations. Stanhope station is home to a souvenir shop and the No. 40 Café, which serves light refreshments. Other attractions in the area include High Force waterfall, Killhope Lead Mining Museum, Raby Castle and Hamsterley Forest. Nearby heritage railways include Locomotion, Shildon (four miles away), Beamish (19 miles) and the Tanfield Railway (20 miles).

Special Events
Events that usually take place on the railway:

Easter event.
Food and drink related trains including Afternoon Tea Trains and Fish & Chip Specials.
Diesel Galas.

Wensleydale Railway

Introduction and History
This east to west trans-Pennine line was constructed in stages across harsh terrain, with Northallerton to Leeming Bar opening in 1848, extending to Leyburn in 1856 and reaching Garsdale in 1878. It was used to carry passengers, farm produce, quarried stone and coal. Passenger services were withdrawn in 1954, after which the line remained open between Northallerton and Redmire for freight. The track between Garsdale and Redmire was lifted in the 1960s. In 1992 British Steel decided it was no longer economic to transport limestone by rail and British Rail then announced its intention to close and sell the line. The sale was delayed when the Ministry of Defence then used the line to occasionally transport military vehicles to and from Redmire. The Wensleydale Railway Association formed in 1990, obtaining a 100-year lease on the line between Northallerton (Castle Hills) and Redmire. The first preserved trains ran between Leeming Bar and Leyburn in 2003, extending to Redmire in 2004 and to Northallerton West station in 2015, although trains don't currently run east of Scruton. During 2022 services had to be cut back to Leyburn in the west as the track to Redmire has reached life expired condition and a £1m appeal has been launched to raise the funds needed for the repairs. In addition, there are long-term aims to extend the line further west towards Garsdale, beginning with the Redmire to Bolton Castle and Aysgarth sections.

Contact Details
Website: www.wensleydale-railway.co.uk
Tel: 01677 425805
Email: Written enquiries can be made from the website.
Address: Leeming Bar Station, Leases Road, Leeming Bar, Northallerton DL7 9AR.

Transport Links
By Rail: Northallerton is the nearest railway station and is five and a half miles from Leeming Bar.
By Road: Car parking is available at Leeming Bar (DL7 9AR), Leyburn (DL8 5ET) and Redmire (DL8 4ES).

Opening Times
The railway usually operates at weekends for the large part of the year and on selected weekdays between April and September.

Line Mileage and Journey Time
0.00	Northallerton West
4.50	Scruton
6.00	Leeming Bar
7.75	Bedale
13.50	Finghall Lane
17.75	Leyburn
22.00	Redmire

A return journey takes about two and a half hours (when trains operate on the full length of the line).

Stock List

Type	Number	Builder	Details
Steam	7537 RICHARD III	Robert Stephenson & Hawthorns	0-6-0T
Diesel	284V	Thomas Hill	4wDH
Diesel	WL4 (804)	Brush Traction	0-6-0DE
Diesel	03144	British Railways	Class 03
Diesel	D9523	British Railways	Class 14
Diesel	33035	BRCW	Class 33
Diesel	37250	English Electric	Class 37
Diesel	47785	Brush Traction	Class 47
DMU	50256, 50746, 51210 & 56343	Metropolitan Cammell	Class 101
DMU	51572 & 56274	British Railways	Class 108
DMU	51353, 51400, 59500 & 59509	Pressed Steel	Class 117
DMU	55032	Pressed Steel	Class 121
DMU	142018 (55559 & 55609)	BREL/Leyland	Class 142
DMU	142028 (55569 & 55619)	BREL/Leyland	Class 142
DMU	142035 (55576 & 55626)	BREL/Leyland	Class 142
DMU	142041 (55582 & 55632)	BREL/Leyland	Class 142
DMU	142060 (55710 & 55756)	BREL/Leyland	Class 142
DMU	142087 (55737 & 55783)	BREL/Leyland	Class 142
DMU	142090 (55740 & 55786)	BREL/Leyland	Class 142
DMU	143623 (55664 & 55689)	Alexander/Barclay	Class 143
DMU	144020 (55820, 55856 & 55843)	Alexander/BREL	Class 144
DMU	975874	BREL/Leyland	Railbus

Attractions

Following a £368 000 National Lottery Heritage Fund grant, the interior and exterior of the Grade II listed Leeming Bar station have recently been restored, enabling visitors to see how it looked during the 1920s. The railway runs through a scenic landscape that is very popular with walkers and the area can be explored from the railway's stations. The Yorkshire Dales National Park is also nearby.

Special Events

Events that usually take place on the railway include:

Wensley Ale.
Afternoon tea services.
Bedale Bonfire Express services during November.
Seasonal trains during December.

Yorkshire Wolds Railway

Introduction and History

The railway between Malton and Driffield opened in 1853, linking the two routes running south from Scarborough, both of which remain in use today. Passenger services between Malton and Driffield ended as early as 1950, although the route continued to carry chalk from local quarries until it was closed in 1958. The Yorkshire Wolds Railway formed in 2008 with the aim of restoring at least part of the route as a heritage railway. Access to the site at Fimber, roughly midway along the railway trackbed, was granted in 2012. The first locomotive arrived in 2013 and the railway opened to the public in 2015, using a short demonstration line. Since then the first stage of the southern extension towards Wetwang has been completed and work to further extend is due to continue through 2023 and beyond.

Contact Details

Website: www.yorkshirewoldsrailway.org.uk
Tel: 01377 338053
Email: info@yorkshirewoldsrailway.org.uk
Address: Yorkshire Wolds Railway, Fimber Halt, Beverley Road, Fimber, YO25 3HG.

Transport Links

By Rail: The nearest railway stations are Driffield (ten miles) and Malton (11 miles).
By Road: Free car parking is available (YO25 3HG).

Opening Times
The railway operates 10.00–16.00 on Sundays and Bank Holidays, beginning on 9 April for the 2023 season and continuing until the end of October. Seasonal trains also run during December.

Line Mileage and Journey Time
The demonstration line has now reached a length of 300 metres and the journey time is relatively short.

Stock List

Type	Number	Builder	Details
Diesel	5576	GEC Traction Ltd	0-4-0DH
Diesel	Patricia (4240017)	Fowler	0-6-0

Attractions
The 2023 season will see the introduction of brake van rides (previously only cab rides in the locomotive were available), increasing the numbers of passengers that can be carried and providing a unique perspective of the line. Restoration of the Fowler diesel is progressing on-site. "Driver for a Fiver" experiences are available and need to be booked in advance. There is a visitor centre inside a restored Mark 1 coach, with artefacts and photographs from when the railway was previously in operation, and a shop selling railway related gifts and refreshments. Nearby attractions include Fimber picnic site, Sledmere House, the Driffield Navigation and the deserted medieval village at Wharram Percy. Pickering, the southern terminus of the North Yorkshire Moors Railway is 20 miles from the Fimber site.

▲ On 27 June 2021, the Yorkshire Wolds Railway's 0-4-0 diesel-hydraulic shunter 5576 is seen giving visitors cab rides along the young heritage railway. **Andy Chard**

WALES

Anglesey Central Railway (proposed)

Llangollen Railway

Gwili Railway

Pontypool & Blaenavon Railway

Llanelli & Mynydd Mawr Railway

Garw Valley Railway (proposed)

Barry Tourist Railway

Region 3 – Wales

Barry Railway

Introduction and History

In 1889 Barry Docks and the railway that served them were built as an alternative to the nearby congested Cardiff Docks. Their primary purpose was the export of minerals, although passengers were also carried on the line to the docks, particularly after Barry Island Pleasure Park opened in 1897. The railway was cut back to Barry Island when Barry Pier station closed in 1976 and main line trains continue to terminate at Platform 1 of Barry Island station today. The Vale of Glamorgan Railway formed in 1994 and the first preserved trains operated from the Barry Island site in 1998. The railway was extended in stages, with heritage trains first crossing the causeway alongside the Barry Island–Barry Docks single line in 2002. The preserved railway terminates at Gladstone Bridge and a second more southerly line runs to a new station, Waterfront, which is adjacent to the site of the former Woodham's scrapyard. In 2022 Transport for Wales (TfW) purchased the site on which the Barry Railway is sited, so that the publicly-owned operator can repurpose the site as a depot for its new trains. The acquisition included the former locomotive shed, for which the heritage railway previously held a long-term lease and TfW has instead made an agreement for the Barry Railway to use the smaller shed at Plymouth Road, Barry Island. TfW has also made provision for the heritage railway to continue operating trains to both Waterfront and Gladstone Bridge, but before services can return, the Barry Railway needs to carry out track repairs and provide a new passenger entrance at Barry Island station.

Contact Details

A new website and updated contact details will be announced in due course.
Address: The Station Buildings, Station Approach, Barry Island, Vale of Glamorgan, CF62 5TH.

Transport Links

By Rail: Main line trains connect with the Barry Railway at Barry Island.
By Road: Parking is available outside Barry Island station (CF62 5TH) and there is free parking nearby.

Opening Times

The railway is not currently open. It is hoped that it will reopen during 2023.

Line Mileage and Journey Time

| 0.00 | Barry Island | | 0.00 | Barry Island |
| 1.00 | Waterfront | | 1.25 | Gladstone Bridge |

Stock List

Type	Number	Builder	Details
Steam	6686	Armstrong Whitworth	0-6-2T
Steam	92245	British Railways	2-10-0
Steam	5539	GWR	2-6-2T
Steam	SUSAN (9537)	Sentinel	4wVBGT
Diesel	08503	British Railways	Class 08
Electro-Diesel	73118	English Electric	Class 73
DMU	50222 & 50338	Metropolitan Cammell	Class 101

Attractions

The goods shed at the Waterfront destination is a recent redevelopment which includes retail and entertainment outlets and a children's playground. The station at Barry Island is also home to Barry War Museum, which opens 14.00–16.00 on Wednesdays and 11.00–16.00 on the second Sunday of the month; admission is free. Other nearby attractions include Barry Island Pleasure Park, Porthkerry Country Park, the beach and coast at Whitmore Bay. The city of Cardiff can be reached by train from Barry Island in 30 minutes.

Gwili Railway

Introduction and History

The Gwili Railway lies on part of the former line between Carmarthen and Aberystwyth in West Wales. It was originally a broad gauge line, opening in 1860 to carry both passengers and local goods. Passenger services ceased in 1964 and the line continued to carry produce such as milk until its closure in 1973. The track was lifted in 1975, the same year in which the Gwili Railway Company was formed. The company acquired an eight-mile section of trackbed between Abergwili Junction and Llanpumsaint and the first preserved trains ran from Bronwydd Arms to Cwmdwyfran in 1978. The railway has since been extended three times, across the River Gwili to Llwyfan Cerrig in 1987, to Danycoed in 2001 and to the former Abergwili Junction in 2017, which is only 1.25 miles from the end of the main line at Carmarthen. Major redevelopment work began at Abergwili Junction in 2022 and when this has been completed in 2023, services will begin and end from the redeveloped station which will include a new car park. There are longer-term plans to further extend the railway.

Contact Details

Website: www.gwili-railway.co.uk
Tel: 01267 238213
Email: info@gwili-railway.co.uk
Address: Gwili Railway, Bronwydd Arms Station, Bronwydd Arms, Carmarthenshire, SA33 6HT.

Transport Links

By Rail: Carmarthen station is just over a mile from Brownwydd Arms.
By Road: Parking will be available at Abergwili Junction once the new car park is complete in 2023. There is also parking at Bronwydd Arms (SA33 6HT). There is no public access at Llwyfan Cerrig or Danycoed Halt.

Opening Times

The railway usually operates at weekends, on selected weekdays between Easter and October and every day during July and August.

▲ GWR 0-6-0PT 5786, which carries the number L92, stands at the platform of the Gwili Railway's Bronwydd Arms station on 30 June 2021. During 2023, the railway's new base at Abergwili Junction is due to be completed.   **Alisdair Anderson**

Line Mileage and Journey Time

0.00 Abergwili Junction
1.50 Bronwydd Arms
3.25 Llwyfan Cerrig
3.75 Danycoed Halt

A return journey takes about 1 hour 30 minutes.

Stock List

Type	Number	Builder	Details
Steam	1345	Peckett	0-4-0ST
Steam	7058	Robert Stephenson & Hawthorns	0-4-0ST
Steam	17 (1338)	Andrew Barclay	0-6-0T
Steam	1369	GWR	0-6-0PT
Steam	3829	Hunslet	0-6-0ST
Steam	7849	Robert Stephenson & Hawthorns	0-6-0ST
Steam	HAULWEN	Vulcan Foundry	0-6-0ST
Steam	28	Hunslet	0-6-2T
Diesel	312433	Ruston & Hornsby	4wDM
Diesel	LWO 2108 (5391)	GEC Traction Ltd	0-6-0DH
Diesel	5014	Peckett	0-6-0DM
Diesel	D2178	British Railways	Class 03
Diesel	08888	British Railways	Class 08
Diesel	43056	BREL	Class 43
DMU	51347, 51401 & 59508	Pressed Steel	Class 117

Attractions

The railway follows a scenic route along the course of the River Gwili. There is a working signal box and gift shop at Bronwydd Arms, a miniature railway at Llwyfan Cerrig and driver footplate experiences can be arranged. The two foot gauge Teifi Valley Railway is about half an hour's drive away. Nearby attractions include Carmarthen with its 800-year-old market, the National Botanic Gardens of Wales and the Brecon Beacons National Park.

Special Events

Events that usually take place on the railway include:

Easter Special.
Teddy Bears Picnic during May.
Driver Experience Days are available.
Halloween Lights of the Valley Train during October & November.
Santa Specials during December.
There are also dining trains, cream team trains and Murder Mystery services.

Llanelli & Mynydd Mawr Railway

Introduction and History

The first section of the four foot gauge horse-drawn tramway carrying ironstone to Llanelly Docks (as it was spelled at that time) opened in 1803. This was later extended to Cynheidre and Cross Hands; however, it fell into disuse as early as 1844. It was officially re-opened in 1883, although trains had been operating before 1883 and it continued to carry minerals and coal until 1989 when Cynheidre Colliery closed. The railway never had a regular passenger service, although it saw regular workmen's services and occasional charter trains. After closure, an initial preservation group was not able to raise sufficient funds to buy the line and it was sold to the local authorities and converted into the Swiss Valley Cycle Route. This is now part of Route 47 of the National Cycle Network. The Llanelli and Mynydd Mawr Railway Company formed in 1999 with the aim of opening a heritage railway. The site of the former Cynheidre Colliery and approximately one mile of trackbed have been purchased. It first opened to the public in late 2017, making it one of Britain's youngest heritage railways. Trains initially operated on a quarter-mile section of track and this has recently been increased to almost half a mile. Work to further extend the railway northwards is due to continue and the long-term aim is to extend the line as far as possible north and south, alongside the existing cycle path.

Contact Details

Website: www.llanellirailway.co.uk
Email: llanellirailway@gmail.com
Address: Llanelli & Mynydd Mawr Railway, Former Cynheidre Colliery, Llanelli, Carmarthenshire, SA15 5YF.

Transport Links

By Rail: The nearest railway station is Llanelli, which is six miles away.
By Road: Free parking is available at Cynheidre (SA15 5YF, note this postcode is for the nearby village, turn right before Cynheidre Village sign if travelling from Llanelli).
By Bike: Route 47 of the National Cycle Network passes the Cynheidre site.

Opening Times

Trains operate on selected dates (predominantly Saturdays), which for 2023 will be 4–5 March, 8–9 April 2023, 20 May, 10 June, 15 July, 12 August, 26 August, 23 September, 28 October and during December for Santa Specials.

Line Mileage and Journey Time

Trains currently operate for 0.45 miles and the journey time is relatively short.

Stock List

Type	Number	Builder	Details
Diesel	10222	Sentinel	0-4-0
Diesel	73130	English Electric	Class 73
DMU	AD9117	Baguley Drewry	4wDM
DMU	55019	GRCW	Class 122
DMU	142006 (55547 & 55597)	BREL/Alexander	Class 142
DMU	143606 (55647 & 55672)	Alexander/Barclay	Class 143
DMU	143607 (55648 & 55673)	Alexander/Barclay	Class 143
DMU	143612 (55653 & 55678)	Alexander/Barclay	Class 143
DMU	153374	Leyland	Class 153
EMU	315856	BREL	Class 315
EMU	483006 (126 & 226)	Metropolitan Cammell	Class 483
EMU	483008 (128 & 228)	Metropolitan Cammell	Class 483

Attractions

During 2021 the first locomotive cabs arrived on site, as The Cab Yard began relocating its collection of locomotive and other railway vehicle cabs to Cynheidre. More cabs are due to arrive in 2023, providing a unique attraction at a heritage railway. Pacer driving experiences can be booked. There is a small heritage centre and a static buffet coach selling refreshments at Cynheidre. Guided tours of the site and stock shed are available by advance arrangement, for which donations are suggested. Nature trails are organised in conjunction with a local wildlife group, to explore the area's plant and animal wildlife. Nearby attractions include Gwili Railway, Llyn Llech Owain Country Park, Llanelli WWT National Wetland Centre and the National Botanic Gardens of Wales.

Special Events

Events that usually take place on the railway include:

Easter event, which will take place on 8 & 9 April in 2023.
Family events during school holidays.
Halloween event, which will be on 28 October in 2023.
Santa Specials during December.

Llangollen Railway

Introduction and History

Llangollen is at the eastern end of the railway which ran across central Wales from Ruabon to Barmouth, opening in full in 1865 and closing to passengers a century later in 1965. It survived for freight use until 1968, soon after which the track was lifted and many of the stations were demolished. The first preservation group formed in 1972 and by 1975 Llangollen station had reopened. The preserved railway was extended to Berwyn in 1985, Deeside in 1990, Glyndyfrdwy in 1992 and to Carrog in 1996. It was further extended to a temporary terminus at Corwen East in 2014, which was formally opened in 2015. At the end of the 2018 running season, the operational section was cut back to Carrog and Corwen East was dismantled, to allow the line to be further extended to a new terminus, Corwen Central. This is a quarter of mile east of the original Corwen station, which closed in 1965 and is now privately owned. The extension to Corwen Central was completed in 2020, but its opening was delayed until early 2023 after the heritage railway encountered financial difficulties.

Contact Details

Website: www.llangollen-railway.co.uk
Tel: 01978 860979
Email: info@llangollen-railway.co.uk
Address: Llangollen Railway, The Station, Abbey Road, Llangollen, LL20 8SN.

Transport Links

By Rail: Ruabon is the nearest railway station and is six miles from Llangollen.
By Road: Corwen Central (LL21 0DN) is the best place to arrive by car as there is ample parking. There is only limited parking at Carrog (LL21 9BD), no parking at Berwyn or Glyndyfrdwy stations and limited disabled parking only at Llangollen (LL20 8SN).

Opening Times

Trains operate on most dates between late February and early November. A variety of timetables operate through the running season, therefore checking the railway's website for the latest information is recommended.

Line Mileage and Journey Time

0.00	Llangollen
1.50	Berwyn
3.25	Deeside Halt
5.25	Glyndyfrdwy
7.25	Carrog
9.75	Corwen Central

A return journey takes at least 1 hour 40 minutes, depending on the starting point.

Stock List

Type	Number	Builder	Details
Steam	7754	GWR	0-6-0PT
Steam	68067	Hudswell Clarke	0-6-0ST
Steam	68030	Hunslet	0-6-0ST
Steam	5619	GWR	0-6-2T
Steam	5532	GWR	2-6-2T
Steam	80072	British Railways	2-6-4T
Steam	3802	GWR	2-8-0
Diesel	2145 Basil	Hunslet	0-4-0DM
Diesel	2782	Yorkshire Engine Co.	0-4-0
Diesel	03162	British Railways	Class 03
Diesel	08195	British Railways	Class 08
Diesel	D5310	BRCW	Class 26
Diesel	31271	Brush Traction	Class 31
Diesel	1566	British Railways	Class 47
DMU	50447, 50454 & 50528	BRCW	Class 104
DMU	56456	Cravens	Class 105
DMU	51933, 56223 & 56504	British Railways	Class 108
DMU	50416 & 56171	Wickham	Class 109
DMU	51618	British Railways	Class 127

Attractions

The railway runs through part of a UNESCO World Heritage Site and an Area of Outstanding Natural Beauty, following the River Dee which is home to migratory salmon, otters and lampreys. It is also close to the Llangollen Canal and the Berwyn Mountains. The new terminus at Corwen includes the 1924-built signal box from Weston Rhyn, which is between Chirk and Gobowen. Corwen Museum and the adjacent Corwen Manor and candle factory are near the town's new station. The market town of Llangollen has been popular with tourists for centuries and there are many walks and rural areas to explore from the railway's stations. Cambrian Heritage Railways is nearby, on the other side of the English border.

Special Events

Events that usually take place on the railway include:

Mother's and Father's Day Events.
Classic Transport Weekend.
Steam, Diesel & DMU Galas.
Halloween Trains during October.
Santa Specials and Mince Pie Specials during December.

Pontypool & Blaenavon Railway

Introduction and History

The railway from Brynmawr to Blaenavon opened in 1869; passenger services commenced in 1870 and the line was subsequently extended south to Pontypool. Passenger traffic ended in 1941 and the last of the coal trains ran from Blaenavon to Pontypool in 1980 when Big Pit closed. Heritage train services began in 1983, when the line between Furnace Sidings and Whistle Inn Halt opened. The railway was extended south to Blaenavon High Level station in 2010 and along the spur to Big Pit in 2011. There are long-term plans to further extend north to Waunavon and Brynmawr and also to the south, sharing the route with the present cycle path. A new carriage shed opened in Sept 2021, providing the railway with valuable undercover storage space.

Contact Details

Website: www.bhrailway.co.uk
Tel: 01495 792263
Email: info@bhrailway.co.uk
Address: Pontypool & Blaenavon Railway, The Railway Station, Furnace Sidings, Garn Yr Erw, Blaenavon, NP4 9SF.

Transport Links

By Rail: The nearest railway stations are Abergavenny and Ebbw Vale Town (both seven miles), however there are good bus connections from Cwmbran (details on P&BR website).
By Road: There is ample free parking at the Furnace Sidings base (NP4 9AX).
By Bike: On route 492 of the National Cycling Network.

Opening Times

Trains usually operate at weekends from Easter until early September, plus on selected weekdays during school holidays and on some dates during October and December.

Line Mileage and Journey Time

0.00	Coed Avon		
0.25	Blaenavon High Level	0.00	Furnace Sidings
1.50	Furnace Sidings	0.50	Big Pit Halt
2.00	Whistle Inn Halt		

A round trip takes about one hour.

Stock List

Type	Number	Builder	Details
Steam	CALEDONIA WORKS (1219)	Andrew Barclay	0-4-0ST
Steam	1823	Andrew Barclay	0-4-0ST
Steam	2015	Andrew Barclay	0-4-0ST
Steam	FORESTER	Andrew Barclay	0-4-0ST

Steam	ROSYTH No.1	Andrew Barclay	0-4-0ST
Steam	1857	Hudswell Clarke	0-6-0T
Steam	9629	GWR	0-6-0PT
Steam	2 (1421)	Avonside	0-6-0ST
Steam	SIR JOHN (1680)	Avonside	0-6-0ST
Steam	EMPRESS	Bagnell	0-6-0ST
Steam	1873 JESSIE	Hunslet	0-6-0ST
Steam	71515	Robert Stephenson & Hawthorns	0-6-0ST
Diesel	Blaenavon No. 14	Hudswell Clarke	0-4-0
Diesel	22497	Fowler	0-6-0DM
Diesel	John Roden (5511)	Hunslet	0-6-0DH
Diesel	170 (7063)	Hunslet	0-8-0DH
Diesel	D5627	Brush Traction	Class 31
Diesel	37023	English Electric	Class 37
Diesel	D6916	English Electric	Class 37
DMU	51351 & 51397	Pressed Steel	Class 117

Attractions

The railway, which is on the edge of the Brecon Beacons National Park, has one of the steepest gradients found on a British standard gauge heritage line. The rolling stock includes a varied collection of steam and diesel locomotives, multiple units and restored vintage saloons which are used on selected dates. "Heritage Railway Experiences" are available, assisting the driver and train guard with their duties. The Pontypool & Blaenavon Model Railway Club is based at the Furnace Sidings site and has railways of several different gauges. The National Coal Mining Museum and Rhymney Brewery are near to Big Pit station. The Railway Shop in Blaenavon town centre has a large range of railway-themed books, toys and models and its proceeds support the P&BR. Blaenavon Heritage Centre and the Ironworks are a 10 and 15 minute walk from Blaenavon High Level respectively. Route 492 of the National Cycle Network follows the present railway and much of the trackbed between Blaenavon and Pontypool.

Special Events

Events that usually take place on the railway include:

Model railway and transport-themed events.
Steam and diesel galas.
Halloween Ghost Trains during October.
Santa Specials during December.

▲ This timeless scene was captured on 16 April 2022; GWR 0-6-2T 5619 leaves the Llangollen Railway's Carrog station with a service for Llangollen that is formed of Mark 1 suburban coaches.
Martyn Tattam

▼ This second view at Carrog station illustrates the variety of different vantage points that heritage railways offer. On 29 August 2021, Class 108 vehicles 56504 & 51933 await departure with the 13.15 to Llangollen.
Aubrey Evans

WEST MIDLANDS

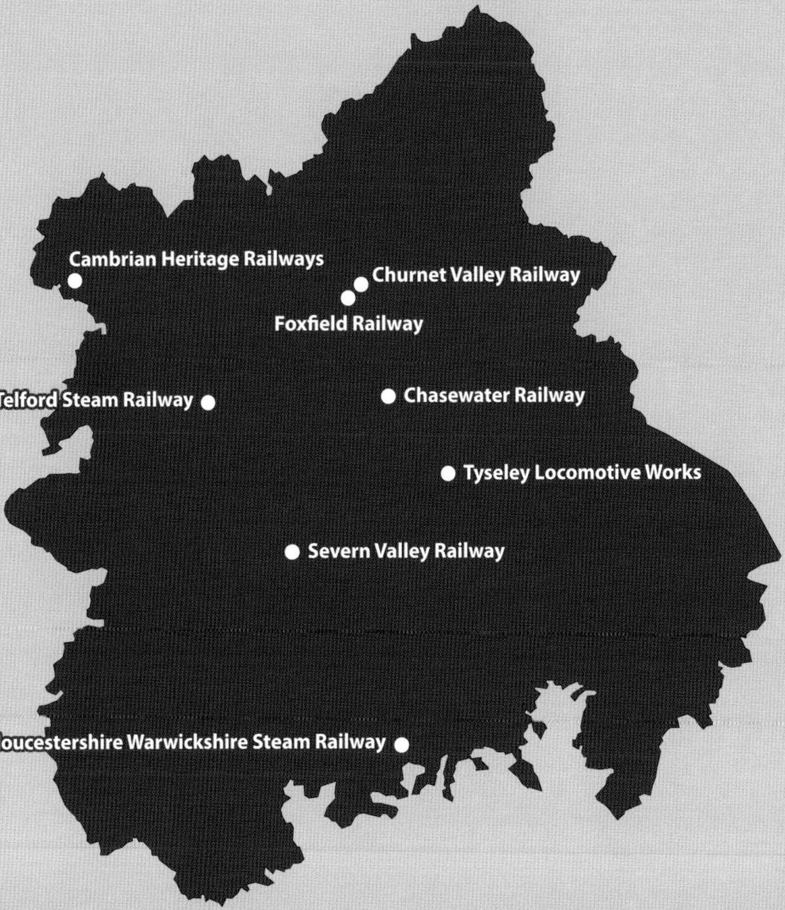

Cambrian Heritage Railways

Churnet Valley Railway

Foxfield Railway

Telford Steam Railway

Chasewater Railway

Tyseley Locomotive Works

Severn Valley Railway

Gloucestershire Warwickshire Steam Railway

▲ Cambrian Heritage Railways' electro-diesel, 73129 "City of Winchester" stands at Weston Wharf after having arrived with the 12.00 from Oswestry on 10 September 2022. The railway's recently acquired Pacers, 144007 (near) & 144006, are visible in the background.   **Andy Chard**

▼ Looking sharp in British Rail Blue livery, 47105, which is based at the Gloucestershire Warwickshire Railway, pauses at Toddington with the 13.30 Broadway–Cheltenham Racecourse on 30 July 2022.   **Andy Chard**

Region 4 – West Midlands

Cambrian Heritage Railways

Introduction and History

The branch line from Gobowen to Oswestry opened in 1848. A separate railway and station opened in Oswestry in 1860, heading south and this included the branch from Llynclys Junction to the quarry at Porthywaen. After the 1923 Grouping, improvements were made to what had become the Cambrian Railways station at Oswestry, enabling the former GWR station to close in 1924. Passenger services between Gobowen and Oswestry ended in 1966; stone trains from Gobowen to Blodwell continued until 1988 and the final weed killing train ran in 1993. A group of enthusiasts formed the Cambrian Railways Society (CRS) in 1972 and leased Oswestry goods yard from British Rail. The society opened a railway museum and from 1997 trains carried passengers on a short stretch of track. In 1998 the separate Cambrian Railways Trust (CRT) formed, aiming to return trains from Gobowen to Blodwell and began negotiations with Railtrack (subsequently Network Rail) to purchase the trackbed. A further group leased the trackbed between Llynclys and Pant after it was purchased by Oswestry Council. They relaid a ¾-mile length of track and started operating trains from 2005. Also in 2005, the local council bought Oswestry station and funding was obtained to restore the building and site. The CRS and CRT merged in 2009 forming Cambrian Heritage Railways, which now operates trains from both the Oswestry and Llynclys sites. The line from Oswestry was extended south to a new terminus at Weston Wharf between 2019 and 2021 and this was formally opened in April 2022. The long-term aim is for heritage trains to operate along the full length of the former freight line from Gobowen to Blodwell Quarry via Oswestry, which would require some major engineering projects.

Contact Details

Website: www.cambrianrailways.com
Tel: 01691 728131
Email: info@cambrianrailways.com
Address: Cambrian Heritage Railways, Old Station Building, Oswald Road, Oswestry, Shropshire, SY11 1RE.

Transport Links

By Rail: From Gobowen station Oswestry is 2.5 miles, Weston Wharf is 4 miles and Llynclys South is 7 miles.
By Road: Chargeable car parking is available at Oswestry (SY11 1RE) and there is free parking at Llynclys South (SY10 8BX).

Opening Times

Trains usually operate from Oswestry on Saturdays, Sundays and selected weekdays from May until early October, plus on selected dates during November and December. Trains from Llynclys South run less frequently and checking before travelling is recommended. The Cambrian Railway Museum in Oswestry opens 11.00–15.00 Tuesdays to Fridays from Easter to September.

Line Mileage and Journey Time

0.00	Oswestry	0.00	Llynclys South
1.5	Weston Wharf	0.75	Penygarreg Halt

Return trips from Oswestry and Llynclys South take about 40 and 25 minutes respectively.

Stock List

Type	Number	Builder	Details
Steam	2261	Andrew Barclay	0-4-0ST
Steam	2131 OLIVER VELTOM	Peckett	0-4-0ST
Steam	1430	Peckett	0-4-0ST
Steam	885	Andrew Barclay	0-6-0ST
Steam	3770 NORMA	Hunslet	0-6-0ST
Diesel	TELEMON	Drewry	0-4-0
Diesel	ALPHA	Hibberd	0-4-0

Diesel	CYRIL	Hibberd	0-4-0
Diesel	D893	Hudswell Clarke	0-4-0
Diesel	11517	Ruston & Hornsby	0-4-0
Diesel	SCOTTIE	Ruston & Hornsby	0-4-0
Diesel	458641	Ruston & Hornsby	0-4-0DE
Diesel	D1230	English Electric	0-6-0
Diesel	H037	English Electric	0-6-0
Diesel	D3019	British Railways	Class 08
Electro-Diesel	E6036 (73129)	English Electric	Class 73
DMU	51512, 51187, 51205 & 56055	Metropolitan Cammell	Class 101
DMU	144006 (55806 & 55829)	Alexander/BREL	Class 144
DMU	144007 (55807 & 55830)	Alexander/BREL	Class 144

Attractions

There are two sites to visit, although both don't always operate passenger trains simultaneously. The Oswestry site is home to the original ornate Cambrian Railways station building, the restored Oswestry South signal box and the Cambrian Railway Museum which is housed within the 150-year-old goods shed and is free to enter. Nearby attractions include Oswestry Town Museum, Pontcysyllte Aqueduct, Chirk Castle and the Llangollen Railway.

Chasewater Railway

Introduction and History

The industrial railways around Cannock Chase opened in the 1860s and were used to transport coal from the area's collieries. This continued until the 1960s when the coal mines and railway network were closed. The first preservation group (Railway Preservation Society, West Midlands District) formed in 1959, creating one of Britain's earliest heritage railway beginnings. The group acquired two derelict coaches and a rail-connected base at Hednesford in 1960 and the first locomotive arrived in 1961. In 1964 a 25-year lease was signed for a new site, on a section of trackbed on the former Aldridge to Brownhills branch. The first heritage trains ran on this in 1968 when Hawthorne Leslie 0-4-0ST "Asbestos" provided brake van rides. By 1970 all the rolling stock had been transferred from Hednesford to the Brownhills site, where regular operating days were taking place. The railway had to close between 1982 and 1985, as the funds needed to repair the line across the causeway were not available. Once this had been overcome and the repairs completed, the railway reopened and it was extended to Norton Lakeside in 1994, Chasewater Heaths in 1995 and Chasetown in 2004.

Contact Details

Website: www.chasewaterrailway.co.uk
Tel: 01543 452623
Email: admin@chasewaterrailway.co.uk
Address: Chasewater Country Park, Brownhills West Station, Pool Lane, Burntwood, Staffordshire, WS8 7NL.

Transport Links

By Rail: The nearest railway station is Landywood, which is five miles away.
By Road: There is a car park at Brownhills West, although visitors may temporarily need to park at Chasewater Country Park (both sites use the postcode WS8 7NL).

Opening Times

Trains usually operate between 11.00 and 16.30 on Saturdays, Sundays and Bank Holidays from March to October. Departure times may differ during special events.

Line Mileage and Journey Time

0.00	Brownhills West
1.00	Norton Lakeside Halt
1.50	Chasewater Heaths
1.75	Chasetown

A return journey takes about one hour.

Stock List

Type	Number	Builder	Details
Steam	2 (2842)	Bagnall	0-4-0ST
Steam	ASBESTOS (2780)	Hawthorn Leslie	0-4-0ST
Steam	750 WALESWOOD	Hudswell Clarke	0-4-0ST
Steam	2937	Neilson & Co	0-4-0ST
Steam	6 (917)	Peckett	0-4-0ST
Steam	431	Hudswell Clarke	0-6-0ST
Steam	HOLLY BANK No.3	Hunslet	0-6-0ST
Steam	S100 (1822)	Hudswell Clarke	0-6-0T
Steam	5 (9632)	Sentinel	4wVBT
Diesel	3097	Bagnall	0-4-0
Diesel	3208	Bagnall	4wDH
Diesel	3027	Baguley	0-4-0
Diesel	3410	Baguley	0-4-0
Diesel	3590	Baguley	0-4-0
Diesel	4100013	Fowler	0-4-0
Diesel	21 (1612)	Hibberd	4wDM
Diesel	DERBYSHIRE STONE No.2 (1891)	Hibberd	4wDM
Diesel	6678	Hunslet	0-4-0
Diesel	27656	North British	0-4-0
Diesel	D2911 (27876)	North British	0-4-0
Diesel	530003 MYFANWY (8366)	Robert Stephenson & Hawthorns	0-4-0
Diesel	111C	Thomas Hill	4wDH
Diesel	305306 (4472)	Ruston & Hornsby	4wDM
Diesel	AD9118	Baguley Drewry	4wDM
Diesel	15097	Simplex	0-4-0
Diesel	15099	Simplex	0-4-0
Diesel	RRM106 (27656)	North British	0-4-0DH
Diesel	01568 HELEN	Thomas Hill	4wDH
Diesel	103C	Thomas Hill	4wDH
Diesel	200V	Thomas Hill	4wDH
Diesel	3119	Bagnall	0-6-0
Diesel	6 (9000)	Hunslet	0-6-0
Diesel	D615	Hudswell Clarke	0-6-0DM
DMU	59444	British Railways	Class 116
DMU	59603	British Railways	Class 127
DMU	142027 (55518 & 55568)	BREL/Leyland	Class 142
DMU	142029 (55520 & 55570)	BREL/Leyland	Class 142
DMU	142030 (55521 & 55571)	BREL/Leyland	Class 142

Attractions

At Brownhills West, there is a tea room which opens 10.00–16.00 seven days a week, a model railway which opens during weekends, a railway museum with free entry and a model shop which opens 10.00–16.00 Thursdays to Sundays. Steam locomotive driving experiences are available and these need to be arranged in advance. The railway takes its name from the canal reservoir which it travels around and across, providing an interesting route. The area has a variety of walks, trails and cycling paths. Norton Lakeside is a Site of Special Scientific Interest and there is a nearby wildfowl reserve, which can also be explored on foot or bicycle (trains can carry bicycles). Nearby attractions include Chasewater Country Park, Wakelake, Beacon Park and the city of Lichfield.

Special Events

Events that usually take place on the railway include:

Diesel Galas.
1940s Weekend.
Wizards and Witches Events.
Halloween Event during October
Santa Specials during December.

Churnet Valley Railway

Introduction and History
The lines that comprise today's Churnet Valley Railway are the remnants of several railways that were built at different times. The route from Macclesfield to Uttoxeter via Leek opened in 1849 and became known as the Churnet Valley Line, taking the name from the river it follows. This carried minerals from local quarries and connected with a number of industrial narrow gauge railways in the area. The line from Stoke-on-Trent to Milton Junction opened in 1864, as part of the Stoke to Congleton route. Milton Junction to Leekbrook Junction near Cheddleton opened in 1867 and Leekbrook Junction to Waterhouses opened in 1905, the line connecting with a narrow gauge line to Hulme End. Passenger services on the Waterhouses branch ended in 1935 and the line was cut back to Cauldon Lowe quarry in 1943. Passenger trains ceased on the Leek–Stoke route in 1956 and on the Macclesfield–Uttoxeter Churnet Valley Line in 1960. The first preservation group formed in the 1970s and Cheddleton became its base from 1977, while freight from Stoke-on-Trent continued to the quarries at Oakamore and Cauldon Lowe until 1988 and 1989 respectively. Preserved trains between Cheddleton and Leek Brook began in 1996 and these were extended south to Consall in 1998 and to Kingsley & Froghall in 2001. The steeply graded line from Leek Brook to Cauldon Lowe reopened in 2010, but was then cut back to today's terminating point at Ipstones in 2014. The railway has the unique and ambitious aim of extending in four different directions; track laying for the northern extension to Leek began in 2019. There are also longer term plans to extend west towards Stoke, south to Oakamore and to reinstate the eastern section between Ipstones and Cauldon Lowe.

Contact Details
Website: www.churnetvalleyrailway.co.uk
Tel: 01538 360522
Email: enquiries@churnetvalleyrailway.co.uk
Address: Churnet Valley Railway, Kingsley and Froghall Station, Froghall, Staffordshire, ST10 2HA.

Transport Links
By Rail: Stoke-on-Trent station is nine miles from Cheddleton and Blythe Bridge is seven miles from Kingsley & Froghall.
By Road: There is free parking at both Cheddleton (ST13 7EE) and Kingsley & Froghall (ST10 2HA) stations.

Opening Times
The railway operates on most weekends through the year and on selected weekdays, with more regular services during school holidays.

Line Mileage and Journey Time
0.00	Ipstones
4.50	Leek Brook
5.50	Cheddleton
7.75	Consall
9.75	Kingsley & Froghall

A return Kingsley & Froghall–Cheddleton journey takes about 1 hour 10 minutes, plus a further 1 hour 10 minutes for a return to Ipstones.

Stock List
Type	Number	Builder	Details
Steam	KATIE	Andrew Barclay	0-4-0ST
Steam	44422	LMS	0-6-0
Steam	2871	Fablok	0-6-0T
Steam	2944	Fablok	0-6-0T
Steam	3278	American Locomotive Co	2-8-0
Steam	6046	Baldwin Locomotive Works	2-8-0
Steam	5197	Lima Locomotive Co	2-8-0
Steam	48173	LMS	2-8-0
Diesel	BRIGHTSIDE	Yorkshire Engine Co.	0-4-0
Diesel	6 ROGER H BENNETT	Yorkshire Engine Co.	0-6-0

Diesel	D3800	British Railways	Class 08
Diesel	D8057	English Electric	Class 20
Diesel	25322	British Railways	Class 25
Diesel	33021	BRCW	Class 33
Diesel	33102	BRCW	Class 33
Diesel	47292	British Railways	Class 47

Attractions

There is a small museum at Cheddleton station, housed within the original 1849 station building and the site has a locomotive shed and goods yard. The railway offers steam footplate rides and driver experience courses. Cheddleton Flint Mill is a short walk away from the station. The region is home to Peak Wildlife Park and the market town of Leek, which is on the edge of the Peak District. The Manifold Way is a cycle and footpath along the trackbed of the former Leek & Manifold Light Railway. Nearby heritage railways include Peak Rail, the Foxfield Railway and the Ecclesbourne Valley Railway.

Special Events

The railway has a large and varied events programme which includes:

Valentine's Express Trains.
Mother's Day Lunch Trains.
A variety of food and drink themed services.
Diesel Galas.
Polar Express Trains during December.

▲ On 23 April 2022, GWR Class 2900 4-6-0 2999 "LADY OF LEGEND" crosses the Severn Valley Railway's Falling Sands Viaduct.   **Tom Marshall**

Foxfield Railway

Introduction and History
The branch line from Blythe Bridge to Foxfield Colliery in Dilhorne, Staffordshire was built in 1893, taking a circuitous route over steep gradients to keep the railway as far away as possible from Dilhorne Hall. The colliery closed in 1965 and the site was taken over by a mineral processing firm which wanted to retain the railway for carrying minerals. At the time, the Foxfield Light Railway Society formed to operate trains over the line, with the agreement of the owning company. No further commercial freight trains operated; however, in 1967 the first heritage trains worked, carrying passengers in converted wagons. Carriages and further locomotives were subsequently acquired and a new station was built at Caverswall Road. The main line connection near Blythe Bridge has been removed and the half-mile section from Caverswall Road to the main line is currently disused. Passenger trains travel as far as Dilhorne Park, where the line continues for another three quarters of a mile to Foxfield Colliery, although at present this is not regularly used.

Contact Details
Website: www.foxfieldrailway.co.uk
Tel: 01782 396210
Email: flrenquiries@foxfieldrailway.co.uk
Address: Foxfield Railway Station, Caverswall Road, Blythe Bridge, Stoke-on-Trent, ST11 9BG.

Transport Links
By Rail: The nearest station is Blythe Bridge, which is half a mile away.
By Road: Free parking is available at Caverswall Road (ST11 9BG).

Opening Times
The railway usually operates on Sundays, Bank Holidays and on selected other dates from April to October.

Line Mileage and Journey Time
0.00   Caverswall Road
2.00   Dilhorne Park

A return journey takes about 45 minutes.

Stock List

Type	Number	Builder	Details
Steam	4101	Dübs & Company	0-4-0CT
Steam	1563	Avonside	0-4-0ST
Steam	HAWARDEN (2623)	Bagnall	0-4-0ST
Steam	1827	Beyer Peacock	0-4-0ST
Steam	3581	Hawthorn Leslie	0-4-0ST
Steam	4388	Kerr Stuart	0-4-0ST
Steam	MOSS BAY	Kerr Stuart	0-4-0ST
Steam	1803	Peckett	0-4-0ST
Steam	11 (2081)	Peckett	0-4-0ST
Steam	HENRY CORT	Peckett	0-4-0ST
Steam	6	Robert Heath	0-4-0ST
Steam	FLORENCE No.2 (3059)	Bagnall	0-6-0ST
Steam	LEWISHAM	Bagnall	0-6-0ST
Steam	WHISTON	Hunslet	0-6-0ST
Steam	WIMBLEBURY	Hunslet	0-6-0ST
Steam	1207	Manning Wardle	0-6-0ST
Steam	ACKTON HALL No.3 (1567)	Peckett	0-6-0ST
Steam	BELLEROPHON	Haydock	0-6-0WT
Steam	2	North Staffordshire Railway	0-6-2T
Steam	9535	Sentinel	4wVBGT
Electric	1130	English Electric	0-4-0
Diesel	3207	Bagnall	0-4-0
Diesel	WD820	English Electric	0-4-0
Diesel	4421	Kerr Stuart	0-4-0

Diesel	275886	Robert Stephenson & Hawthorns	4wDM
Diesel	242915	Ruston & Hornsby	4wDM
Diesel	408496	Ruston & Hornsby	4wDM
Diesel	424841	Ruston & Hornsby	0-4-0
Diesel	2262	Simplex	4wDM
Diesel	3150	Bagnall	0-6-0
Diesel	LUDSTONE (2868)	Yorkshire Engine Co.	0-6-0
DMU	142055 (55705 & 55751)	BREL/Leyland	Class 142

Attractions

The restored Foxfield Colliery is open to visitors on selected dates only and can be reached on foot from Dilhorne Park or by shuttle bus from Caverswall Road. The railway showcases its industrial history with a large collection of industrial locomotives and wagons. Driving experiences are available, using either steam or diesel locomotives. There is a miniature railway which has steep gradients and a variety of steam, petrol and battery locomotives. This is approximately one quarter of a mile long and operates on selected Sundays. At the railway's Caverswall Road base there is a museum with a large collection of railway exhibits, a souvenir & model railway shop, a real ale bar and station buffet. Nearby attractions include the Churnet Valley Railway, World of Wedgewood and Potteries Museum & Art Gallery in Stoke-on-Trent.

Special Events

As 2023 will be the centenary of the end of the North Staffordshire Railway, which was known as "The Knotty", a festival will be held on the Foxfield Railway to mark this. Other events that usually take place on the railway include:

Easter Weekend event.
Cream Tea Trains.
Vintage and Vehicle Rallies.
Victorian Weekend.
Wizard Adventure.
North Pole Express trains during December.

Gloucestershire Warwickshire Steam Railway

Introduction and History

The railway from Stratford-upon-Avon to Cheltenham via Honeybourne opened in 1906. Passenger services were withdrawn in 1960, although freight and occasional trains to the Cheltenham races continued until 1976 when the line closed. The Cheltenham & Stratford Railway Association was created in 1977, with the aim of preserving the line. Initially, the group leased the trackbed and were given access to it from 1981. In 1984 the first preserved trains operated on a 0.4 mile section of track that was laid from Toddington. Also in 1984, the 15-miles of trackbed between Cheltenham and Broadway, along with the remaining buildings along this, were purchased from British Rail. The operational section was extended in stages, reaching Winchcombe in 1987, Gotherington in 1997, Cheltenham Race Course in 2003 and Broadway in the opposite direction in 2018. There are long-term aspirations to extend the railway four miles further north to Honeybourne, where it would connect with the national rail network and also to extend a further three quarters of a mile south to the outskirts of Cheltenham.

Contact Details

Website: www.gwsr.com
Tel: 01242 621405
Email: info@gwsr.com
Address: GWSR, Churchward House, Winchcombe Railway Station, Cheltenham, GL54 5LD.

Transport Links

By Rail: The nearest main line railway station is Cheltenham Spa, which is 2.5 miles from Cheltenham Race Course station. Stagecoach services D and E operate regularly between Cheltenham Spa and Cheltenham Race Course stations on Mondays to Saturdays.
By Road: There are car parks at Cheltenham Race Course (GL50 4SH) and Toddington (GL54 5DT), pay & display parking at Broadway (WR12 7DH) and limited or no parking at the other stations.

Opening Times

Trains operate at weekends for the majority of the year, on Tuesdays to Thursdays from April to October and during December and early January for seasonal services.

Line Mileage and Journey Time

0.00	Broadway
4.75	Toddington
5.75	Hayles Abbey Halt
7.25	Winchcombe
10.50	Gotherington
14.00	Cheltenham Race Course

A return journey takes up to three hours.

Stock List

Type	Number	Builder	Details
Steam	1976	Peckett	0-4-0ST
Steam	76077	British Railways	2-6-0
Steam	2807	GWR	2-8-0
Steam	2874	GWR	2-8-0
Steam	3850	GWR	2-8-0
Steam	4270	GWR	2-8-0T
Steam	7820	British Railways	4-6-0
Steam	7903	British Railways	4-6-0
Steam	35006	Southern Railway	4-6-2
Diesel	4210130	Fowler	0-4-0DM
Diesel	11230	Drewry	0-6-0
Diesel	372	Yorkshire Engine Co.	0-6-0
Diesel	D2182	British Railways	Class 03
Diesel	D2280	Robert Stephenson & Hawthorns	Class 04
Diesel	D8137	English Electric	Class 20
Diesel	20228	English Electric	Class 20
Diesel	5081	British Railways	Class 24
Diesel	D5343	BRCW	Class 26
Diesel	37215	English Electric	Class 37
Diesel	D6948	English Electric	Class 37
Diesel	45149	British Railways	Class 45
Diesel	47105	Brush Traction	Class 47
Diesel	47376	Brush Traction	Class 47
DMU	51360, 51363, 51372, 51405, 59505 & 59510	Pressed Steel	Class 117
DMU	55003	GRCW	Class 122

Attractions

There is a viewing area for the yard and locomotive depot at Toddington. The two foot gauge Toddington Narrow Gauge Railway has steam and diesel locomotives and begins from Toddington station car park, travelling for approximately half a mile. A Royal Mail coach houses model railway displays at Winchcombe station; this opens most weekends and during special events. English Heritage Hailes Abbey is near to Hayles Abbey Halt (request stop). Cheltenham Racecourse is adjacent to its namesake station. Other nearby attractions include Berkeley Castle, Blenheim Palace, Sudeley Castle, the Cotswolds and several market towns.

Special Events

Events that usually take place on the railway include:

Easter Eggspress.
Wartime in the Cotswolds.
Classic Vehicle and Bus Rallies.
Summer Diesel Gala.
Autumn Mixed Traffic Gala.
Various food and drink themed events, including the Steam & Real Ale Weekend.
Santa Express Trains during December.

Severn Valley Railway

Introduction and History
The railway from Kidderminster to Bridgnorth and Shrewsbury opened in 1862. It closed as a through route in 1963, although freight traffic continued from Kidderminster to Alveley, near Highley, until 1969. The section from Kidderminster to Bewdley survived until early 1970, after which it was cut back to Foley Park, to where freight trains from Kidderminster worked until 1982. The Severn Valley Railway Society formed in 1965, with the initial aim of acquiring five and a half miles of the railway from Bridgnorth to Alveley. This was successful and the first heritage trains operated between Bridgnorth and Hampton Loade in 1970. In the early 1970s the railway sold shares to raise funds to purchase the section from Highley to Foley Park from British Rail. This was also successful and the line was extended to Bewdley in 1974. After freight services to Foley Park ceased, the final 1.5-mile section from Foley Park to Kidderminster was acquired and the new Kidderminster Town station built, allowing through trains from Bridgnorth to return to Kidderminster from 1984. The main line connection at Kidderminster has been reinstated, over which through trains occasionally pass.

Contact Details
Website: www.svr.co.uk
Tel: 01562 757900
Email: contact@svrlive.com
Address: Severn Valley Railway, Number One, Comberton Place, Kidderminster, DY10 1QR.

Transport Links
By Rail: Kidderminster main line station is adjacent to Kidderminster Town (SVR) station.
By Road: There is pay & display parking at Kidderminster (DY10 1QX), Bewdley (DY12 1BG) and Bridgnorth (WV16 5DT). Parking at Arley, Highley & Hampton Loade is very limited and not recommended.

Opening Times
The railway operates during weekends and Bank Holidays from March to December and on a variety of weekdays.

Line Mileage and Journey Time
0.00	Kidderminster Town
3.50	Bewdley
5.00	Northwood Halt
7.00	Arley
9.25	Highley
10.25	Country Park Halt
11.50	Hampton Loade
16.00	Bridgnorth

A return journey takes about three hours.

Stock List
Type	Number	Builder	Details
Steam	1450	GWR	0-4-2T
Steam	4085 DUNROBIN	Sharp Stewart	0-4-4T
Steam	1501	British Railways	0-6-0PT
Steam	5764 (L95)	GWR	0-6-0PT
Steam	7714	GWR	0-6-0PT
Steam	813	Hudswell Clarke	0-6-0ST
Steam	2047	Manning Wardle	0-6-0ST
Steam	71516	Robert Stephenson & Hawthorns	0-6-0ST
Steam	686	Hunslet	0-6-0T
Steam	47383	Vulcan Foundry	0-6-0T
Steam	600	North British	2-10-0
Steam	Catch Me Who Can	Trevithick 200	2-2-0
Steam	43106	British Railways	2-6-0
Steam	46443	British Railways	2-6-0
Steam	7325	GWR	2-6-0

Steam	42968	LMS	2-6-0
Steam	82045	82045 Steam Locomotive Trust	2-6-2T
Steam	4150	GWR	2-6-2T
Steam	4566	GWR	2-6-2T
Steam	5164	GWR	2-6-2T
Steam	80079	British Railways	2-6-4T
Steam	2857	GWR	2-8-0
Steam	48773	North British	2-8-0
Steam	75069	British Railways	4-6-0
Steam	4930	GWR	4-6-0
Steam	7802	GWR	4-6-0
Steam	7812	GWR	4-6-0
Steam	7819	GWR	4-6-0
Steam	45110	Vulcan Foundry	4-6-0
Steam	34027	Southern Railway	4-6-2
Diesel	319290	Ruston & Hornsby	0-4-0
Diesel	D2960	Ruston & Hornsby	0-4-0
Diesel	D2961	Ruston & Hornsby	0-4-0
Diesel	D3802 (08635)	British Railways	Class 08
Diesel	08896	British Railways	Class 08
Diesel	D3022	British Railways	Class 08
Diesel	13201	British Railways	Class 08
Diesel	D3586	British Railways	Class 08
Diesel	09107	British Railways	Class 09
Diesel	D4100	British Railways	Class 09
Diesel	12099	British Railways	Class 11
Diesel	D9551	British Railways	Class 14
Diesel	D8568	Clayton	Class 17
Diesel	20048	English Electric	Class 20
Diesel	31466	Brush Traction	Class 31
Diesel	33108	BRCW	Class 33
Diesel	D7029	Beyer Peacock	Class 35
Diesel	37308	English Electric	Class 37
Diesel	40106	English Electric	Class 40
Diesel	D821	British Railways	Class 42
Diesel	50007	English Electric	Class 50
Diesel	50031	English Electric	Class 50
Diesel	50033	English Electric	Class 50
Diesel	50035	English Electric	Class 50
Diesel	50044	English Electric	Class 50
Diesel	50049	English Electric	Class 50
Diesel	D1013	British Railways	Class 52
Diesel	D1015	British Railways	Class 52
Diesel	D1062	British Railways	Class 52
DMU	50933, 51941, 52064, 56208 & 59250	British Railways	Class 108

Attractions

The SVR is one of Britain's longest heritage railways and has a very large collection of locomotives, which is often embellished for its steam and diesel galas. There are plenty of exhibits at the Engine House Visitor & Education Centre at Highley and the locomotive works at Bridgnorth can be viewed from the station footbridge. Route 45 of the National Cycle Network travels through Bewdley and along the route of the former Wyre Forest railway line and continues north from Bridgnorth on the former railway to Coalport. Nearby attractions include Severn Valley Country Park, West Midland Safari Park, The Museum of Carpet, Wyre Forest and Hartlebury Castle & Museum.

Special Events

Events that usually take place on the railway include:

Steam and Diesel Galas.
Step Back to the 1940s.
Scream Trains during October.
Steam in Lights during November.
Santa Trains during December.

In addition, Footplate Experiences and Photo Charters can be booked on selected dates.

▲ As it is prepared for the day's work ahead, GWR Class 1500 0-6-0PT 1501 and its reflection are captured in the morning sun on 21 November 2021. **Martyn Tattam**

Telford Steam Railway

Introduction and History

The region is rich in industrial history, with the railways having played an important role in transporting raw materials and locally manufactured goods. The first wooden wagonways in the area were replaced by a cast iron plateway as early as 1769, connecting the mines and sites supplying raw materials to the iron works. The railway between Wellington and Horsehay opened in 1859 and was subsequently extended south-west to Craven Arms in 1867. The Horsehay Company Ltd was established in 1886 and occupied the site of today's steam railway. It fabricated, assembled and disassembled bridges, and had an extensive industrial railway network to aid this, before the bridges were transported to destinations throughout the British Empire. The line through Horsehay & Dawley closed to passenger services in 1962 and freight from Lightmoor Junction continued to use it until 1979. The first preservation group, the Telford Horsehay Steam Trust, formed in 1976, restoring its first steam locomotive in 1981. The heritage railway opened to the public in 1984 and was extended north to Lawley Village in 2015. Initial work has begun on a 1.5-mile southern extension from Horsehay & Dawley, which will connect to the disused Ironbridge branch at the former Lightmoor Junction. Once that has been completed, the railway could then continue along the branch to Coalbrookdale and Buildwas. As the Ironbridge branch remains connected to the Wolverhampton to Telford line at Madeley Junction, this could provide the railway with a main line connection.

Contact Details

Website: www.telfordsteamrailway.co.uk
Tel: 01952 503880
Email: enquiries@telfordsteamrailway.co.uk
Address: Telford Steam Railway, The Old Loco Shed, Bridge Road, Horsehay, Telford, TF4 2NF.

Transport Links

By Rail: The nearest railway station is Telford Central, which is 2.5 miles away.
By Road: Free parking is available outside the old loco shed or in the main yard (use postcode TF4 2NF).

Opening Times

The railway opens on selected weekends from April to late September and on selected other dates.

Line Mileage and Journey Time

0.00	Lawley Village		0.00	Lawley Village
1.25	Spring Village		1.00	Horsehay & Dawley

A return journey on both spurs of the railway starting from Spring Village takes 50 minutes.

Stock List

Type	Number	Builder	Details
Steam	1944	Andrew Barclay	0-4-0F
Steam	3240 BEATTY	Hawthorn Leslie	0-4-0ST
Steam	1990	Peckett	0-4-0ST
Steam	9366	Sentinel	0-4-0VBT
Diesel	27414 TOM	North British	0-4-0
Diesel	183062	Ruston & Hornsby	0-4-0
Diesel	313394	Ruston & Hornsby	0-4-0
Diesel	382824	Ruston & Hornsby	0-4-0
Diesel	525947	Ruston & Hornsby	0-4-0
Diesel	08757	British Railways	Class 08
Diesel	37263	English Electric	Class 37
DMU	50531	BRCW	Class 104
DMU	51950 & 52062	British Railways	Class 108
DMU	142004 (55545 & 55595)	BREL/Leyland	Class 142
DMU	142058 (55708 & 55754)	BREL/Leyland	Class 142
DMU	144013 (55813 & 55836)	Alexander/BREL	Class 144

Attractions

Steam trains run on most operating days and diesel services on the other dates. The railway's base includes a model railway, a miniature railway, a gift shop and tea room. A variety of hands-on railway experiences are available, including a guard experience and locomotive driving experiences. The Phoenix Model Engineering Society operate a miniature railway alongside Telford Steam Railway and this usually opens on the last Sunday of each month and Bank Holiday Mondays. Nearby attractions include Wonderland Telford, Cosford RAF Museum, Bllsts Hill Victorian Town and Ironbridge Gorge museums.

Special Events

Events that usually take place on the railway include:

Easter events
1940s Weekend.
Anything Goes Gala during September.
Ghost Trains.
Polar Express Trains during November and December.

Tyseley Locomotive Works

Introduction and History

The steam locomotive depot at Tyseley opened in 1908 and has remained in continuous use as a traction maintenance depot since. When former GWR locomotive 7029 'Clun Castle' was purchased by a rail enthusiast in 1966, it was moved to Tyseley, which became its new home. The final British Railways steam locomotives allocated to Tyseley left the depot in 1967 and as preservationists acquired further steam locomotives, these were brought to Tyseley. The heritage operation grew and became known as Birmingham Railway Museum, while continuing to share the site, as it does with Tyseley DMU depot today. The first main line steam train ran in 1999 and the organisation subsquently split into two, with Tyseley Locomotive Works storing and maintaining steam locomotives and Vintage Trains promoting main line trains; Vintage Trains became a train operating company in its own right in 2018. Tyseley Locomotive Works usually opens to the public on one or two weekends each year, during which trains provide rides along a short stretch of track.

Contact Details

Website: www.vintagetrains.co.uk
Tel: 0121 708 4960
Email: bookings@vintagetrains.co.uk
Address: Tyseley Locomotive Works, 670 Warwick Road, Birmingham, B11 2HL.

Transport Links

By Rail: Tyseley railway station is adjacent to the works, a short walk away.
By Road: No on-site parking is available and visitors are encouraged to travel by public transport.

Opening Times

In 2023, the annual open day will take place in June.

Line Mileage and Journey Time

Trains carry passengers for approximately one quarter of a mile and the journey time is relatively short.

Stock List

Type	Number	Builder	Details
Steam	No 1 (2004)	Peckett	0-4-0ST
Steam	No.1 Cadbury	Avonside	0-4-0T
Steam	9600	GWR	0-6-0PT
Steam	7760	North British	0-6-0PT
Steam	L94 (7752)	North British	0-6-0PT
Steam	41708	Midland Railway	0-6-0T
Steam	Fred (7289)	Robert Stephenson & Hawthorns	0-6-0ST
Steam	4121	GWR	2-6-2T

Steam	4588	GWR	2-6-2T
Steam	2885	GWR	2-8-0
Steam	4709	New build	2-8-0
Steam	7029	British Railways	4-6-0
Steam	4936	GWR	4-6-0
Steam	4965	GWR	4-6-0
Steam	5043	GWR	4-6-0
Steam	5080	GWR	4-6-0
Steam	5593	North British	4-6-0
Steam	6880	Betton Grange Society	4-6-0
Steam	71000	British Railways	4-6-2
Diesel	299099	Ruston & Hornsby	0-4-0
Diesel	347747	Robert Stephenson & Hawthorns	0-6-0DM
Diesel	08616	British Railways	Class 08
Diesel	13029	British Railways	Class 08
Diesel	47773	Brush Traction	Class 47
DMU	144014 (55814, 55850 & 55837)	Alexander/BREL	Class 144
DMU	144019 (55819, 55855 & 55842)	Alexander/BREL	Class 144
DMU	144023 (55823, 55859 & 55846)	Alexander/BREL	Class 144

Attractions

Tyseley Locomotive Works has an operational turntable and is home to a large collection of locomotives, including new-build projects and the annual open day provides the public with a rare opportunity to see these. Nearby attractions include Blakesley Hall and the city of Birmingham. The Severn Valley Railway is 20 miles away.

▲ On 1 October 2021, 24081 passes Dropping Wells Farm with the 10.55 Bridgnorth–Kidderminster Severn Valley Railway service.   **Tom McAtee**

EAST MIDLANDS

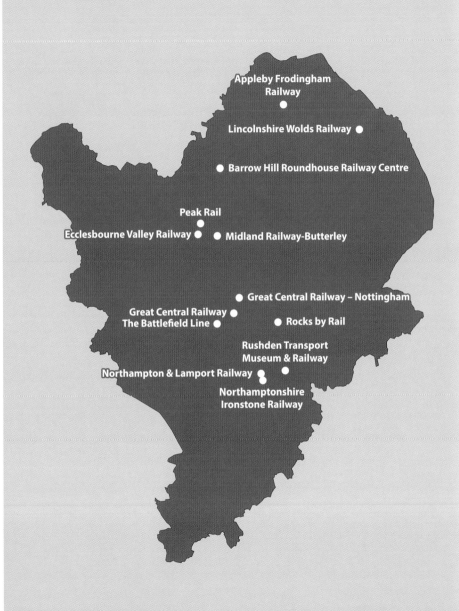

Appleby Frodingham Railway

Lincolnshire Wolds Railway

Barrow Hill Roundhouse Railway Centre

Peak Rail

Ecclesbourne Valley Railway

Midland Railway-Butterley

Great Central Railway – Nottingham

Great Central Railway
The Battlefield Line

Rocks by Rail

Rushden Transport
Museum & Railway

Northampton & Lamport Railway

Northamptonshire
Ironstone Railway

Region 5 – East Midlands

Appleby Frodingham Railway – Scunthorpe

Introduction and History

The steelworks at Scunthorpe and the extensive railway complex within them were established in the mid-19th Century. The site remains an operational steelworks today and contains more than 100 miles of working track, over which railtours run on selected dates. Since 1990, these have been operated by the Appleby Frodingham Railway, using either a diesel multiple unit or a steam or diesel locomotive and brake van combination, giving a very different experience to that of other heritage railways. A Class 144 Pacer was acquired in 2020 and the site is now one of the few that provides second generation DMU driving experiences.

Contact Details

Website: www.afrps.co.uk
Tel: 07889 297271
Email: glenn@afrps.co.uk
Address: Appleby Frodingham Railway, PO Box 1, Scunthorpe, DN16 1BP.

Transport Links

By Rail: The nearest railway station is Scunthorpe, which is one mile from the site.
By Road: Parking is available at the steelworks, which is accessed from Brigg Road, Scunthorpe (DN16 1XA).

Opening Times

Railtours of the steelworks operate during the daytime on selected Saturdays and on selected evenings. A donation is requested to cover the costs.

Line Mileage and Journey Time

The railway is not linear and each tour tends to follow a different route around the steelworks. The distance travelled varies; it is usually at least 10 miles and takes around four hours (slightly less for evenings tours).

Stock List

Type	Number	Builder	Details
Steam	8 (2369)	Andrew Barclay	0-4-0ST
Steam	1 (1438)	Peckett	0-4-0ST
Steam	3 (1919)	Avonside	0-6-0ST
Steam	3138	Fablok	0-6-0T
Diesel	1 (2661)	Yorkshire Engine Co.	0-6-0
Diesel	Horsa (8368)	Bagnall	0-4-0
Diesel	1 (2877)	Yorkshire Engine Co.	0-6-0
DMU	56207 & 59245	British Railways	Class 108
DMU	144017 (55817, 55853 & 55840)	Alexander/BREL	Class 144

Attractions

The railtours are unique for a heritage railway, providing visitors with the opportunity to see an operational steelworks. Note that for safety reasons children under the age of 10 cannot travel on brake van tours and children under 5 cannot travel on any tour. Steam locomotive and Pacer driver experiences are available. A restored buffet coach is used to provide refreshments. Other nearby attractions include North Lincolnshire Museum in Scunthorpe, Elsham Hall, Gardens & Country Park and Normanby Hall Country Park.

▲ Avonside 0-6-0ST 1919 and Hunslet 0-6-0ST 3846 stand in the platform of the Appleby Frodingham Railway Scunthorpe with a brake van special on 26 June 2021. **Gordon Edgar**

▼ 03066 provides rides at Barrow Hill Roundhouse on 28 August 2022, with steam loco 1501 out of sight on the rear of the train. **Robert Pritchard**

Barrow Hill Roundhouse Railway Centre

Introduction and History

The railway through Chesterfield and Staveley opened in 1841 as part of the North Midland Railway's route from Derby to Rotherham and Leeds. A locomotive depot was built at Staveley in 1865, followed by the roundhouse in 1870. After 121 years of continuous use, British Rail closed the roundhouse in 1991 and the condition of the buildings and the site then deteriorated. In 1989 the Barrow Hill Engine Shed Action Group formed with the aim of saving the roundhouse from demolition. The group lobbied for the building to be given Grade II listed status and this was granted in 1991. The project received funding from several organisations and much restoration work was completed. The site first opened to the public in 1998, with diesel-hauled brake van rides being provided. It now has a museum and a large collection of locomotives, some of which reside there long-term, while others travel to and from other locations. The roundhouse remains connected to the main line, enabling occasional charter trains to arrive at the site for special events.

Contact Details

Website: www.barrowhill.org
Tel: 01246 472450
Email: enquiries@barrowhill.org
Address: Barrow Hill Limited, Campbell Drive, Barrow Hill, Chesterfield, S43 2PR.

Transport Links

By Rail: The nearest station is Chesterfield, which is four miles away. There is a free bus from Chesterfield station and town centre on some special event days.
By Road: There is ample free parking on site (S43 2PR).

Opening Times

The roundhouse and museum open 10.00–16.00 on Saturdays and Sundays from March to mid-December.

Line Mileage and Journey Time

Trains operate on a section of the former Springwell branch on selected dates. This runs north from the roundhouse site for approximately half a mile and the journey time is relatively short. Harry Needle Railroad Company is based at Barrow Hill. Members of its locomotive fleet will be present, but are omitted from the stocklist as this is a commercial operator whose locomotives regularly move to and from the site.

Stock List

Type	Number	Builder	Details
Steam	HENRY (2491)	Hawthorn Leslie	0-4-0ST
Steam	8217	GER	0-6-0
Steam	68006	Hunslet	0-6-0ST
Steam	VULCAN (3272)	Vulcan Foundry	0-6-0ST
Steam	158A	Midland Railway	2-4-0
Steam	506	Great Central Railway	4-4-0
Steam	1000	Midland Railway	4-4-0
Electric	81002	BRCW	Class 81
Electric	82008	Beyer Peacock	Class 82
Electric	E3035	English Electric	Class 83
Electric	85006	British Railways	Class 85
Electric	91117	BREL	Class 91
Diesel	12589 HARRY	Robert Stephenson & Hawthorns	0-4-0DM
Diesel	D2868	Yorkshire Engine Co.	Class 02
Diesel	02003	Yorkshire Engine Co.	Class 02
Diesel	03066	British Railways	Class 03
Diesel	07012	Ruston & Hornsby	Class 07
Diesel	08799	British Railways	Class 08
Diesel	D4092	British Railways	Class 10
Diesel	D5910	Baby Deltic Project	Class 23
Diesel	26007	BRCW	Class 26
Diesel	27066	BRCW	Class 27

Diesel	45060	British Railways	Class 45
Diesel	45105	British Railways	Class 45
Diesel	45118	British Railways	Class 45
Diesel	46010	British Railways	Class 46
Diesel	55019	English Electric	Class 55
Diesel	D9009	English Electric	Class 55
Diesel	D9015	English Electric	Class 55
EMU	62364 & 76762	BREL	Class 421
EMU	62321	BREL	Class 423

Attractions
The roundhouse, which is now over 150 years old, has a 24-road turntable and is the only surviving operational roundhouse in Great Britain. The shear legs (lifting gear) can be seen, along with a large display of locomotives, an operational signal box, display rooms and various railway exhibits. The Deltic Preservation Society's maintenance depot and museum is adjacent to the roundhouse and are usually open on Saturdays and during some special events. Peak Rail, the Midland Railway-Butterley and the Ecclesbourne Valley Railway are all under 20 miles away. Other attractions in the area include Cliffe Park, Abbeydale Industrial Hamlet, Chesterfield and Sheffield.

Special Events
A varied mix of events intermittently take place at the roundhouse, including live music, plays, lectures and exhibitions. A Real Ale Festival is planned for 18–20 May 2023.

▲ 20110 approaches the Battlefield Line's Shackerstone station with the 13.05 from Shenton on 22 May 2022. **Andy Chard**

The Battlefield Line

Introduction and History

The Battlefield Line was part of the Ashby & Nuneaton Joint Railway which opened in 1873, linking Nuneaton to the Leicestershire coalfields. Before the 1923 Grouping, it was jointly operated by the London & North Western and the Midland Railways. British Rail ran the final passenger train over the line in 1965, after which it closed. The preservation era began in 1969 when the Shackerstone Railway Society formed, shortly before the track was lifted in 1970. The first heritage train worked from Shackerstone to Market Bosworth in 1973 and in 1992 the line was extended to Shenton. The railway takes its name from Bosworth Battlefield near Shenton, where the final battle of the War of the Roses took place in 1485.

Contact Details

Website: www.battlefieldline.co.uk
Tel: 01827 880754
Email: enquiries@battlefieldline.co.uk
Address: The Shackerstone Railway Society Ltd, Shackerstone Station, Leicestershire, CV13 6NW.

Transport Links

By Rail: Nuneaton and Hinckley railway stations are seven and six miles from Shenton respectively. Polesworth and Atherstone stations are both nine miles from Shackerstone.
By Road: There is ample parking at all three stations, which is free at Shakerstone (CV13 0BS) and Market Bosworth (CV13 0PF); charges apply at Shenton (CV13 6DJ).
By Boat: Narrowboats can moor at Ashby Canal Bridge 52 (a ten minute walk to Shackerstone station), Bridge 42 at Bosworth Marina (a five minute walk to Market Bosworth station) and Shenton Aqueduct or Bridge 35 (both a five minute walk to Shenton station).

Opening Times

Trains operate during weekends from late March and on selected Wednesdays during school holidays.

Line Mileage and Journey Time

0.00 Shackerstone
2.50 Market Bosworth
4.25 Shenton

A return journey takes just under one hour.

Stock List

Type	Number	Builder	Details
Steam	1859 SIR GOMER	Peckett	0-6-0ST
Steam	TEDDY (2012)	Peckett	0-4-0ST
Diesel	263001 NANCY	Ruston & Hornsby	0-4-0
Diesel	268881	Ruston & Hornsby	0-4-0DE
Diesel	281271	Ruston & Hornsby	0-4-0DM
Diesel	422 HOT WHEELS	Andrew Barclay	0-6-0
Diesel	594 BIG MOMMA	Andrew Barclay	0-6-0
Diesel	1901	English Electric	0-6-0
Diesel	D2867	Yorkshire Engine Co.	Class 02
Diesel	04110	Robert Stephenson & Hawthorns	Class 04
Diesel	08653	British Railways	Class 08
Diesel	08682	British Railways	Class 08
Diesel	08701	British Railways	Class 08
Diesel	08706	British Railways	Class 08
Diesel	08905	British Railways	Class 08
Diesel	12083	British Railways	Class 11
Diesel	2002 (20063)	English Electric	Class 20
Diesel	20087	English Electric	Class 20
Diesel	D7523	British Railways	Class 25
Diesel	33008	BRCW	Class 33
Diesel	33053	BRCW	Class 33
Diesel	33208	BRCW	Class 33

Diesel	33201	BRCW	Class 33
Diesel	37906	English Electric	Class 37
Diesel	40118	English Electric	Class 40
Diesel	45015	British Railways	Class 45
Diesel	58012	BREL	Class 58
Diesel	58048	BREL	Class 58
Battery	905	English Electric	0-4-0
DMU	51131	British Railways	Class 116
DMU	51321	BRCW	Class 118
DMU	55005	GRCW	Class 122
DEMU	975386	British Railways	Class 202
EMU	65321 & 77112	British Railways	Class 416

Attractions

Footplate rides and dining and driver experiences are available on various dates. There is a gift and model railway shop at Shackerstone. Bosworth Battlefield is one mile from Shenton. The Ashby Canal runs alongside the railway and boats can be hired and moored at the marina, which is a short walk from Market Bosworth station. Other attractions nearby include Conkers World of Adventure & Discovery, Ashby de la Zouch, Tamworth Castle and Twycross Zoo.

Special Events

Events that usually take place on the railway include:

Mother's Day Champagne Teas.
Easter eggstravaganza.
Mother's Day and Father's Day events.
Rails & Ales festival during the summer.
Family Fun Weekend during the August Bank Holiday weekend.
Santa Specials during December.

Ecclesbourne Valley Railway

Introduction and History

The branch from Duffield to Wirksworth opened in 1867 and passenger services were withdrawn 80 years later in 1947. The line was then used to carry freight and Wirksworth station was demolished in 1967 so the site could be developed as a stone terminal. The branch continued to carry local stone until traffic ended in 1989. The track then remained in place and the route opened as a heritage railway in 2002. Initially heritage trains ran for half a mile from Wirksworth and they now make the 18-mile round trip to Duffield and up the unusually steep 1 in 27 incline of the Ravenstor extension when this is in use on special event days.

Contact Details

Website: www.e-v-r.com
Tel: 01629 823076
Email: ticketoffice@e-v-r.com
Address: Ecclesbourne Valley Railway, Station Road, Coldwell Street, Wirksworth, DE4 4FB.

Transport Links

By Rail: On arrival at Duffield, use the footbridge to cross to Platform 3 for the EVR.
By Road: Car parking is available at Wirksworth (DE4 4FB) and Duffield (DE56 4EQ) where there is a smaller car park for both the EVR and national rail users.

Opening Times

Trains operate during most weekends and on selected other days throughout the year.

Line Mileage and Journey Time

0.00	Ravenstor
0.50	Wirksworth
4.00	Idridgehay
5.25	Shottle
9.00	Duffield

A return journey takes about 1 hour 30 minutes.

Stock List

Type	Number	Builder	Details
Steam	2217 Henry Ellison	Andrew Barclay	0-4-0
Steam	3 (2360)	Andrew Barclay	0-4-0
Steam	68012	Bagnall	0-6-0ST
Steam	102	Hudswell Clarke	0-6-0T
Steam	80080	British Railways	2-6-4T
Diesel	402803	Ruston & Hornsby	0-4-0
Diesel	MEGAN	Thomas Hill	0-4-0
Diesel	Tom	Thomas Hill	0-4-0
Diesel	265V	Thomas Hill	0-4-0
Diesel	10275	Rolls Royce Sentinel	0-6-0
Diesel	D9525	British Railways	Class 14
Diesel	D9537	British Railways	Class 14
Diesel	31601	Brush Traction	Class 31
Diesel	33103	BRCW	Class 33
Diesel	47192	British Railways	Class 47
Electro-Diesel	73001	English Electric	Class 73
Electro-Diesel	73210	English Electric	Class 73
DMU	50170, 50253, 51505 & 59303	Metropolitan Cammell	Class 101
DMU	50599 & 51567	British Railways	Class 108
DMU	51073	GRCW	Class 119
DMU	55027, 55031 & 55034	Pressed Steel	Class 121
DMU	55006	GRCW	Class 122
DMU	79018 & 79612	British Railways	Derby Lightweight
DMU	79900	British Railways	Derby Lightweight
EMU	68500 & 68506	British Railways	Class 489

Attractions

At Wirksworth there is a museum which opens on the days that trains operate and a 7¼ gauge railway which has recently been extended and this operates on Saturdays and special event days. There is also a two foot gauge line at Wirksworth, but this has been out of use since 2019 and there are no immediate plans to reopen it. The railway has a large collection of heritage multiple units and offers both steam and diesel footplate experiences. The region has many attractions including the Peak District, Matlock, Matlock Bath and Carsington Water. Other nearby railway attractions include Peak Rail, Crich Tramway Village, Midland Railway-Butterley and Steeple Grange Light Railway.

Special Events

Events that usually take place on the railway include:

Diesel and railcar themed events.
Classic Bus & Coach Rally.
Dining services include afternoon tea and ploughman's lunch trains.
Steam train journey with ghost stories.
The Train Through Christmas Countryside.

Great Central Railway

Introduction and History

The Great Central Railway from London Marylebone to Rugby, Leicester and Nottingham opened to freight in 1898 and to passenger services in 1899, providing a new route from the North to the South East. Express trains ended in 1960 and the smaller stations, including Rothley and Quorn and Woodhouse, closed in 1963. Through services ended in 1966 when the line south of Rugby was severed and it closed fully in 1969, when Rugby–Nottingham Arkwright Street services ceased. The first preservation group, the Main Line Steam Trust, formed in the early 1970s and acquired the station and trackbed at Loughborough. The first heritage trains worked in 1973, with steam-hauled services to Quorn. In 1976 the section from Loughborough to Rothley was secured and with the assistance of the local council, the trackbed from Loughborough to Belgrave & Birstall to the south was acquired. A new station at Leicester North was built immediately south of the former Belgrave & Birstall station, with trains terminating there from 1990. The line became Britain's only double track heritage railway in 2000, with the facility for test trains to operate at 60 mph, although the maximum speed for heritage passenger trains is 25 mph. In 2015 the branch from Swithland to the former quarry site at Mountsorrel reopened and infrequent services operate to a newly constructed halt there. Work is progressing to merge with the Nottingham Heritage Railway, creating an 18-mile line; the bridge over the Network Rail line near Leicester was reinstated in 2017, repairs to the bridge across the Grand Union Canal followed and the 125-year old railway bridge over the A60 was replaced in November 2022. This new bridge over the A60 will carry two lines, one for the reunited heritage railway and one for the main line connection at Loughborough Chord Junction.

Contact Details

Website: www.gcrailway.co.uk
Tel: 01509 632323
Email: sales@gcrailway.co.uk
Address: Great Central Railway, Great Central Road, Loughborough, LE11 1RW.

Transport Links

By Rail: Loughborough (main line station) is one mile from Loughborough Central.
By Road: Parking is available at Loughborough (LE11 1RW, roadside parking), Quorn & Woodhouse (LE12 8AG), Rothley (LE7 7LD) and Leicester North (LE4 3BR).

Opening Times

Trains operate every weekend through the year and on selected weekdays. Services on the Mountsorrel branch only run on selected dates.

Line Mileage and Journey Time

0.00	Loughborough Central	0.00	Rothley
2.00	Quorn and Woodhouse	1.50	Mountsorrel Halt
4.75	Rothley		
7.75	Leicester North		

A return journey takes about 1 hour 30 minutes.

Stock List

Type	Number	Builder	Details
Steam	3809	Hunslet	0-6-0ST
Steam	4 (7684)	Robert Stephenson & Hawthorns	0-6-0T
Steam	47406	Vulcan Foundry	0-6-0T
Steam	92214	British Railways	2-10-0
Steam	46521	British Railways	2-6-0
Steam	78018	British Railways	2-6-0
Steam	78019	British Railways	2-6-0
Steam	63601	Great Central Railway	2-8-0
Steam	48305	LMS	2-8-0
Steam	48624	Southern Railway	2-8-0
Steam	45305	Armstrong Whitworth	4-6-0
Steam	73156	British Railways	4-6-0
Steam	6990	British Railways	4-6-0

Steam	7027	British Railways	4-6-0
Steam	45491	LMS	4-6-0
Steam	777	North British	4-6-0
Steam	70013	British Railways	4-6-2
Steam	34039	Southern Railway	4-6-2
Steam	9370	Sentinel	4wVBT
Diesel	4210079	Fowler	0-4-0DM
Diesel	D2989	Ruston & Hornsby	Class 07
Diesel	08907	British Railways	Class 08
Diesel	13101	British Railways	Class 08
Diesel	D3690	British Railways	Class 08
Diesel	10119	British Railways	Class 10
Diesel	D8098	English Electric	Class 20
Diesel	D5185	British Railways	Class 25
Diesel	D5401	BRCW	Class 27
Diesel	D6535	BRCW	Class 33
Diesel	D6700	English Electric	Class 37
Diesel	37714	English Electric	Class 37
Diesel	D123	British Railways	Class 45
Diesel	1705	Brush Traction	Class 47
Diesel	50017	English Electric	Class 50
DMU	50193, 50203, 50266, 50321, 51427 & 56342	Metropolitan Cammell	Class 101
DMU	59575	Metropolitan Cammell	Class 111
DMU	51396 & 59506	Pressed Steel	Class 117
DMU	59276	British Railways	Class 120
DMU	55009	GRCW	Class 122
EMU	70576	British Railways	Class 411

Attractions

There is a museum at Loughborough Central and a walkway from which the signal box and part of the engine shed can be seen (the shed itself is restricted). Quorn and Woodhouse has a tea room housed in an authentic recreated air raid shelter. The railway offers a large variety of dining trains, plus steam and diesel driving experiences. The Charnwood Forest Garden Railway is adjacent to Rothley station and operates at weekends and Bank Holidays. Nearby attractions include the Nottingham Heritage Railway, Stonehouse Family Farm & Motor Museum, Charnwood Museum, Bradgate Park and Gorse Hill City Farm in Leicester.

Special Events

The programme of events for 2023 illustrates the breadth of events that take place on the railway:

1–2 January: New Year Trains.
27–29 January: Winter Steam Gala.
21–23 February: Paw Patrol.
24 Feb–24 March: Railway Closed for Major Engineering Work (cafes open at Quorn & Rothley).
5 March: Swapmeet (no trains).
18–19 Mar: 16mm & Model Engineers Weekend (Trains at Leicester N, Rothley & Mountsorrel only).
March 25–26 (date TBC): Railways At Work Gala.
7–10 April: Easter Vintage Festival.
12–14 April: Family Holiday Event.
April 22–23: Spring Diesel Gala.
6 May: Quorn Bus Rally.
13–14 May: Vintage Vehicle Rally.
2–4 June: 1940s Weekend.
17–18 June: 50th Anniversary Celebrations.
25 June: Swapmeet.
4–6 August: Summer Family Event.
12–13 August: Summer Vintage Vehicle Festival.
22–24 August: Summer Family Event.
1–3 September: Diesel Gala.
3 September: Swapmeet.
14–17 September: Beer Festival.

5–8 October: Autumn Steam Gala.
3 November: Bonfire Night.
18–19 November: Last Hurrah Gala.
25 November: Christmas Train Services Commence.
31 December: The Night Rider.

Lincolnshire Wolds Railway

Introduction and History
Trains first worked on the railway from Grimsby to Louth in 1847 and it was opened to passengers in 1848. All stations on the route except North Thoresby were closed to passengers in 1961, followed by North Thoresby and Louth, which closed in 1970 when the line was singled and reduced to a freight branch from Grimsby. This remained in use until 1980, when British Rail closed the line and then promptly demolished the stations and lifted the track. The first preservation group formed in the late 1970s, initially opposing the proposed closure, and in 1984 it established a base at Ludborough station. Since then, the LWR has purchased five miles of trackbed between Ludborough and a site on the outskirts of Louth, where a new station is planned. The first heritage trains between Ludborough and North Thoresby began in 2009. The line is currently being extended south towards the outskirts of Louth, the first stage being the 0.75-mile section to Pear Tree Lane Crossing, near the site of the former Utterby Halt. The long-term aim is to extend both north and south, restoring as much of the route between Grimsby and Louth as possible.

Contact Details
Website: www.lincolnshirewoldsrailway.co.uk
Tel: 01507 363881
Email: marclwr@hotmail.com
Address: Lincolnshire Wolds Railway, Ludborough Station, Station Road, Ludborough, Lincolnshire, DN36 5SQ.

Transport Links
By Rail: Grimsby Town is the nearest railway station and is nine miles from the Ludborough base.
By Road: Free parking is available at Ludborough station (use postcode DN36 5SH).

Opening Times
Trains operate on most Sundays from mid-March until October and on selected other dates.

Line Mileage and Journey Time
0.00   Ludborough
1.75   North Thoresby

A return journey takes 40 minutes.

Stock List

Type	Number	Builder	Details
Steam	SPITFIRE	Andrew Barclay	0-4-0ST
Steam	1749 FULSTOW	Peckett	0-4-0ST
Steam	LION	Peckett	0-4-0ST
Steam	7597	Robert Stephenson & Hawthorns	0-6-0T
Steam	1313	Motala Verkstad	4-6-0
Diesel	4210131	Fowler	0-4-0DM
Diesel	4210145	Fowler	0-4-0DM
Diesel	423657	Robert Stephenson & Hawthorns	0-4-0DE
Diesel	5308	Hunslet	4wDM
Diesel	375713	Ruston & Hornsby	0-4-0DM
Diesel	414303	Ruston & Hornsby	0-4-0DM
Diesel	421418	Ruston & Hornsby	0-4-0DM
Diesel	DEBBIE (3151)	Bagnall	0-6-0
Diesel	D3167	British Railways	Class 08

Attractions

There is a railway museum at Ludborough with a collection of artefacts from the route's history and a café which is located within a Mark 1 coach. Guided tours around the LWR's engine shed are available on selected Sundays and these usually begin at 12.30 and 14.30. Footplate rides and signal box experiences can be arranged for an additional charge. The railway is near to the market town of Louth, the coastal resort of Cleethorpes and the larger town of Grimsby.

Special Events

The following events are due to take place during 2023 & 2024:

19 March: Mother's Day Special.
9–10 April: Easter Egg Hunt, children receive a gift.
28–29 May: Pirate Fancy Dress.
18 June: Father's Day trains.
16 July: Vintage vehicles & engines display.
20 August: Teddy Bear Day (bring your own teddy).
9–10 September: Heritage Weekend.
16–17 September: Life in the 1940s.
29 October: Halloween Spooktacular.
9–10 & 16–18 December: Santa Specials.
1 January 2024: New Year's Day trains.

▲ British Rail Standard Class 9F 92134 approaches the Great Central Railway's Rothley station with a freight train on 5 October 2021.   **Gordon Edgar**

Midland Railway-Butterley

Introduction and History

The railway between Pye Bridge and Ambergate opened in 1875, linking the present-day routes from Chesterfield to Nottingham and Derby to Matlock. Passenger services ended in 1947 and the line closed in 1968 after freight traffic ceased. The track was then lifted and Butterley station was demolished. In the late 1960s Derby Corporation and Derbyshire County Council planned to create a museum dedicated to the Midland Railway and three steam locomotives were purchased. A site was found on the closed Pye Bridge–Ambergate line; however, the organisations withdrew from the project due to a lack of funds. The Midland Railway Project was a volunteer group which collected and restored railway items. It revived the project in the early 1970s. Butterley became its base and Swanwick Junction was to be the site of the museum. The first open day was held in 1975. One mile of track was laid and the first preserved trains departed from the newly-constructed Butterley station in 1981. The railway has since been extended west to Hammersmith, where the A38 severs the trackbed, and east to Ironville, where the main line connection has been reinstated. New stations have been constructed and there has been considerable development of the railway's heritage attractions.

Contact Details

Website: www.midlandrailway-butterley.co.uk
Tel: 01773 570140
Email: enquiries@midlandrailway-butterley.co.uk
Address: Butterley Station, Ripley, Derbyshire, DE5 3QZ.

Transport Links

By Rail: The nearest station is Alfreton, which is four miles away.
By Road: Free parking is available at Butterley (DE5 3QZ).

Opening Times

The railway operates on most weekends through the year and on selected weekdays.

Line Mileage and Journey Time

0.00   Hammersmith
0.25   Butterley
1.00   Swanwick Junction
2.75   Ironville Junction
3.00   End of Line

A return journey from Butterley takes 45–70 minutes, depending on the starting point and which timetable is operating.

Stock List

Type	Number	Builder	Details
Steam	4 (454)	Naismyth Wilson	0-4-0
Steam	STANTON No.24 (1875)	Andrew Barclay	0-4-0CT
Steam	109	Markham & Co	0-4-0ST
Steam	3 (3597)	Hawthorn Leslie	0-4-0ST
Steam	VICTORY (1547)	Peckett	0-4-0ST
Steam	WHITEHEAD	Peckett	0-4-0ST
Steam	7214	Robert Stephenson & Hawthorns	0-4-0ST
Steam	1 (7817)	Robert Stephenson & Hawthorns	0-4-0ST
Steam	3883 (2868) LORD PHIL	Hunslet	0-6-0ST
Steam	47445	Hunslet	0-6-0T
Steam	47564	Hunslet	0-6-0T
Steam	47357	North British	0-6-0T
Steam	23 (BR No. 47327)	North British	0-6-0T
Steam	80098	British Railways	2-6-4T
Steam	92212	British Railways	2-10-0
Steam	73129	British Railways	4-6-0
Steam	5551	LMS-Patriot Project	4-6-0
Steam	6233	LMS	4-6-2
Steam	46203	LMS	4-6-2

Electric	27000	British Railways	Class 77
Diesel	441	Andrew Barclay	0-4-0DH
Diesel	No. 4 (416)	Andrew Barclay	0-4-0DH
Diesel	16038	Fowler	0-4-0DM
Diesel	ALBERT	Hudswell Clarke	0-6-0DM
Diesel	MANTON	Hudswell Clarke	0-6-0DM
Diesel	RS12	Simplex	4wDM
Diesel	RS9	Simplex	4wDM
Diesel	D2858	Yorkshire Engine Co.	Class 02
Diesel	D2138	British Railways	Class 03
Diesel	08331	British Railways	Class 08
Diesel	08590	British Railways	Class 08
Diesel	12077	British Railways	Class 11
Diesel	20227	English Electric	Class 20
Diesel	D7671	British Railways	Class 25
Diesel	5580	Brush Traction	Class 31
Diesel	31108	Brush Traction	Class 31
Diesel	31418	Brush Traction	Class 31
Diesel	D5814	Brush Traction	Class 31
Diesel	40012	English Electric	Class 40
Diesel	D4	British Railways	Class 44
Diesel	45133	British Railways	Class 45
Diesel	D182	British Railways	Class 46
Diesel	47761	British Railways	Class 47
Diesel	47401	Brush Traction	Class 47
Diesel	D1516	Brush Traction	Class 47
Diesel	D1048	British Railways	Class 52
DMU	51118 & 56097	GRCW	Class 100
DMU	51907 & 56490	British Railways	Class 108
DMU	50015, 50019, 56006 & 56015	British Railways	Class 114
DMU	59659, 51669 & 51849	British Railways	Class 115
DMU	51591, 51610, 51625 & 59609	British Railways	Class 127
DMU	141113 (55513 & 55533)	BREL/Leyland	Class 141
DMU	142011 (55552 & 55602)	BREL/Leyland	Class 142
DMU	142013 (55554 & 55604)	BREL/Leyland	Class 142
EMU	29666 & 29670	Metropolitan Cammell	MSJ&A

Attractions

There is plenty to explore at Swanick Junction; the West Shed Experience (railway museum), the demonstration signal box, the Victorian railwayman's church, the Road Transport Building and the National Fork Truck Heritage Centre. There are a variety of smaller railways at Swanick – the Golden Valley Light Railway, the Historical Model Railway Society, a miniature railway and a narrow gauge railway. At Butterley there is a garden railway, a model railway and carriage shed. Butterley Country Park is adjacent to the railway and other nearby attractions include Crich Tramway Village and Duffield Castle.

Special Events

Events that usually take place on the railway include:

Diesel Gala.
Victorian Train Weekend.
Wizards & Spooks during October.
Fireworks Night during November.
Santa Specials during December.

Northampton & Lamport Railway

Introduction and History

The railway between Northampton and Market Harborough opened in 1859 to carry passengers and local goods. Passenger services were withdrawn in 1960, but through passenger traffic returned between January and May 1969 and again from 1972 to 1973. The first preservation group formed in 1981 and organised a final charter train to travel the length of the line before it closed in August 1981. The group's name was later changed to the Northampton & Lamport Railway and a base was established at Pitsford and Brampton, the first station north of Northampton. The first heritage trains ran in late 1995 and the railway formally opened in 1996. The line has recently been extended south by half a mile to a new station called Boughton which involved restoring an 8-arch low viaduct and constructing a new terminus. This new section is due to be formally opened in 2023, subject to the Department for Transport issuing the required Light Railway Order. There are longer-term plans to extend the line north, initially to a small halt with a run round loop at Merry Tom Crossing, which will require repairs to the bridge across the River Nene.

Contact Details

Website: www.nlr.org.uk
Tel: 01604 820327
Email: enquiries@nlr.org.uk
Address: Northampton & Lamport Railway, Pitsford & Brampton Station, Pitsford Road, Chapel Brampton, NN6 8BA.

▲ As most heritage railways consist of single track lines, there are very few locations where scenes like this can be captured. On 29 January 2022 BR Standard Class 5MT 73156 heads towards Quorn with a van train on the Great Central Railway, while Class 2MT 78018 approaches with a passenger service for Loughborough. **Martyn Tattam**

Transport Links

By Rail: The nearest station is Northampton, which is five miles away.
By Road: Free parking is available Pitsford & Brampton Station.
By Bike: Arrive on the Brampton Valley Way, a foot and cycle path which follows the railway and trackbed between Northampton and Market Harborough.

Opening Times

Trains usually operate on Sundays and Bank Holidays from mid-March to late-October, and during November and December for seasonal services. During the operating season Pitsford & Brampton station opens on some Wednesdays and Saturdays when trains aren't in service, although this is subject to volunteer availability, so checking before travelling is recommended.

Line Mileage and Journey Time

0.00   Northern limit
0.65   Pitsford & Brampton
1.50   Boughton

A round trip takes about 40 minutes.

Stock List

Type	Number	Builder	Details
Steam	776	Andrew Barclay	0-4-0ST
Steam	2323	Andrew Barclay	0-4-0ST
Steam	3718	Hawthorn Leslie	0-4-0ST
Steam	2104	Peckett	0-4-0ST
Steam	3193 (75142)	Hunslet	0-6-0ST
Steam	45 (5470)	Kitson	0-6-0ST
Steam	1378 WESTMINSTER	Peckett	0-6-0ST
Steam	3862	GWR	2-8-0
Steam	5967	GWR	4-6-0
Diesel	21	Fowler	0-4-0
Diesel	1	Ruston & Hornsby	4wDM
Diesel	764	Ruston & Hornsby	0-4-0
Diesel	53	Ruston & Hornsby	0-6-0
Diesel	31289	Brush Traction	Class 31
Diesel	47205	British Railways	Class 47

Attractions

At Pitsford & Brampton station, visitors can browse the gift shop and second-hand book shop. The Brampton Valley Way foot and cycle path follows the course of the present-day railway and the disused sections between Northampton and Market Harborough. Other attractions in the area include Abington Museum, Delapre Abbey and the large town of Northampton.

Special Events

Events that usually take place on the railway include:

Mothering Sunday Specials.
Easter Egg Specials.
Kids for a Quid on selected dates.
Father's Day Specials.
Halloween Event during October.
Santa Specials during December.
Mince Pie Specials on New Years' Eve and New Years' Day.

Northamptonshire Ironstone Railway

Introduction and History
When iron ore deposits were discovered in the area during the mid-19th Century, these were excavated and initially transported using a network of industrial narrow gauge railways. These later fell into disuse after the minerals became uneconomical to extract. The Rushden Railway Society formed in December 1971 with the intention of purchasing and restoring two industrial Peckett steam locomotives that were previously used in the ironstone industry. At the same time, residential development was planned for the area and Northampton Development Corporation wanted to preserve the disused ironstone railway and the nearby Iron Age fort. The society gained access to the site, gradually restored it and laid the standard gauge railway. There are 1.5 miles of track on the site and there are plans to increase the length of the operational section, enabling longer passenger rides.

Contact Details
Website: www.northantsironstonerailway.co.uk
Tel: 01604 702031
Email: info@northantsironstonerailway.co.uk
Address: Northamptonshire Ironstone Railway, Hunsbury Hill Road, Camp Hill, Northampton, NN4 9UW.

Transport Links
By Rail: Northampton is the nearest station and is three miles away.
By Road: Parking is available at the railway (NN4 9UW).

Opening Times
The railway operates on alternate Sundays from April to October. The site can be viewed on days when trains are not in service.

Line Mileage and Journey Time
Passenger trains run on a quarter mile section, providing a half-mile round trip and the journey time is relatively short.

Stock List

Type	Number	Builder	Details
Steam	2130	Peckett	0-4-0ST
Steam	BELVEDERE	Sentinel	4wVBGT
Steam	MUSKETEER	Sentinel	4wVBGT
Diesel	46 (242868) HEATHER	Ruston & Hornsby	4wDM
Diesel	394014	Ruston & Hornsby	4wDM
Diesel	4220001 CHARLES WAKE	Fowler	0-4-0
Diesel	4220016 FLYING FALCON	Fowler	0-4-0
Diesel	4200022	Fowler	0-4-0
Diesel	3967	Hibberd	0-4-0
Diesel	D697	Hudswell Clarke	0-4-0
Diesel	394014	Ruston & Hornsby	0-4-0
Diesel	321734	Robert Stephenson & Hawthorns	4wDM
EMU	70284, 70510 & 70296	British Railways	Class 411
EMU	69304	British Railways	Class 422

Attractions
The standard gauge industrial railway has some sharp curves, steep gradients and uses a variety of different vehicles to provide passenger rides. There is a small museum and workshop which are free to visit. Cab rides and "Driver for a fiver" are available when trains are operating. Full and half day steam locomotive driving experiences can be booked in advance. The railway shares the site with Hunsbury Hill Country Park, which includes a children's play area and an Iron Age fort. Nearby attractions include Abington Park Museum, Abington Park, Delapre Abbey and the Northampton & Lamport Railway which is eight miles away.

Special Events
Events that usually take place on the railway include:

Easter Event.
Christmas train rides during December.

Nottingham Heritage Railway

Introduction and History

The railway from London Marylebone to Rugby and Nottingham opened in 1898 and details of the route's history and decline are given in the Great Central Railway listing above. The section from Loughborough to Ruddington survived beyond the 1969 closure as an unsignalled single line to serve the British Gypsum site at Hotchley Hill and the Ministry of Defence (MoD) depot on the spur at Ruddington. Freight traffic continued until the mid-1980s when the MoD depot closed and the route was never formally closed by British Rail. In the early 1990s a group of transport enthusiasts created a museum on the former MoD site and operated trains on a short section of track. Negotiations began to return trains to the route and purchase the line from British Rail. Gypsum traffic then resumed, but the railway had been severed at East Leake, separating the freight and heritage operations. The line was reconnected, allowing passenger services to return to Rushcliffe Halt in 2003. On weekdays gypsum trains travelled to the plant at Hotchley Hill (East Leake), using the main line connection at Loughborough and heritage trains operated during weekends. No trains ran during 2022, as the bridge that carries the line over the A60 was found to be in need of replacement. The bridge was demolished in late 2022 and trains are due to return in 2023. There is also a longer-term project to reconnect to the Great Central Railway at Loughborough (see the GCR listing above). Nottingham Express Transit (tram service) occupies the former railway north of Ruddington, preventing a northern extension.

Contact Details

Website: www.gcrn.co.uk
Tel: 0115 940 5705
Email: info@gcrn.co.uk
Address: Nottingham Heritage Railway, Mere Way, Ruddington, Nottinghamshire, NG11 6JS.

Transport Links

By Rail: Nottingham railway station is six miles from Ruddington and East Midlands Parkway is six miles from Rushcliffe Halt.
By Road: Parking is available at Ruddington (NG11 6JS) and Rushcliffe Halt (LE12 6HX).

Opening Times

The railway usually operates on Sundays and Bank Holidays from April to October and on selected other dates, including Saturdays from June to August and during December.

Line Mileage and Journey Time

0.00   Ruddington Fields
4.25   Rushcliffe Halt
9.00   Loughborough (line end)

A return journey takes 1 hour 30 minutes.

Stock List

Type	Number	Builder	Details
Steam	Julia (1682)	Hudswell Clarke	0-6-0ST
Steam	1762	Manning Wardle	0-6-0ST
Steam	2009	Manning Wardle	0-6-0ST
Steam	5 (2015)	Manning Wardle	0-6-0ST
Steam	1631	American Locomotive Co.	2-8-0
Steam	2138	American Locomotive Co.	2-8-0
Steam	2364	Baldwin Locomotive Works	2-8-0
Steam	8274	North British	2-8-0
Steam	61264	LNER	4-6-0
Diesel	D2959	Ruston & Hornsby	0-4-0
Diesel	No.2 MARBLAEGIS	Ruston & Hornsby	0-4-0
Diesel	H014	Sentinel	0-6-0DH
Diesel	03118	British Railways	Class 03
Diesel	08220	British Railways	Class 08
Diesel	08694	British Railways	Class 08
Diesel	08784	British Railways	Class 08
Diesel	08922	British Railways	Class 08

Diesel	D8154	English Electric	Class 20
Diesel	D5830	Brush Traction	Class 31
Diesel	37009	English Electric	Class 37
Diesel	43044	British Railways	Class 43
Diesel	43159	British Railways	Class 43
DMU	50645 & 50926	British Railways	Class 108
DMU	51138 & 51151	British Railways	Class 116
DMU	59501	Pressed Steel	Class 117
DMU	144003 (55803 & 55826)	Alexander/BREL	Class 144

Attractions

There is plenty to explore at Ruddington, including a miniature railway, a large model railway, the standard gauge railway workshop, a children's play area, café and gift shop. Nottingham Area Bus Society is also based at the Ruddington site and has a large collection of vintage buses and coaches. Steam and diesel driving experiences are available along the route. The railway is home to the Inter City 125 Group which is raising funds to build a new depot at Ruddington to house its high speed trains (HST). The Great Central Railway is located near the southern end of the line. Attractions in nearby Nottingham include Green's Mill & Science Centre, Stonebridge City Farm, the National Justice Museum and City of Caves.

Special Events

Events that usually take place on the railway include:

Easter Eggspress Steam Specials.
Steam and Diesel Galas.
Heritage vehicle and transport themed events.
Model Railway event.
Firework Spectacular in November.
Santa & Christmas Specials during December.

▲ 31601 entered preservation relatively recently in 2018 and is based at the Ecclesbourne Valley Railway. On 8 June 2021 it is seen passing Rolands Crossing near Wirksworth with the 10.55 Wirksworth–Duffield. **Steve Donald**

Peak Rail

Introduction and History

The railway from Derby to Ambergate opened in 1840 and was extended north to Rowsley in 1849, including the section that Peak Rail now occupies. The further extension north across the more challenging terrain between Rowsley and Manchester was later completed in 1860. Local passenger services ceased in 1967 when Matlock Bath, Darley Dale, Rowsley, Bakewell and Millers Dale stations closed and the line between Matlock and Millers Dale closed in 1968, when St Pancras–Manchester express services ended. The northern section of the route has remained in continuous use with freight services to Peak Forest. The Peak Railway Preservation Society formed in 1975 and initially opened the Buxton Steam Centre with a short running track, which later closed. Peak Rail relocated to Darley Dale in the 1980s and the first heritage trains worked to Matlock Riverside in 1991. The line was extended north to a new station at Rowsley South in 1997 and south to Matlock in 2011, when the route was reconnected with the main line network. During 2022 services were cut back to Matlock Riverside rather than running into Matlock's Platform 2 so that locomotives can run round at Matlock Riverside, as opposed to having to work in top and tail format to Matlock. There are plans to extend further north to the original station in Rowsley and also to Bakewell. It has long been hoped that the railway could one day return to Buxton, although this would require a number of major engineering and financial obstacles to be overcome.

Contact Details

Website: www.peakrail.co.uk
Tel: 07979 496488
Email: peakrail@peakrail.co.uk
Address: Peak Rail, Matlock Station, Matlock, Derbyshire, DE4 3NA.

Transport Links

By Rail: When trains run to Matlock, cross from the main line Platform 1 to Platform 2 for Peak Rail. Through tickets are available from East Midlands Railway ticket offices.
By Road: Pay & display parking is available at Matlock (DE4 3NA) and free parking at Darley Dale (DE4 2EQ) and Rowsley South (DE4 2LF).
By Bike: The traffic-free Monsal Trail follows the railway from Matlock to Rowsley and beyond.

Opening Times

The railway operates on Saturdays, Sundays and a small number of weekdays from April until October inclusive.

Line Mileage and Journey Time

0.00	Rowsley South
1.25	Darley Dale
3.00	Matlock Riverside
3.50	Matlock

A return journey takes about one hour.

Stock List

The stock list includes locomotives belonging to the Heritage Shunters Trust, which has a large collection of diesel shunting locomotives and is based at Rowsey South.

Type	Number	Builder	Details
Steam	DUNLOP No.6 (2648)	Bagnall	0-4-0ST
Steam	3138	Hawthorn Leslie	0-6-0ST
Steam	AUSTIN No. 1 (5459)	Kitson	0-6-0ST
Steam	7063	Robert Stephenson & Hawthorns	0-4-0ST
Steam	150 (3892)	Robert Stephenson & Hawthorns	0-6-0ST
Steam	72	Vulcan Foundry	0-6-0ST
Steam	65	Hudswell Clarke	0-6-0T
Steam	6634	GWR	0-6-2T
Steam	5553	GWR	2-6-2T
Steam	5224	GWR	2-8-0T
Diesel	144V	Thomas Hill	4wDH
Diesel	9120	Baguley Drewry	4wDM

Diesel	146C	Fowler	0-4-0
Diesel	4220015	Fowler	0-4-0
Diesel	4240015	Fowler	0-6-0
Diesel	9222	Hunslet	0-4-0
Diesel	No. 5 (7161)	Hunslet	0-4-0DH
Diesel	RS8	ICI South Central Workshops	0-4-0
Diesel	27097	North British	0-4-0
Diesel	319284	Ruston & Hornsby	0-4-0
Diesel	3 (423658)	Ruston & Hornsby	0-4-0
Diesel	L2 (312989)	Ruston & Hornsby	0-4-0DE
Diesel	1 (421439)	Ruston & Hornsby	0-4-0DE
Diesel	BIGGA (102C)	Thomas Hill	0-4-0
Diesel	WD7229	Vulcan Foundry	0-4-0
Diesel	2679	Yorkshire Engine Co.	0-4-0
Diesel	2 JAMES (2675)	Yorkshire Engine Co.	0-4-0
Diesel	2480	Yorkshire Engine Co.	0-4-0DE
Diesel	319284	Ruston & Hornsby	0-4-0DM
Diesel	CLIVE (486)	Andrew Barclay	0-6-0
Diesel	803	Brush Traction	0-6-0
Diesel	D1197	English Electric	0-6-0
Diesel	E1	Hudswell Clarke	0-6-0DM
Diesel	6295	Hunslet	0-6-0
Diesel	Louise (6950)	Hunslet	0-6-0
Diesel	27932	North British	0-6-0
Diesel	10180	Sentinel	0-6-0
Diesel	2895	Yorkshire Engine Co.	0-6-0
Diesel	2940	Yorkshire Engine Co.	0-6-0

▲ Class 44 D8 pauses at Peak Rail's picturesque Darley Dale station with the 13.30 Rowsley–Matlock Riverside on 23 April 2022.   **Andy Chard**

Diesel	D1387	Hudswell Clarke	0-4-0DH
Diesel	D2953	Andrew Barclay	Class 01
Diesel	D2854	Yorkshire Engine Co.	Class 02
Diesel	D2866	Yorkshire Engine Co.	Class 02
Diesel	03027	British Railways	Class 03
Diesel	03099	British Railways	Class 03
Diesel	03113	British Railways	Class 03
Diesel	03180	British Railways	Class 03
Diesel	D2139	British Railways	Class 03
Diesel	D2199	British Railways	Class 03
Diesel	D2272	Robert Stephenson & Hawthorns	Class 04
Diesel	D2284	Robert Stephenson & Hawthorns	Class 04
Diesel	D2289	Robert Stephenson & Hawthorns	Class 04
Diesel	D2337	Robert Stephenson & Hawthorns	Class 04
Diesel	D2205	Vulcan Foundry	Class 04
Diesel	D2229	Vulcan Foundry	Class 04
Diesel	D2587	Hunslet	Class 05
Diesel	06003	Andrew Barclay	Class 06
Diesel	07001	Ruston & Hornsby	Class 07
Diesel	08016	British Railways	Class 08
Diesel	08830	British Railways	Class 08
Diesel	09001	British Railways	Class 09
Diesel	D9524	British Railways	Class 14
Diesel	D7659	Beyer Peacock	Class 25
Diesel	37152	English Electric	Class 37
Diesel	D8	British Railways	Class 44
Diesel	46035	British Railways	Class 46
Diesel	D1501 (47402)	Brush Traction	Class 47
Diesel	50029	English Electric	Class 50
Diesel	50030	English Electric	Class 50
Diesel	73138	English Electric	Class 73
Diesel	PWM650	Ruston & Hornsby	Class 97
Diesel	PWM654	Ruston & Hornsby	Class 97
EMU	HAZEL & CAR No. 87	Metropolitan Cammell	5 Bel
EMU	62266	British Railways	Class 423

Attractions

The picturesque Darley Dale station has a small museum displaying the history of the line. The Rowsley site has a 60-foot working turntable and is the home of the Heritage Shunters Trust with its extensive collection of shunting locomotives and the Renown Repulse Restoration Group which is restoring two Class 50s (50029 & 50030). There are many attractions in Matlock Bath and the surrounding Peak District, including the Peak District Lead Mining Museum and Chatsworth House to the north. Nearby heritage railways include the Ecclesbourne Valley Railway, the Churnet Valley Railway and the Midland Railway-Butterley.

Special Events

Events that usually take place on the railway include:

Luxury dining trains.
Mother's Day & Father's Day lunch trains.
Kids Go Free on selected dates.
Steam, diesel and heritage shunter galas.
Car and heritage vehicle themed events.
Halloween event during October.
Santa & Steam Specials during December.

Rocks by Rail

Introduction and History

Rocks by Rail, also known as The Living Ironstone Museum, demonstrates historic mineral extraction techniques and includes an operational standard gauge railway. The site was connected to the Midland Railway branch line from Ashwell Junction to Cottesmore, which was completed in 1882 to transport quarried iron ore, and this remained in use until 1974. The three-foot gauge tramway and rope incline allowed loaded stone and minerals to be let down the steep slope and into rail wagons for onward transport to steelworks. The railway today is used to demonstrate the techniques used and carries passengers in restored brake vans.

Contact Details

Website: www.rocks-by-rail.org
Tel: 07974 171068
Email: curator@rocks-by-rail.org
Address: Rocks By Rail Living Ironstone Museum, Cottesmore, Oakham LE15 7FF.

Transport Links

By Rail: The nearest railway station is Oakham, which is five miles away.
By Road: The site has ample car parking (at LE15 7FF) and is near to the village of Cottesmore.

Opening Times

The railway operates on alternate Sundays and Bank Holidays between Easter and mid-October. The site also opens for "non-operational viewing days" on Tuesdays and Thursdays during this period.

Line Mileage and Journey Time

The railway line is three quarters of a mile long and the journey time is relatively short.

Stock List

Type	Number	Builder	Details
Steam	1931	Andrew Barclay	0-4-0ST
Steam	2088 SIR THOMAS ROYDEN	Andrew Barclay	0-4-0ST
Steam	3865 SINGAPORE	Hawthorn Leslie	0-4-0ST
Steam	287	Hunslet	0-4-0ST
Steam	1759 ELIZABETH	Peckett	0-4-0ST
Steam	1257 UPPINGHAM	Peckett	0-4-0ST
Steam	2350 BELVOIR	Andrew Barclay	0-6-0ST
Steam	1972 STAMFORD	Avonside	0-6-0ST
Steam	2668 CRANFORD No.2	Bagnall	0-6-0ST
Steam	1308 RHOS	Hudswell Clarke	0-6-0ST
Steam	No. 9 (2521)	Yorkshire Engine Co.	0-6-0ST
Diesel	4220007 KETTON No. 1	Fowler	0-4-0
Diesel	10201 BETTY	Rolls Royce Sentinel	0-4-0
Diesel	10204 JEAN	Rolls Royce Sentinel	0-4-0
Diesel	10207 GRAHAM	Rolls Royce Sentinel	0-4-0
Diesel	306092	Ruston & Hornsby	0-4-0
Diesel	421436 ELIZABETH	Ruston & Hornsby	0-4-0
Diesel	544997 ERIC TONKS	Ruston & Hornsby	0-4-0
Diesel	207103 IMP	Ruston & Hornsby	0-4-0
Diesel	178V	Thomas Hill	4wDH
Diesel	186V MR D	Thomas Hill	4wDH
Diesel	OMB 1382 (2872)	Yorkshire Engine Co.	0-6-0
Diesel	DE5 (2791)	Yorkshire Engine Co.	0-6-0

Attractions

Rocks by Rail is located within a 19-acre reclaimed quarry site which has a variety of walks, picnic spots and nature trails. The passenger brake van rides are usually steam-hauled and diesel locomotives are used on some days. Diesel locomotive "Driver for a Fiver" sessions are available on selected dates. The museum has a collection of industrial steam and diesel locomotives and wagons, plus an exhibition building and workshop where visitors can see those under restoration. There is a cab and model of the huge dragline crane "Sundew", which was the largest of its type in the world when built. Nearby attractions include Rutland Water which has an aqua park and nature reserve, and the market towns of Oakham, Melton Mowbray and Stamford.

Special Events
Events that usually take place on the railway include:

Easter Event.
Themed exhibitions.

Rushden Transport Museum & Railway

Introduction and History
Rushden station was the only intermediate station on the short branch from Wellingborough to Higham Ferrers, which opened in 1894 and closed to passenger services in 1959. The line remained open for freight and seasonal passenger traffic until the final train ran in 1969. This consisted of a Class 25 collecting 12 wagons from Higham station and the track was lifted not long after this. Rushden Historical Transport Society (RHTS) formed in 1976 and leased Rushden station in 1984. Rushden Transport Museum opened in 1986 and in 1996 the site was purchased by the RHTS. The first heritage train ran from Rushden in 2009, exactly 50 years after passenger services ended and the running line was subsequently increased to a length of half a mile. In June 2017 RHTS acquired Rushden Goods Shed from Northamptonshire County Council and this has been restored as a community and events venue. In 2019 train services were suspended and they returned in September 2021, using one of the railway's recently acquired Class 142 Pacers. There are plans to extend the line a further half-mile to a new halt near Higham Ferrers.

Contact Details
Website: www.rhts.co.uk
Tel: 0300 3023 150
Email: secretary@rhts.co.uk
Address: Rushden Transport Museum, Station Approach, Rushden, Northamptonshire, NN10 0AW.

Transport Links
By Rail: The nearest railway station is Wellingborough, which is six miles from Rushden.
By Road: There is limited car parking at Rushden station (NN10 0AW); however, free parking is available nearby on Rectory Road and at the small car park on John Clark Way.

Opening Times
Trains only operate on selected dates, such as when special events take place.

Line Mileage and Journey Time
The railway runs for half a mile from Rushden station and a journey (consisting of two return trips) takes around 15 minutes.

Stock List

Type	Number	Builder	Details
Steam	EDMUNDSONS	Andrew Barclay	0-4-0ST
Steam	2654	Bagnall	0-6-0ST
Diesel	10159	Sentinel	4wDH
Diesel	WD 70048	Andrew Barclay	0-4-0DM
Diesel	10433	Vulcan Foundry	0-4-0DM
Diesel	03179	British Railways	Class 03
Diesel	31206	Brush Traction	Class 31
DMU	55029	Pressed Steel	Class 121
DMU	142084 (55734 & 55780)	BREL/Leyland	Class 142
DMU	142091 (55741 & 55787)	BREL/Leyland	Class 142

Attractions

The Rushden site is home to the Victorian railway station, the Transport Museum, a Gresley buffet coach and a real ale bar which opens seven days a week. Other attractions in the area include Wellingborough Museum, Irchester Country Park, Irchester Narrow Gauge Railway Museum and the Northampton & Lamport Railway which is 20 miles away.

Special Events

Events that usually take place on the railway include:

A variety of food and drink themed events.
Model Weekend.
Halloween Ghost Trains.
Christmas event.

▲ Not long after it arrived at its new home, Peak Rail, D1501 (47402) heads away from Darley Dale on a hot 13 August 2022 with an afternoon service for Matlock. **Martyn Tattam**

EASTERN

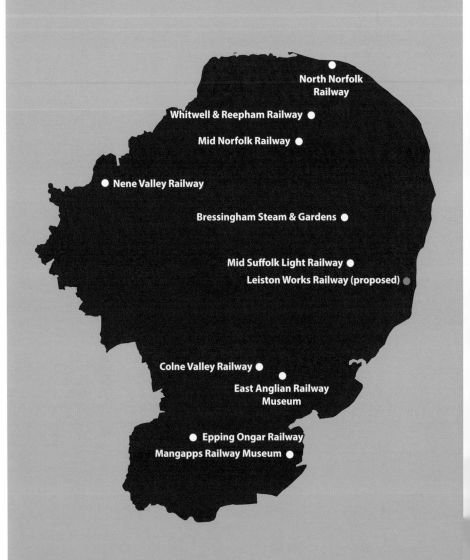

North Norfolk
Railway

Whitwell & Reepham Railway

Mid Norfolk Railway

Nene Valley Railway

Bressingham Steam & Gardens

Mid Suffolk Light Railway
Leiston Works Railway (proposed)

Colne Valley Railway

East Anglian Railway
Museum

Epping Ongar Railway
Mangapps Railway Museum

Region 6 – Eastern

Bressingham Steam & Gardens

Introduction and History
Bressingham was established by Alan Bloom after he purchased the 220-acre estate of Bressingham Hall in 1946. The first of several traction engines arrived in 1961 and the first narrow gauge railway was laid in 1965. The site now houses a steam museum, gardens, a garden centre and a number of different railways, all of which are open to the public. The railways consist of a standard gauge demonstration line (approximately 0.25 miles long), the Fen Railway (2 foot gauge, 1.5 miles), the Garden Railway (10¼ inch gauge, 0.75 miles) and the Waveney Valley Railway (15 inch gauge, 1.5 miles).

Contact Details
Website: www.bressingham.co.uk
Tel: 01379 686900
Email: info@bressingham.co.uk
Address: Bressingham Steam & Gardens, Low Road, Bressingham, Diss, Norfolk, IP22 2AA.

Transport Links
By Rail: The nearest railway station is Diss, which is three and a half miles away.
By Road: Free parking for cars and coaches is available on site (IP22 2AA).

Opening Times
The gardens and railways are open from late-March until late-October and on selected other dates. Note that the standard gauge railway does not operate on every opening day.

Line Mileage and Journey Time
The standard gauge demonstration line runs for approximately 0.25 miles and the journey time is relatively short. The three other railways are all much longer (see above).

Stock List

Type	Number	Builder	Details
Steam	6841 WILLIAM FRANCIS	Beyer Peacock	0-4-0+0-4-0
Steam	1472	Andrew Barclay	0-4-0F
Steam	25 (6087)	Neilson & Co	0-4-0ST
Steam	GRANVILLE (BR No. 30102)	LSWR	0-4-0T
Steam	32662	LBSCR	0-6-0T
Steam	87	GER	0-6-0T
Steam	5865	Norwegian State Railways	2-10-0
Steam	490	GER	2-4-0
Steam	377 KING HAAKON VII	Norwegian State Railways	2-6-0
Steam	80 THUNDERSLEY	LT&SR	4-4-2T
Diesel	1 (497753)	Ruston & Hornsby	0-4-0DH
Diesel	11103 (D297)	Vulcan Foundry	0-4-0DM

Attractions
Bressingham has four different railways, each with a different gauge and which together give over four miles of railway journeys. There is a collection of working and static steam and traction engines, gardens to visit and an adjacent garden centre. Visitors can ride on the 1897-built Gallopers carousel, which has been meticulously restored. Bressingham is also the home of the Dad's Army Appreciation Society and a Dad's Army Museum. Other attractions in the region include Banham Zoo, the market town of Diss and the fens and coastlines of Norfolk.

Special Events
Events that usually take place at Bressingham include:

Father's Day event.
Traction Engine Gathering.
Transport themed events.
Christmas at Bressingham.

Colne Valley Railway

Introduction and History

The railway from Chappel & Wakes Colne on the present-day Sudbury branch, to Haverhill, opened in stages. It reached Halstead in 1860, extending to Castle Hedingham in 1861, to Yeldham in 1862, to Haverhill in 1863 and it was connected to the Stour Valley Railway at Haverhill in 1865. Passenger services were withdrawn in 1960, followed by freight in 1965 and much of the railway infrastructure was demolished soon after. The land at the Hedingham site was bought in 1973; a heritage railway organisation was formed and the first preserved trains ran in 1976. The surviving Hedingham railway station was carefully moved from its original location one mile away and has been renamed Castle Hedingham.

Contact Details

Website: www.colnevalleyrailway.co.uk
Tel: 01787 461174
Email: info@colnevalleyrailway.co.uk
Address: Colne Valley Railway, Yeldham Road, Castle Hedingham, CO9 3DZ.

Transport Links

By Rail: Sudbury and Braintree are the nearest railway stations and both are nine miles away.
By Road: Ample free car parking is available at Castle Hedingham station (CO9 3DZ).

Opening Times

The railway operates every Sunday, most Saturdays and on selected weekdays from April to October inclusive. It also runs during December for Santa Special services.

Line Mileage and Journey Time

Castle Hedingham is in the centre of the railway, which operates for slightly less than one mile and a return trip takes about half an hour.

Stock List

Note that the steam locomotives 45163, 45293 and 35010 are on an adjacent privately-owned site and can't be viewed or accessed from the Colne Valley Railway.

Type	Number	Builder	Details
Steam	1875	Avonside	0-4-0ST
Steam	1	Hawthorn Leslie	0-4-0ST
Steam	190	Hunslet	0-6-0ST
Steam	WD200 (3800)	Hunslet	0-6-0ST
Steam	60 JUPITER	Robert Stephenson & Hawthorns	0-6-0ST
Steam	45163	Armstrong Whitworth	4-6-0
Steam	45293	Armstrong Whitworth	4-6-0
Steam	35010	Southern Railway	4-6-2
Diesel	3147	Hibberd	4wDM
Diesel	12228	Hunslet	0-4-0DH
Diesel	281266	Ruston & Hornsby	0-4-0DM
Diesel	D2041	British Railways	Class 03
Diesel	D2184	British Railways	Class 03
Diesel	43071	British Railways	Class 43
Diesel	43073	British Railways	Class 43
Diesel	43082	British Railways	Class 43
DMU	51339 & 51382	Pressed Steel	Class 117
DMU	55033	Pressed Steel	Class 121
EMU	75023	British Railways	Class 307
EMU	75881	British Railways	Class 308
EMU	71205 & 78037	BREL	Class 312
Electric	1	Robert Stephenson & Hawthorns	Bo-Bo

Attractions

Following the recent arrival of three High Speed Train (HST) power cars, the line is one of the few heritage railways where passengers can travel on a HST (on selected dates). In addition to the standard gauge line, there is a 7¼ inch gauge miniature railway with steam and diesel locomotives, a model railway and a museum. Visitors can see inside the working signal box on most dates or explore the nearby woodland walk. Train driver experience courses are available on selected dates. Heritage railways within the region include the East Anglian Railway Museum, the Mid Suffolk Light Railway and the Epping Ongar Railway. Other attractions in the area include Hedingham Castle, Long Melford Country Park and Coggeshall Grange Barn.

Special Events
13–14 May 2023: Miniature Railway Gala.
18 June 2023: Unusual Trains.
October 2023: Gala event.
December: Santa Specials.

East Anglian Railway Museum

Introduction and History
The Stour Valley Railway Preservation Society formed in 1968 to save and preserve the railway from Sudbury to Long Melford. This was not successful and the line now terminates at Sudbury. However, in 1969 the society instead leased the derelict goods yard, shed, signal box and station buildings at nearby Chappel & Wakes Colne from British Rail. In 1970 a Hunslet steam locomotive first carried passengers along a short stretch of relaid track and in the years that followed, the buildings were restored, as were various items of rolling stock. In 1983 the engine restoration workshop was built. In 1986 the society became the East Anglian Railway Museum focusing on the railway history of the area and in 1987 the site was purchased from British Rail. Today it is easily accessible by rail, with one platform of Chappel & Wakes Colne being the museum's home and the other platform is used by Marks Tey to Sudbury main line services.

Contact Details
Website: www.earm.co.uk
Tel: 01206 242524
Email: information@earm.co.uk
Address: East Anglian Railway Museum, Chappel & Wakes Colne Station, Colchester, Essex, CO6 2DS.

Transport Links
By Rail: Cross the footbridge at Chappel & Wakes Colne station.
By Road: Free car parking is available at the museum (CO6 2DS).

Opening Times
The site and museum open on Saturdays, Sundays and Wednesdays all year round, except on Christmas Day, Boxing Day and during occasional special events such as the beer festival. The railway operates on some of the opening dates and checking the website for the latest information is recommended.

Line Mileage and Journey Time
The demonstration line runs for around a quarter of a mile and the journey time is relatively short.

Stock List

Type	Number	Builder	Details
Steam	11 (1047)	Andrew Barclay	0-4-0ST
Steam	2542 JUBILEE	Bagnall	0-4-0ST
Steam	2039	Peckett	0-4-0ST
Steam	LAMPORT No.3	Bagnall	0-6-0ST
Steam	54 (7031)	Robert Stephenson & Hawthorns	0-6-0ST
Steam	69621	GER	0-6-2T
Diesel	144 JOHN PEEL	Andrew Barclay	0-4-0
Diesel	D72229	Drewry	0-4-0
Diesel	4220039 7	Fowler	0-4-0
Diesel	2029	Simplex	0-4-0

▲ On 18 September 2021, Class 04 D2279 and Class 101 51213 & 56358 were in action at Chappel and Wakes Colne Station. The platform in the foreground is used by the East Anglian Railway Museum and that in the background is served by main line services between Marks Tey and Sudbury.
Tony Christie

▼ D5631 (31207) is seen near Dead Man's Bridge on the North Norfolk Railway with an empty stock working comprised of vintage carriages that are destined for Weybourne on 21 June 2022.
Glen Batten

Diesel	D2279	Robert Stephenson & Hawthorns	Class 04
DMU	51213 & 56358	Metropolitan Cammell	Class 101
DMU	79963	Waggon und Maschinenbau	Railbus
EMU	77092	BREL	Class 317

Attractions

The museum has a wealth of railway-related attractions, including the heritage centre with various interactive exhibits, the restored goods shed which is filled with railway memorabilia, the restoration shed where locomotives and rolling stock are restored and the active Grade I listed signal box. There is miniature railway which has recently been rebuilt. Driving Experiences are available. If arriving by train from Marks Tey, you will cross Chappel Viaduct, which is one of the largest viaducts and brick-built structures in the country. The Colne Valley Railway is 12 miles away and the Epping Ongar Railway is relatively nearby. Other nearby attractions include Clare Castle Country Park, Long Melford Country Park and Colchester Zoo.

Special Events

Events that usually take place include:

Days out with Thomas.
Beer Festival.
October Diesel Days.
Halloween Steam.

Epping Ongar Railway

Introduction and History

The railway from London reached Ongar in 1865 and was steam-hauled until 1957, when the route become part of London Underground's Central Line. Passenger numbers declined until the Underground line between Epping and Ongar closed in 1994. Fortunately, much of the infrastructure remained in place, facilitating its transition into a heritage railway and the line reopened as such in 2004. The railway doesn't currently operate into Epping (London Underground) station, but there are plans to extend there, which would provide a direct rail connection.

Contact Details

Website: www.eorailway.co.uk
Tel: 01277 365200
Email: enquiries@eorailway.co.uk
Address: Epping Ongar Railway, Ongar Station, Station Approach, Ongar, Essex, CM5 9BN.

Transport Links

By Rail: London Underground Central Line services terminate at Epping station, at which visitors can transfer to the connecting heritage bus service.
By Road: There is no public parking at Ongar or North Weald stations, except limited disabled spaces which must be booked in advance. Chargeable parking is available at Epping Underground station (CM16 4HW).

Opening Times

Trains usually operate on Saturdays, Sundays and Bank Holidays from April to October and on selected other weekdays. The railway also operates between late November and early January for Light Fantastic and Santa Special services.

Line Mileage and Journey Time

0.00	Ongar
1.75	Blake Hall
3.50	North Weald
5.75	Epping Ongar Boundary
6.00	Epping

A return journey takes about 1 hour 30 minutes.

Stock List

Type	Number	Builder	Details
Steam	3437	Hawthorn Leslie	0-6-0ST
Steam	3837	Hawthorn Leslie	0-6-0ST
Steam	56 (7667)	Robert Stephenson & Hawthorns	0-6-0ST
Steam	63 CORBY (7761)	Robert Stephenson & Hawthorns	0-6-0ST
Steam	4141	GWR	2-6-2T
Steam	5521	GWR	2-6-2T
Steam	4953	GWR	4-6-0
Diesel	RH398616	Ruston & Hornsby	0-4-0
Diesel	03119	British Railways	Class 03
Diesel	03170	British Railways	Class 03
Diesel	13180 (08114)	British Railways	Class 08
Diesel	D9520	British Railways	Class 14
Diesel	20001	English Electric	Class 20
Diesel	31438	Brush Traction	Class 31
Diesel	D6729	English Electric	Class 37
Diesel	45132	British Railways	Class 45
Diesel	47635	British Railways	Class 47
DMU	51342 & 51384	Pressed Steel	Class 117
DMU	56287	Pressed Steel	Class 121
DEMU	60110 & 60810	British Railways	Class 205

Attractions
Railway related activities include driver and signal box experiences and the "Epping Fryer" evening fish and chip specials. The Penny Salon Micro Gallery can be found at Ongar station; North Weald Airfield and Museum is a short walk from North Weald station and Epping Forest is also nearby. Other heritage railways in the area include the Colne Valley Railway and Mangapps Railway Museum.

Special Events
Events that usually take place on the railway include:

Easter Egg Hunt.
Steam and Diesel Galas.
1940s Weekend.
Family Fun Days.
Epping Ongar Light Fantastic during the winter months.
Santa Specials during December.

Mangapps Railway Museum

Introduction and History
The Mangapps Railway Museum is situated on a private site and, unlike most heritage railways and museums, it is not on the site of a former railway. All the station buildings, signal boxes, infrastructure and rolling stock have been brought from other locations. The site includes a museum with a large collection of railway exhibits, many of which are from East Anglia and the former Great Eastern Railway. An operational railway line has been created and this is used by a variety of locomotives, including examples of industrial steam, industrial diesel and main line diesels.

Contact Details
Website: www.mangapps.co.uk
Tel: 01621 784898
Address: Mangapps Railway Museum, Southminster Road, Burnham-on-Crouch, Essex, CM0 8QG.

Transport Links
By Rail: The nearest station is Burnham-on-Crouch, which is just over one mile away.
By Road: There is ample free parking on-site (CM0 8QG).

Opening Times
The railway usually operates on Saturdays, Sundays and Bank Holidays from March to October and every day during August and some other school holidays.

Line Mileage and Journey Time
The railway consists of two spurs and a return journey takes about 20 minutes.

0.00	Mangapps	0.00	Mangapps Yard
0.40	Old Heath	0.25	Southminster Road
0.55	Line End		

Stock List

Type	Number	Builder	Details
Steam	1619	Andrew Barclay	0-4-0ST
Steam	8 (2157)	Andrew Barclay	0-4-0ST
Steam	2613	Bagnall	0-6-0PT
Steam	MINNIE	Fox Walker	0-6-0ST
Diesel	ELLAND No 1	Hudswell Clarke	0-4-0
Diesel	11104	Drewry	0-6-0
Diesel	03018	British Railways	Class 03
Diesel	03020	British Railways	Class 03
Diesel	03081	British Railways	Class 03
Diesel	03089	British Railways	Class 03
Diesel	D2158	British Railways	Class 03
Diesel	03399	British Railways	Class 03
Diesel	D2325	Robert Stephenson & Hawthorns	Class 04
Diesel	31105	Brush Traction	Class 31
Diesel	31233	Brush Traction	Class 31
Diesel	33018	BRCW	Class 33
Diesel	33110	BRCW	Class 33
DMU	51381	Pressed Steel	Class 117
EMU	75033 & 75250	British Railways	Class 302

Attractions
The Mangapps site has two stations, a large number of steam and diesel locomotives, a variety of wagons and a museum housing a substantial collection of railway artefacts. The displays include a variety of locomotive nameplates, station signs and signalling equipment. There is a demonstration signal box, where the lever frame and sub-floor workings are visible. Other attractions in the area include National Trust Danbury Commons & Blakes Wood, Northey Island and Dengie National Nature Reserve.

Special Events
Events that usually take place include:

Summer Gala event when a variety of locomotives haul passenger trains.
End of season Steam Up.

Mid Norfolk Railway

Introduction and History

The railway between Wymondham and Dereham opened in 1847. It was extended to King's Lynn in 1848 and to Wells-next-the-Sea in 1857. The decline began when passenger services between Dereham and Wells ended in 1964 and the line from Wymondham to Dereham was singled in 1965. Passenger services between Dereham and King's Lynn ceased in 1968, followed by Wymondham–Dereham in 1969. Freight north of Wymondham continued but was progressively cut back, running to Fakenham until 1980, to Ryburgh until 1983 and to North Elmham until 1989, when the branch north of Wymondham closed. A group that formed in 1974 had been campaigning for passenger trains to return and this resulted in at least one charter train operating on the line each year between 1978 and 1988. The group leased Hardingham station and yard in 1983, at which it initially established a museum and base. This closed in 1989 and a number of groups then merged in 1990, creating the beginning of today's Mid Norfolk Railway. The first heritage trains ran from Yaxham in 1995 and services returned to Dereham in 1997. In 1998 the Wymondham–Dereham section was purchased and through trains from the main line were reinstated. The railway was extended north to Hoe Crossing in 2013 and to Worthing Crossing in 2018. Passenger services between Dereham and Hoe Crossing began in 2022, providing the first regular passenger services north of Dereham since 1964. The line to North Elmham station remains in-situ but does not yet see regular trains. The railway owns the trackbed which continues north to County School, where there are visitor attractions (see below) and there are long term aims to further extend the line to Fakenham.

Contact Details

Website: www.midnorfolkrailway.co.uk
Tel: 01362 851723
Email: info@mnr.co.uk or to contact the museum at Dereham: museum@mnr.org.uk
Address: Dereham Railway Station, Station Road, Dereham, Norfolk, NR19 1DF.

Transport Links

By Rail: Wymondham railway station is just under one mile from Wymondham Abbey station.
By Road: Free parking is available at Dereham station (NR19 1DF) and parking is very limited at Wymondham Abbey.

Opening Times

The railway operates on Saturdays, Sundays and Bank Holidays from March until October, plus on selected weekdays and during November & December for Polar Express Trains. In addition, County School station usually opens 10.00–16.00 during summer weekends.

Line Mileage and Journey Time

0.00	Wymondham Abbey
3.00	Kimberley Park
6.25	Thuxton
8.75	Yaxham
10.50	Dereham
12.25	Hoe Level Crossing
14.25	Worthing Hoe Road Crossing
15.00	North Elmham (regular services don't yet reach this point)
16.50	County School station (the line from North Elmham is not in operational condition)

A return journey takes about 1 hour 45 minutes.

Stock List

Type	Number	Builder	Details
Steam	2 (7818)	Robert Stephenson & Hawthorns	0-4-0ST
Steam	9596	Sentinel	4wVBGT
Steam	22 (3846)	Hunslet	0-6-0ST
Steam	80078	British Railways	2-6-4T
Diesel	BSC1 (D1049)	English Electric	0-6-0DH
Diesel	03197	British Railways	Class 03
Diesel	D2334	Robert Stephenson & Hawthorns	Class 04
Diesel	31255	Brush Traction	Class 31

Diesel	33202	BRCW	Class 33
Diesel	47367	Brush Traction	Class 47
Diesel	47580	Brush Traction	Class 47
Diesel	47596	Brush Traction	Class 47
Diesel	50019	English Electric	Class 50
DMU	56301	GRCW	Class 100
DMU	51226, 51434, 51499, 51503, 56347 & 59117	Metropolitan Cammell	Class 101
DMU	51942 & 56270	British Railways	Class 108
DMU	51370, 51412 & 59520	Pressed Steel	Class 117
DMU	142038 (55579 & 55629)	BREL/Leyland	Class 142
DMU	142061 (55711 & 55757)	BREL/Leyland	Class 142
DMU	144018 (55818, 55854 & 55841)	Alexander/BREL	Class 144
EMU	75120	British Railways	Class 307
EMU	68004	British Railways	Class 419

Attractions

The Mid Norfolk is one of Britain's longer heritage railways and is actively extending northwards. There is a museum, gift shop and tea room at Dereham. At County School, there is a another museum and team room, and in 2022 the dual gauge (5-inch & 3.5-inch) Wensum Valley Light Railway began operating there on selected Sundays. Steam and diesel driver experience days can be arranged on the standard gauge line. The narrow gauge Bure Valley Railway and Bressingham Steam & Gardens are all nearby. Other attractions in the area include Lenwade Dinosaur Adventure and Gressenhall Farm and Workhouse. Wymondham Abbey is a short walk from the railway's southern terminus and there is plenty to explore in Wymondham and Dereham.

Special Events

14 May 2023: Vintage Bus Day.
23–25 June 2023: Steam Weekend.
5–6 August 2023: 1940s Weekend.
22–24 September 2023: Diesel Gala.

Other events that usually take place on the railway include a variety of Dining Trains, a Model Railway Exhibition, a Summer Craft Fair and Polar Express Trains during November and December.

Mid Suffolk Light Railway

Introduction and History

The light railway, with its reduced speed limit and different safety requirements to the main line network, opened to goods traffic between Haughley near Stowmarket and Laxfield in 1904 and to passenger services in 1908. It was intended for the railway to continue to Halesworth on the present-day Ipswich–Lowestoft line, but a lack of finances meant that it only reached Laxfield. The railway was effectively bankrupt before it opened and was never profitable, leading to its closure in 1952 and the track was lifted in 1953. In 1991 a group of railway enthusiasts formed and initially created a railway museum close to the current Brockford site. The station at Brockford was re-established, a short stretch of track was laid and the first heritage trains worked in 2002. The line is currently being extended to a new station which will be called Aspall Halt. The work may be completed in 2023 and will double the length of the line.

Contact Details

Website: www.mslr.org.uk
Tel: 01449 766899 or 01449 766874
Email: enquiries@mslr.org.uk
Address: Mid Suffolk Railway, Brockford Station, Wetheringsett, Stowmarket, Suffolk, IP14 5PW.

Transport Links

By Rail: The nearest railway station is Stowmarket, which is nine miles away.
By Road: Free car parking is available at Brockford (IP14 5PW).

Opening Times

The railway operates on Sundays and Bank Holidays from late May until early September and on selected weekdays.

Line Mileage and Journey Time

Train currently run for a quarter of a mile from Brockford and a return journey takes about 20 minutes. When the line to Aspall Halt opens, it will run for a length of just over half a mile.

Stock List

Type	Number	Builder	Details
Steam	2565	Bagnall	0-4-0ST
Steam	1604	Hudswell Clarke	0-4-0ST
Steam	12 Marcia (1631)	Peckett	0-4-0T
Steam	985	LNER	0-4-0T
Steam	2525	Cockerill	0-4-0WT
Steam	1700 WISSINGTON	Hudswell Clarke	0-6-0ST
Diesel	294266	Ruston & Hornsby	0-4-0
Diesel	ALSTON	Ruston & Hornsby	0-4-0
Diesel	20337	Fowler	0-4-0DM

Attractions

Unlike many other heritage railways, there is no ex-British Rail coaching stock. Instead, vintage carriages are used, including the recently restored Victorian four-wheel coach and the 1865 Great Eastern Railway First Class smoking coach No. 140. Visitors can explore the Arts Council accredited museum which tells the story of the railway and see the carriage and wagon workshop which houses active renovation projects. Tours of the workshop are available, subject to staffing. There is also a café, shop and a restored real ale bar coach. Attractions in the region include Suffolk Owl Sanctuary and the Food Museum in Stowmarket. The East Anglian Railway Museum and Colne Valley Railway are both about 35 miles away.

Special Events

Events that will take place during 2023:

9–10 April: Easter Steam Up.
30 April–1 May: Bank Holiday Steam.
28–29 May: Middy in the 1940s.
26–27 August: Model Mania.
2–3 September: Country Railway Gala.
2–3, 9–10 & 16–17 December: Santa Specials.

Nene Valley Railway

Introduction and History

The railway from Blisworth (near Northampton), on the present-day West Coast Main Line, to Peterborough opened in 1845, when it became the first railway to reach Peterborough. Wansford subsequently grew in importance, becoming a junction with four lines converging after the railway to Stamford was built in 1867 and the route to Seaton in 1879. Passenger trains from Peterborough to Rugby via Seaton ceased in 1966, although freight continued to the quarry at Nassington until 1971 (this was 1.5 miles west of Yarwell Junction). In 1969 a group that was to become the Peterborough Railway Society (PRS) formed and after the Peterborough Development Corporation purchased the railway in 1974, it was leased to the PRS. The first preserved trains ran between Orton Mere and Wansford in 1977, using continental locomotives and rolling stock, a theme which continues with some of the railway's rolling stock today. The railway was extended from Orton Mere to Peterborough in 1986 and from Wansford to Yarwell Junction in 2007. The main line connection remains and is used for transferring visiting locomotives and by occasional railtours (although at the time of writing in early 2023 this was temporarily out of use while funds were being raised for repairs). There are aspirations to extend the railway towards Elton on the line that ran south from Yarwell Junction to Blisworth (as opposed to the western line from Yarwell to Rugby via Nassington).

Contact Details
Website: www.nvr.org.uk
Tel: 01780 784444
Email: adminassistant@nvr.org.uk
Address: Nene Valley Railway Ltd, Wansford Station, Stibbington, Peterborough, PE8 6LR.

Transport Links
By Rail: The nearest railway station is Peterborough, which is just over one mile away.
By Road: Free parking is available at Wansford (PE8 6LR) station. Alternatively, there is chargeable parking at Orton Mere (PE2 7DA), at Nene Park adjacent to Overton station (PE2 5UU) or at Pleasure Fair Meadow car park near Peterborough NVR station (PE2 9NR).

Opening Times
Trains operate during weekends and on selected weekdays for the majority of the year.

Line Mileage and Journey Time
0.00   Peterborough NVR
1.50   Orton Mere
2.50   Overton
6.25   Wansford
7.25   Yarwell Junction

A return journey takes about 1 hour 30 minutes, slightly less when the railcar is operating.

▲ This interesting looking locomotive is 2-2-0WT "The Blue Circle" which was built by Aveling & Porter in 1926. On 20 August 2022, it operates a brake van service at Wansford on the Nene Valley Railway. **Alisdair Anderson**

Stock List

Type	Number	Builder	Details
Steam	1626	Cockerill	0-4-0VBT
Steam	4612	GWR	0-6-0PT
Steam	DEREK CROUCH	Hudswell Clarke	0-6-0ST
Steam	75006	Hunslet	0-6-0ST
Steam	JACKS GREEN	Hunslet	0-6-0ST
Steam	656	Danske Statsbaner	0-6-0T
Steam	THOMAS	Hudswell Clarke	0-6-0T
Steam	5485	Fablok	0-8-0T
Steam	THE BLUE CIRCLE	Aveling & Porter	2-2-0WT
Steam	64305	DB, Germany	2-6-2T
Steam	1178	Motala Verkstad	2-6-2T
Steam	73050	British Railways	4-6-0
Steam	101	Motala Verkstad	4-6-0
Steam	34081	British Railways	4-6-2
Diesel	BARABEL	Sentinel	0-4-0
Diesel	D1123	English Electric	0-4-0DH
Diesel	304469	Ruston & Hornsby	0-4-0DM
Diesel	DL83	Sentinel	0-6-0
Diesel	323.674-2	Gmeinder & Co.	4wDH
Diesel	2895	Hibberd	Petrol loco
Diesel	2896	Hibberd	4wDM
Diesel	77120	American Locomotive Co.	Bo-BoDE
Diesel	9529	British Railways	Class 14
Diesel	43045	British Railways	Class 43
Diesel	43060	British Railways	Class 43
Diesel	45041	British Railways	Class 45
DMU	1212	Hagglund and Soner	Swedish Railcar
DMU	143602 (55651 & 55668)	Alexander/Barclay	Class 143

Attractions

The 5-inch gauge Wansford Miniature Railway opened in 2021; this has steam & battery locomotives, and two stations, a turntable and signals. The viewing platform at Wansford gives access to the restoration work in progress and shed tours are available (advance arrangement may be needed). Wansford also has a second-hand book carriage, a café and a gift shop. The railway offers driving experiences, for which advance booking is required. At nearby Peterborough is the city's Cathedral and Railworld, which has a variety of railway and wildlife exhibits. Ferry Meadows is close to Overton station and Thorpe Meadows, with a sculpture walk and rowing lake, is also nearby.

Special Events

Events that usually take place on the railway include:

Steam and Diesel Galas.
Thomas-themed events.
The Jolly Fisherman (fish & chip specials).
The Wizard's Express during October.
Santa Express Trains during December.

North Norfolk Railway

Introduction and History

The railway between Cromer and Melton Constable opened in 1887 as part of the Midland & Great Northern Joint Railway network. The route became known as the Poppy Line, due to the abundance of the distinct flowers in the area. Despite public protest beforehand, the line was closed in 1959. The North Norfolk Railway (NNR) was one of Britain's earlier heritage railways, forming in 1965. The first two steam locomotives were delivered in 1967 and in 1973 the Royal Train episode of Dad's Army was filmed at Weybourne station. Services between Sheringham and Holt began in 1975. A major milestone was achieved in 2010 when Sheringham East level crossing was reinstated, reconnecting the NNR with the national rail network. Fundraising is in progress to rebuild the station building and canopy at Sheringham, which BR destroyed during the 1960s. There is a long-term plan to join the NNR with the Mid Norfolk Railway, creating the Norfolk Orbital Railway, a rail circuit that would include the current routes of both railways.

Contact Details

Website: www.nnrailway.co.uk
Tel: 01263 820800
Email: enquiries@nnrailway.co.uk
Address: North Norfolk Railway, Station Approach, Sheringham, Norfolk, NR26 8RA.

Transport Link

By Rail: Main line connection at Sheringham; the two stations are adjacent, separated by a road.
By Road: Car parking is available at Sheringham (NR26 8RA, charges apply), Weybourne (NR25 7HN) and Holt (NR25 6AJ) stations. Parking space at Weybourne is limited.

Opening Times

The line has one of the most intensive timetables of any heritage railway, with trains operating daily from April to October and during weekends for most of the rest of the year.

Line Mileage and Journey Time

0.00	Sheringham
2.75	Weybourne
3.25	Kelling Heath Halt
5.00	Holt

A return journey takes about 50 minutes.

Stock List

Type	Number	Builder	Details
Steam	564	GER	0-6-0
Steam	1982	Hunslet	0-6-0ST
Steam	1744	North British	0-6-2T
Steam	92203	British Railways	2-10-0
Steam	90775	North British	2-10-0
Steam	76084	British Railways	2-6-0
Steam	53809	Robert Stephenson & Co	2-8-0
Steam	8572	Beyer Peacock	4-6-0
Diesel	D2051	British Railways	Class 03
Diesel	D2063	British Railways	Class 03
Diesel	D3935	British Railways	Class 08
Diesel	D3940	British Railways	Class 08
Diesel	12131	British Railways	Class 11
Diesel	20227	English Electric	Class 20
Diesel	D5631	Brush Traction	Class 31
Diesel	D6732	English Electric	Class 37
DMU	51188, 51192, 51228, 56062 & 56352	Metropolitan Cammell	Class 101
DMU	50479 & 56182	BRCW	Class 104

Attractions

The William Marriott Museum, which tells the story of East Anglia's railways, and a model railway are located at Holt station. The NNR's locomotive yard, a railway bookshop and another model railway can be found at Weybourne. A variety of visitor experiences can be booked in advance, including Steam Driving, Diesel Driving and Signalling Experiences. The Mid Norfolk Railway and the narrow gauge Bure Valley Railway are about eight and ten miles from the NNR respectively. Sheringham town centre, the Norfolk Coastal Path, Sheringham Park and several other National Trust sites are near to the railway.

Special Events
Events that usually take place on the railway include:

A variety of dining trains.
Steam, Diesel & Mixed Traction Galas.
Vintage Transport Day.
1940s Weekend.
Norfolk Lights Express between November and early January.
Santa & Mince Pie Specials.

Whitwell & Reepham Railway

Introduction and History
The Midland & Great Northern Joint Railway (M&GNJR) from Norwich City to Melton Constable opened in 1882 and Whitwell & Reepham station was situated roughly half way along the rural route. The Great Eastern Railway had opened a more conveniently located station in Reepham in 1881, creating competition from the beginning. After declining use, passenger services to Whitwell & Reepham ceased in 1959, although freight continued until 1981, running via Themelthorpe Curve, which British Rail had built in 1960. The final weedkilling train passed through Whitwell & Reepham in 1983 and track lifting began the following year. From 1993, much of the trackbed became part of Marriott's Way, a traffic-free cycle and footpath named after William Marriott, Chief Engineer of the M&GNJR, which runs through both former stations in Reepham. The derelict Whitwell & Reepham station site was offered for sale by Norfolk County Council in 2006 and bought by a rail enthusiast who restored it and relaid railway track in the yard behind the station; the line extends for a short distance to the south. The first heritage trains ran when the station reopened in 2009 and it now has a growing collection of rolling stock. There are plans to extend the railway north towards Themelthorpe Curve.

Contact Details
Website: www.whitwellstation.com
Tel: 01603 871694
Email: info@whitwellstation.com
Address: Whitwell & Reepham Station, Whitwell Road, Reepham, Norfolk, NR10 4GA.

Transport Links
By Rail: The nearest stations are on other heritage railways. Aylsham on the narrow gauge Bure Valley Railway is 9 miles away, Dereham on the Mid Norfolk Railway (see above) is 11 miles away and Norwich station is 15 miles away.
By Road: Free parking is available at Whitwell & Reepham.
By Bike: Whitwell & Reepham station is situated on the Marriott's Way route. Cycle hire is available nearby.

Opening Times
The station usually opens six days a week (Tuesday–Sunday) and is closed on Mondays. Diesel trains run between 10.00 & 17.00 during weekends, operating on demand rather than to a timetable. On the first Sunday of the month the site opens at 08.00 to serve breakfast and steam trains run every half hour between 12.30 & 16.00. The opening times occasionally vary, such as when special events take place.

Line Mileage and Journey Time
The railway runs for a quarter of a mile from Whitwell & Reepham and the journey time is relatively short.

Stock List

Type	Number	Builder	Details
Steam	2199 VICTORY	Andrew Barclay	0-4-0ST
Steam	945 ANNIE	Andrew Barclay	0-4-0ST
Steam	AGECROFT No.3 (7681)	Robert Stephenson & Hawthorns	0-4-0ST
Diesel	1 (3733)	Baguley	0-4-0
Diesel	D2700	North British	0-4-0
Diesel	466629 TIPOCKITY	Ruston & Hornsby	0-4-0
Diesel	518494 SWANWORTH	Ruston & Hornsby	0-4-0
Diesel	D1171	Hudswell Clarke	0-6-0
EMU	70527	British Railways	Class 411

Attractions

The site includes the restored station building, signal box and a museum with exhibits relating to the station and railway's history. There is a model railway club which is based at the site. Steam driving experiences can be arranged. Whitwell & Reepham station is situated on the 26-mile-long traffic-free Marriott's Way through rural Norfolk. The region is also home to the North Norfolk Railway, the Mid Norfolk Railway, the historic city of Norwich and several coastal destinations.

Special Events

Events that take place on the railway include:

Easter Egg Hunt.
Mother's Day Event.
Classic Car Evenings.
1940s Weekend.

▲ On 9 September 2021, the North Norfolk Railway's Class 100 vehicle 56301 is seen outposted at County School station, which does not yet see regular passenger services. **Brad Joyce**

SOUTH-EAST

Region 7 – South-East

Bluebell Railway

Introduction and History

The railway was the first of two routes between Oxted and Lewes and was built by the London, Brighton & South Coast Railway, opening in 1882. Closure of the East Grinstead–Lewes route was proposed in 1954 and effected in 1958, with the Haywards Heath–Horsted Keynes route surviving until 1963. A preservation group formed in 1959 and in 1960 the Bluebell Railway became one of the first standard gauge preserved railways in the world to operate trains, initially from Sheffield Park to Bluebell Halt, with the line extending north to Horsted Keynes in 1962, Kingscote in 1994 and East Grinstead in 2013. The East Grinstead extension required vast quantities of 30-foot deep landfill rubbish to be excavated from the railway cutting, before the line could continue over the impressive Imberhorne Viaduct to re-join the national rail network. The railway also owns the trackbed between Horsted Keynes and Ardingly, where today's freight line from Haywards Heath via Copyhold Junction currently ends. There are plans to reinstate this line, which would involve relaying two miles of track and bypassing the aggregates terminal at Ardingly. That would create a through line towards Haywards Heath and a second main line connection. There is also a long-term aspiration to extend south from Sheffield Park to Lewes.

Contact Details

Website: www.bluebell-railway.com
Tel: 01825 720800
Email: enquiries@bluebell-railway.com
Address: The Bluebell Railway, Sheffield Park Station, East Sussex, TN22 3QL.

Transport Links

By Rail: There is a rail connection at East Grinstead; the main line and Bluebell stations are adjacent, with a short walk between the two being required.
By Road: There is plenty of parking space at Sheffield Park (TN22 3QL) and Horsted Keynes (RH17 7BB). There is pay and display parking near to East Grinstead (RH19 1EB) and there is no road access at Kingscote.

Opening Times

Trains operate during weekends from February to December and on the majority of weekdays from April.

Line Mileage and Journey Time

0.00	Sheffield Park
4.50	Horsted Keynes
8.50	Kingscote
10.75	East Grinstead

A return journey takes 1 hour 40 minutes from Sheffield Park or about two hours from East Grinstead.

Stock List

Type	Number	Builder	Details
Steam	3 CAPTAIN Baxter	Fletcher Jennings	0-4-0T
Steam	96 NORMANDY	LSWR	0-4-0T
Steam	263	SECR	0-4-4T
Steam	65	SECR	0-6-0
Steam	592	SECR	0-6-0
Steam	30541	Southern Railway	0-6-0
Steam	4 (641)	Manning Wardle	0-6-0ST
Steam	55 STEPNEY	LBSCR	0-6-0T
Steam	FENCHURCH (32636)	LBSCR	0-6-0T
Steam	58850	North London Railway	0-6-0T
Steam	31027	SECR	0-6-0T
Steam	178	SECR	0-6-0T
Steam	323 BLUEBELL	SECR	0-6-0T

Steam	32473	LBSCR	0-6-2T
Steam	92240	British Railways	2-10-0
Steam	1638	Southern Railway	2-6-0
Steam	31618	Southern Railway	2-6-0
Steam	84030	Bluebell Railway SC2P	2-6-2T
Steam	80064	British Railways	2-6-4T
Steam	80100	British Railways	2-6-4T
Steam	80151	British Railways	2-6-4T
Steam	9017	GWR	4-4-0
Steam	928	Southern Railway	4-4-0
Steam	32424	Bluebell Railway Atlantic Group	4-4-2
Steam	488	LSWR	4-4-2T
Steam	6989	British Railways	4-6-0
Steam	73082	British Railways	4-6-0
Steam	75027	British Railways	4-6-0
Steam	847	Southern Railway	4-6-0
Steam	34059	Southern Railway	4-6-2
Steam	21C123 (BR No.34023)	Southern Railway	4-6-2
Diesel	957	Howard	0-4-0
Diesel	10241	Rolls Royce Sentinel	0-4-0
Diesel	D4106	British Railways	Class 09
Diesel	D6570	BRCW	Class 33

Attractions

The Bluebell Railway has one of the largest collection of British steam locomotives after the National Railway Museum. This, along with the engine shed and museum at Sheffield Park and carriage & wagon works with its viewing gallery at Horsted Keynes, give plenty of railway interest. Attractions in the region include Sheffield Park & Garden and Standen House & Garden (both National Trust), Bluebell Vineyard which is two miles from Sheffield Park and Sackville College at East Grinstead. The Royal Botanic Gardens' Wakehurst site is a few miles from Horsted Keynes.

Special Events

Events that usually take place on the railway include:

Steam and Diesel Galas.
Transport-themed events.
Steamlights Trains between November and January.
Santa Specials during December.

Buckinghamshire Railway Centre

Introduction and History

The Buckinghamshire Railway Centre is based at Quainton Road station which opened in 1868 on the line from London to Verney Junction via Aylesbury. It grew in significance after becoming part of the Great Central Railway in 1899. However, passenger services no longer stopped at the station from 1963 and the route was closed to passenger traffic in 1966. The Quainton Road Society was formed in 1969 and in 1971 it absorbed the London Railway Preservation Society with its collection of railway exhibits. Visitors have been able to travel on steam-hauled trains from Quainton Road since as early as 1970. Today the 25-acre site has one of the country's largest collections of locomotives, rolling stock and railway memorabilia and a short operational heritage railway. The station was recently disconnected from the national rail network as part of the preparatory work for HS2.

Contact Details

Website: www.bucksrailcentre.org
Tel: 01296 655720
Email: office@bucksrailcentre.org
Address: Buckinghamshire Railway Centre, Station Road, Quainton, Aylesbury, Bucks, HP22 4BY.

Transport Links

By Rail: Aylesbury Vale Parkway is the nearest railway station and is less than five miles away.
By Road: There is ample free parking for cars and coaches (HP22 4BY).

Opening Times

The Centre opens on Sundays and on selected weekdays between April and October. During that period steam trains operate on Sundays and some weekdays during school holidays. In addition, the café opens 09.30–13.30 Monday to Fridays.

Line Mileage and Journey Time

There are two operational lines on the site, both of which run for one third of a mile and the journey time is relatively short.

Stock List

Type	Number	Builder	Details
Steam Railcar	5208	Sentinel-Cammell	Steam Railcar
Steam	1477	Andrew Barclay	0-4-0F
Steam	2243	Andrew Barclay	0-4-0F
Steam	2469	Bagnall	0-4-0ST
Steam	1742	Hudswell Clarke	0-4-0ST
Steam	3717	Hawthorn Leslie	0-4-0ST
Steam	1159	Peckett	0-4-0ST
Steam	1903	Peckett	0-4-0ST
Steam	2105	Peckett	0-4-0ST
Steam	807	Aveling & Porter	0-4-0T
Steam	1900	Peckett	0-4-0T
Steam	3567	Aveling & Porter	0-4-0WT
Steam	No. 1	Metropolitan Railway	0-4-4T
Steam	GERVASE	Sentinel	0-4-0VBGT
Steam	7715	GWR	0-6-0PT
Steam	2138	Andrew Barclay	0-6-0ST
Steam	3890	Hunslet	0-6-0ST

▲ 0-6-0 Number 65 was built in 1896 and now resides at the Bluebell Railway, where it is seen at work at the line's Sheffield Park station on 6 August 2021.   **Alisdair Anderson**

Steam	3782 ARTHUR	Hunslet	0-6-0ST
Steam	2498	Yorkshire Engine Co.	0-6-0ST
Steam	1334	Hudswell Clarke	0-6-0T
Steam	24564	North British	0-6-0T
Steam	3020	LNWR	2-2-2
Steam	30585	LSWR	2-4-0WT
Steam	7200	GWR	2-8-2T
Steam	6984	British Railways	4-6-0
Steam	3405	North British	4-8-4
Diesel	20067	Fowler	0-4-0
Diesel	2102	Hibberd	0-4-0
Diesel	3271	Hibberd	0-4-0
Diesel	3765	Hibberd	0-4-0
Diesel	2067	Hunslet	0-4-0
Diesel	K4428	Hunslet	0-4-0
Diesel	425477	Ruston & Hornsby	0-4-0
Diesel	463153	Ruston & Hornsby	0-4-0
Diesel	459518	Ruston & Hornsby	0-6-0
Diesel	D2298	Robert Stephenson & Hawthorns	Class 04
DMU	51886, 51899 & 59761	British Railways	Class 115

Attractions

The museum and visitor centre have extensive exhibits including a royal dining coach from 1901 and one of the most complete sets of British Rail goods vehicles. Visitors can ride the 1 km long miniature railway and see the projects awaiting renovation in the restoration sheds. The Travelling Post Office tells the story of moving mail by rail. There is a second-hand bookshop and steam engine driver experiences are available. Nearby attractions include Quainton Windmill, Waddesden Manor, Discover Bucks Museum and the town of Aylesbury.

Special Events

Events that usually take place on the railway include:

Spring Steam Gala.
Day out with Thomas.
Bus Rally.
Classic Car event.
Panto Express trains run during November and December.

Chatham Dockyard Railway

Introduction and History

Chatham Dockyard is a Royal Navy dockyard that was established in the mid-16th Century. Its first railway was a 3 foot 6 inch-gauge horse-drawn tramway that was completed in the 19th century. A standard gauge line was then built in 1865 to move materials across the site and to serve the shipbuilding yards. This was connected to the main line network in 1877. A narrow gauge railway and locomotives were introduced in 1871, however, this had ceased operating by the 1930s. At its peak, it is estimated that there were approximately 17 miles of railway within the Royal Navy dockyard but by the time it closed in 1984, this had been reduced to two miles. Today's visitor attraction is a maritime museum that opened in 1985 and the Chatham Dockyard Railway operates demonstration trains through the site. The trains are not able to carry passengers.

Contact Details

Website: www.dockyardrailway.co.uk
Dockyard website: www.thedockyard.co.uk or
www.100objectskent.co.uk/museum/chatham-historic-dockyard-trust/
Tel: 01634 823800
Email: nkils2@hotmail.co.uk or info@chdt.org.uk
Address: Chatham Historic Dockyard, Main Gate, Chatham, ME4 4TY.

Transport Links

By Rail: The nearest stations are Chatham and Gillingham (Kent); both are just over a mile away.
By Road: Parking is available at the dockyard site (ME4 4TY).

Opening Times
The dockyard opens daily from February to early November and trains operate on selected weekends.

Line Mileage and Journey Time
The dockyard has nearly two miles of track and demonstration trains use about one mile of this including the section to Anchor Wharf. It takes about half an hour for trains to make a return journey.

Stock List

Type	Number	Builder	Details
Steam	INVICTA (2220)	Andrew Barclay	0-4-0ST
Steam	AJAX (7042)	Robert Stephenson & Hawthorns	0-4-0ST
Steam	575 (2675)	Grafton	0-4-2
Steam	558 (2641)	Grafton	0-4-2
Steam	482 (2525)	Grafton	0-4-2
Steam	1942 (2547)	Grafton	0-4-2
Diesel	WD42	Andrew Barclay	0-4-0
Diesel	THALIA (2503)	Drewry	0-4-0
Diesel	ROCHESTER CASTLE (FH3738)	Hibberd	4wDM

Attractions
The dockyard railway operates demonstrations using steam cranes, steam and diesel locomotives and wooden wagons, most of which pre-date the 1923 railway Grouping. Special steamings can be arranged in advance for photographers, railway enthusiasts or private functions. Trains travel through the dockyard, which is a maritime museum covering an 80-acre site, with warships, a historic RNLI lifeboat collection and the Victorian ropery. Additional attractions nearby include Fort Amherst, Chatham Snowsports Centre and Diggerland Kent.

Special Events
Events that are due to take place at the railway:

Two steam locomotives are expected to visit during 2023.
1940s Weekend during September 2023.

Chinnor & Princes Risborough Railway

Introduction and History
The branch line from Princes Risborough to Watlington opened in 1872, with intermediate stations at Chinnor and Aston Rowant. Passenger services ceased in 1957 although trains carrying goods and parcels continued until early 1961, after which the track beyond Chinnor was lifted. The station and platform at Chinnor were demolished during the 1970s; trains continued to work to Chinnor Cement Works until 1989, when Class 47 47258 hauled the final revenue-earning service in December 1989. The Chinnor & Princes Risborough Railway Association then took over the route in 1990 and in 1994 it purchased the freehold for the line, built a new station and ran its first trains from Chinnor. The railway was extended in 1995 and again in 1996 when it reached the former main line junction at Princes Risborough. In 2018 the line was extended into Platform 4 of Princes Risborough station, returning connecting passenger services to the branch for the first time since 1957. There are aspirations to extend the railway south-west along the former Watlington branch in the future.

Contact Details
Website: www.chinnorrailway.co.uk
Tel: 07979 055366 (between 10.00–16.00).
Email: Written enquiries can be made from the website.
Address: Chinnor & Princes Risborough Railway, Station Approach, Station Road, Chinnor, OX39 4ER.

Transport Links
By Rail: The heritage railway operates from Platform 4 of Princes Risborough station.
By Road: Parking is available opposite Chinnor station (use postcode OX39 4BZ).

Opening Times
Trains usually operate on Sundays from April to October and on selected other dates for special events.

Line Mileage and Journey Time
0.00   Princes Risborough
3.75   Chinnor

A return journey between Chinnor and Princes Risborough takes about an hour. In addition, on occasional special event days, passenger rides are available on the quarter mile spur that runs south from Princes Risborough.

Stock List

Type	Number	Builder	Details
Steam	6412	GWR	0-6-0PT
Diesel	IRIS (459515)	Ruston & Hornsby	0-6-0
Diesel	D2069	British Railways	Class 03
Diesel	D3993 (08825)	British Railways	Class 08
Diesel	D3018	British Railways	Class 08
Diesel	97205 (31163)	Brush Traction	Class 31
Diesel	37227	English Electric	Class 37
Diesel	43054	British Railways	Class 43
Diesel	43066	British Railways	Class 43
DMU	51375 (977992)	Pressed Steel	Class 117
DMU	55023 & 55024	Pressed Steel	Class 121
EMU	61736, 61737 & 70573	British Railways	Class 411
EMU	69013	British Railways	Class 412

Attractions
The railway's Chinnor base is home to the Cambrian Tea Room and a shop selling railway books, models and souvenirs. Nearby attractions include Chinnor Windmill, Chinnor Beehive Lime Kiln and Chinnor St. Andrews Church. The historic market town of Princes Risborough is less than a mile from its station and has several 17th and 18th Century buildings, including the National Trust-owned Manor House. The railway is on the edge of the Chiltern Hills, an Area of Outstanding Natural Beauty, which has many walks, hills and woodlands that can be explored.

Special Events
Events that usually take place on the railway:

Mothering Sunday event.
Father's Day event in June.
Spooks & Ghouls event.
Santa Steam Specials during December.

Cholsey & Wallingford Railway

Introduction and History
The branch line from Cholsey to Wallingford opened 1866. It was originally planned for the railway to continue to Watlington and meet the branch from Princes Risborough, part of which forms the Chinnor & Princes Risborough Railway today, but this was not built. Passenger services ceased in 1959; freight trains to Wallingford continued until 1965, after which the station was closed and the land sold. Freight traffic continued to the malting plant to the south of Wallingford until 1981. A final railtour ran from London Paddington to Wallingford in May 1981, before British Rail closed the junction at Cholsey. The C&WR Preservation Society was then formed and heritage services began in 1985 from a temporary platform at Wallingford. The railway returned to Cholsey station in 1994, with trains working into a dedicated bay platform, although there is no main line rail connection. Wallingford station has recently benefited from a series of improvement works, including the installation of the Victorian canopy from Maidenhead station and a platform extension.

Contact Details
Website: www.cholsey-wallingford-railway.com
Tel: 01491 835067
Email: Written enquiries can be made from the website.
Address: Cholsey & Wallingford Railway, Wallingford Station, 5 Hithercroft Road, Wallingford, Oxfordshire, OX10 9GQ.

Transport Links
By Rail: Heritage trains depart from Platform 5 at Cholsey station. Through tickets to Wallingford can be purchased from GWR stations (the Wallingford Rover).
By Road: Parking is available at Wallingford (OX10 9GQ) and there is a small pay & display car park outside Cholsey station (OX10 9QD).

Opening Times
Trains operate on selected weekends and bank holidays through the year and are steam hauled on some dates.

Line Mileage and Journey Time
0.00   Cholsey
2.25   Wallingford

A return journey takes about 45 minutes.

▲ This quintessentially English scene shows GWR 0-6-0PT 6412 passing Bledlow Village Cricket Club on 14 August 2022 hauling a GWR autocoach on the Chinnor & Princess Risborough Railway.
Martyn Tattam

Stock List

Type	Number	Builder	Details
Steam	12 (6515)	Sentinel	4wVBT
Steam	NORTHERN GAS BOARD No. 1 (2142)	Peckett	0-4-0ST
Diesel	3270	Hibberd	0-4-0
Diesel	08123	British Railways	Class 08
Diesel	08022 LION	British Railways	Class 08
Diesel	08060 UNICORN	British Railways	Class 08

Attractions

The railway has a number of locomotives with an industrial and shunting history. Wallingford station has a museum coach, a café and shop with many railway-related items and second-hand books. In Wallingford, there is a 15th Century marketplace, a castle, views of the River Thames and a local museum. Cholsey Church is the burial place of Agatha Christie and is a short walk from Cholsey station. Didcot Railway Centre is six miles away and the Chinnor & Princes Risborough Railway is 16 miles away.

Special Events

Events that usually take place on the railway include:

Easter Running Days.
Cream Tea Specials.
1940s Event.
Polar Express Trains during November and December.

Didcot Railway Centre

Introduction and History

There has been a railway at the Didcot site since 1839, when the Great Western Railway's (GWR) broad gauge line from Reading to Steventon first arrived. In 1844 the GWR built a northern branch line to Oxford and opened Didcot station on the site of the newly created junction. It has remained an important junction, depot and stabling point since. The depot became surplus to British Rail's requirements and closed in 1965; however, in 1967 the Great Western Society gained access to the site and has since used it to restore, exhibit and demonstrate an array of rolling stock and items of railway interest. The railway centre is located within the busy triangle of railway lines at Didcot and includes several short railway lines on which a variety of traction is used to haul passenger trains.

Contact Details

Website: www.didcotrailwaycentre.org.uk
Tel: 01235 817200
Email: info@didcotrailwaycentre.org.uk
Address: Didcot Railway Centre, Didcot, Oxfordshire, OX11 7NJ.

Transport Links

By Rail: The subway inside Didcot Parkway railway station leads directly to the Centre.
By Road: Car parking is available outside Didcot Parkway (OX11 7NJ) or at the nearby larger Foxhall Road site (OX11 7NR) and both are chargeable. Note that as the Railway Centre is entirely surrounded by railway lines, the route to the Centre includes crossing a footbridge or using the station subway, both of which involve stairs. There is a battery-powered stairclimber which can be booked in advance.

Opening Times

The Centre opens on most Saturdays & Sundays and regular weekdays from Spring until October.

Line Mileage and Journey Time

The main section of standard gauge line used to carry passengers is one third of a mile long and the journey time is relatively short.

Stock List

Type	Number	Builder	Details
Steam Railcar	93	GWR	Steam Railmotor
Steam	1340	Avonside	0-4-0ST
Steam	1338	Kitson	0-4-0ST
Steam	I BONNIE PRINCE CHARLIE	Robert Stephenson & Hawthorns	0-4-0ST
Steam	5	George England	0-4-0WT
Steam	1466	GWR	0-4-2T
Steam	3650	GWR	0-6-0PT
Steam	3738	GWR	0-6-0PT
Steam	1363	GWR	0-6-0ST
Steam	2409	Hunslet	0-6-0ST
Steam	6697	Armstrong Whitworth	0-6-2T
Steam	FIRE FLY (replica)	Fire Fly Trust	2-2-2
Steam	5322	GWR	2-6-0
Steam	4144	GWR	2-6-2T
Steam	5572	GWR	2-6-2T
Steam	6106	GWR	2-6-2T
Steam	3822	GWR	2-8-0
Steam	5227	GWR	2-8-0T
Steam	7202	GWR	2-8-2T
Steam	IRON DUKE	Resco Railways	4-2-2
Steam	6998	British Railways	4-6-0
Steam	1014	Great Western Society	4-6-0
Steam	2999	Great Western Society	4-6-0

▲ Didcot Railway Centre has one of the few original steam sheds to have survived into the preservation era, allowing authentic scenes from the past such as this to be recreated. On 2 June 2022, the newly-overhauled Castle Class 4079 "PENDENNIS CASTLE" takes centre stage.   **Martyn Tattam**

Steam	7808	GWR	4-6-0
Steam	4079	GWR	4-6-0
Steam	5051	GWR	4-6-0
Steam	5900	GWR	4-6-0
Steam	6023	GWR	4-6-0
Gas Turbine	18000	Brown Boveri	A1A-A1A
Diesel	DL26	Hunslet	0-6-0
Diesel	604	British Railways	Class 08
Diesel	D9516	British Railways	Class 14
Diesel	D1023	British Railways	Class 52
DMU	22	GWR	Railcar

Attractions

The 21-acre site has a wealth of railway-related exhibits and a large collection of locomotives, which includes steam, diesel and gas turbine engines. The passenger line uses a varied selection of traction and the roster showing what is due to work on each date is shown on the website. Visitors can see the engine shed, carriage display shed, transfer shed with broad and standard gauge railways and the signalling centre with a modern panel and mechanical levers which can be pulled. The site is close to the centre of Didcot; the city of Oxford is 12 miles away and nearby heritage railways include Cholsey & Wallingford (6 miles away), Chinnor & Princes Risborough (19 miles) and Swindon & Cricklade (29 miles).

Special Events

Events that usually take place at the Centre include:

Halloween event.
Steam Into Christmas.

East Kent Railway

Introduction and History

The East Kent Light Railway, as it was originally known, was built in stages between 1911 and 1917, primarily to carry coal. It ran from Shepherdswell to Wingham and Richborough. The first passengers were carried in 1916; however, passenger services between Eastry and Sandwich Road ended as early as 1928 and the remaining passenger services ceased in 1948. The stretch between Shepherdswell and Tilmanstone Colliery continued to carry coal until 1986 and closed in 1987. The preservation era began in 1985 when the East Kent Railway Society formed and the first heritage trains ran in 1993. There are plans to extend the railway south along the trackbed towards Coldred.

Contact Details

Website: www.eastkentrailway.co.uk
Tel: 01304 832042
Email: Written enquiries can be made from the EKR website.
Address: East Kent Railway Trust, Station Road, Shepherdswell, Dover, CT15 7PD.

Transport Links

By Rail: The main line station at Shepherdswell is next to the EKR station.
By Road: There is plenty of free parking at Shepherdswell station (CT15 7PD).

Opening Times

The railway operates on most Sundays, on selected Saturdays and Bank Holidays, and during December for Santa services. In addition, the grounds are open Tuesdays to Sundays (closed Mondays).

Line Mileage and Journey Time

0.00	Shepherdswell
1.75	Eythorne

A return journey takes just under one hour.

Stock List

Type	Number	Builder	Details
Steam	2087	Peckett	0-4-0ST
Steam	2004 ST DUNSTAN	Avonside	0-6-0ST
Steam	9622	Sentinel	4wVBGT
Diesel	4160002	Fowler	0-4-0
Diesel	01530	Thomas Hill	0-4-0
Diesel	427	Ruston & Hornsby	0-6-0
Diesel	08502	British Railways	Class 08
Diesel	08676	British Railways	Class 08
Diesel	08685	British Railways	Class 08
Diesel	08804	British Railways	Class 08
Electric	42 (Kearsley No.1)	Hawthorn Leslie	Bo-Bo
DMU	142017 (55558 & 55608)	BREL/Leyland	Class 142
DMU	142036 (55577 & 55627)	BREL/Leyland	Class 142
DEMU	60100 & 60800	British Railways	Class 205
DEMU	54000	BREL	Class 210
EMU	11161 & 11187	Southern Railway	4 Cor
EMU	65917, 65974 & 72287	ABB	Class 365
EMU	70273	British Railways	Class 411
EMU	62385 & 76747	BREL	Class 421
EMU	76875	BREL	Class 423
EMU	70904, 76397 & 76398	British Railways	Class 423
EMU	61280	British Railways	Class 489

Attractions

The railway has a varied selection of traction, including steam and diesel locomotives, and multiple units. Visitors can ride on the standard gauge line and the 7¼ inch gauge Woodland Miniature Railway at Shepherdswell. There is also a model railway with layouts of four different gauges, two signal boxes which house historical information on the EKR and a nature trail to explore. There are various other attractions in the area, with Canterbury, Sandwich and the Kent Coast all nearby.

Special Events

Events that usually take place at the railway include:

Dining Trains serving Cream Teas and Fish & Chip Suppers.
Beer Festival.
Santa by Train.

Fawley Hill

Introduction and History

Fawley Hill is the home of Lady McAlpine and was built in 1960 by the late Sir William McAlpine. In 1961, Hudswell Clarke 0-6-0ST number 31 was bought for scrap value by Sir William and became the first of many railway items that were brought to Fawley Hill. A 100-metre section of standard gauge track was laid in the 1960s and since then the line has been increased to a length of approximately one mile. The railway only operates on selected dates and is available for hire and use. Some of the larger items that have been brought to the site include Somersham station from Cambridgeshire, a Midland Railway signal box and a footbridge from the Isle of Wight's Ryde–Shanklin line. There is a museum with a large collection of exhibits, which began as a home for Sir William's traction engines and car collection.

Contact Details

Website: www.fawleyhill.co.uk and www.fawleymuseum.org
Tel: 01491 574873
Email: events@fawleyhill.com or invitations@fawleymuseum.co.uk (see Opening Times below)
Address: Fawley Hill, Fawley, Henley-on-Thames, Bucks, RG9 6JA.

Transport Links
By Rail: The nearest station is Henley-on-Thames, which is three miles away.
By Road: There is on-site parking for visitors.

Opening Times
Fawley Hill is a private estate, which only opens on a few days each year and entry has to be requested in advance by contacting invitations@fawleymuseum.co.uk. Entrance at other times is only by prior arrangement for private functions.

Line Mileage and Journey Time
The railway is nearly one mile long and the journey time is relatively short.

Stock List

Type	Number	Builder	Details
Steam	31	Hudswell Clarke	0-6-0ST
Diesel	3817	Hibberd	4wDM
Diesel	3894 ERNIE	Hibberd	4wDM
Diesel	D2120	British Railways	Class 03

Attractions
Fawley Hill has the steepest standard gauge railway in the world, with a gradient of 1 in 13 at its steepest point. The site and museum have a large collection of railway artefacts and some of the larger exhibits include the Great Eastern Railway Chairman's private wooden saloon and two Royal Train carriages; Her Majesty's private carriage and the nursery coach for Prince Charles and Princess Anne. There are two "O" gauge railways and Iron Henge, which is a large circle of supports from the undercroft of St Pancras station. Fawley Hill has an animal sanctuary with over 20 different animal types, which have been transferred from several zoos and animal sanctuaries. Animal feeding trips can be arranged in advance. The museum, Victorian railway station and waiting room can all be used as a venue for weddings and events.

Isle of Wight Steam Railway

Introduction and History
The railway from Ryde to Newport opened in 1875 and was one of several lines on the Isle of Wight which during their lives tended to use older rolling stock than those on the mainland. The final steam trains ran in 1966 and the railway from Ryde to Newport and Cowes then closed. In 1967 a group of enthusiasts formed the Wight Locomotive Society and purchased steam locomotive 24 "Calbourne", which remains at the railway today. In 1971 the Isle of Wight Railway Company formed with the aim of acquiring the line between Wooton and Havenstreet. This was successful and the first preserved trains ran in 1971. In 1991 the railway was extended to Smallbrook Junction, where it connects with the Ryde–Shanklin line. There are plans to reinstate the connection to the Ryde–Shanklin Island Line at Smallbrook Junction, which would allow through running to Ryde. In addition, there are aspirations to extend the railway west towards Newport.

Contact Details
Website: www.iwsteamrailway.co.uk
Tel: 01983 882204
Email: info@iwsteamrailway.co.uk
Address: The Railway Station, Havenstreet, Near Ryde, Isle of Wight, PO33 4DS.

Transport Links
By Rail: Change at Smallbrook Junction on the Ryde–Shanklin route (Island Line). Note, there is no road or footpath access at Smallbrook Junction.
By Road: Free car parking is available at Havenstreet (PO33 4DS).

Opening Times
The railway operates on most days from late-March until the end of September, plus on selected dates during November, December and January for seasonal services.

Line Mileage and Journey Time

0.00   Smallbrook Junction
1.75   Ashey
3.25   Havenstreet
4.75   Wooton

A return journey takes about one hour.

Stock List

Type	Number	Builder	Details
Steam	INVINCIBLE	Hawthorn Leslie	0-4-0ST
Steam	24	LSWR	0-4-4T
Steam	192	Hunslet	0-6-0ST
Steam	198	Hunslet	0-6-0ST
Steam	38 AJAX	Andrew Barclay	0-6-0T
Steam	2 YARMOUTH	LBSCR	0-6-0T
Steam	8 (BR No. 32646)	LBSCR	0-6-0T
Steam	W11 (BR No. 32640)	LBSCR	0-6-0T
Steam	41313	British Railways	2-6-2T
Steam	41298	British Railways	2-6-2T
Diesel	235	Andrew Barclay	0-4-0
Diesel	D2059	British Railways	Class 03
Diesel	D2554	Hunslet	Class 05
EMU	483007 (127 & 227)	Metropolitan Cammell	Class 483

▲ During the year they celebrated their 150th birthdays, the Kent & East Sussex Railway's two LB&SCR Class A1 0-6-0Ts 2678 and 2670 are seen working at Tenterden on 3 June 2022.

Alisdair Anderson

Attractions

There is plenty to explore at the railway's Havenstreet base, including the Train Story Discovery Centre, a museum, Haven Falconry Bird of Prey Centre, a railway gift & model shop, the carriage & wagon workshop and a picnic & children's play area. Attractions in the area include Appley Park, Dinosaur Isle, Butterfly World and there are hundreds of miles of walking and cycling routes on the island.

Special Events

Events that usually take place on the railway include:

Real Ale Festival and food-themed events.
A 1940s themed event.
Transport events, such as Motor Shows and Steam Shows.
Seasonal Santa Specials and Mince Pie Specials.

Kent & East Sussex Railway

Introduction and History

The first section of the Kent & East Sussex Light Railway opened between Robertsbridge and Rolvenden in 1900. It was extended to Tenterden Town in 1903 and to Headcorn in 1905, when it met the main line from Tonbridge to Ashford. After declining use, the Tenterden to Headcorn section closed in 1954 and the track was lifted soon afterwards. The branch from Robertsbridge to Tenterden continued to see freight and occasional charter trains until 1961 when it was closed. During the 1960s, a preservation group worked towards reinstating the railway; however, the Robertsbridge to Bodiam section had to be abandoned due to the number of roads crossing the line. The heritage railway between Tenterden and Rolvenden opened in 1974 and this was extended to Wittersham Road in 1977, Northiam in 1990 and to Bodiam in 2000. Plans are under way to extend and reconnect the railway to the main line under the auspices of the Rother Valley Railway (see the Proposed Railways section).

Contact Details

Website: www.kesr.org.uk
Tel: 01580 765155
Email: enquiries@kesr.org.uk
Address: Tenterden Town Station, Station Road, Tenterden, Kent, TN30 6HE.

Transport Links

By Rail: Robertsbridge station is five miles from Bodiam and the nearest stations to Tenterden are Ham Street (eight miles) and Headcorn (nine miles).
By Road: Parking is available at Tenterden Town (TN30 6HE) and Northiam (TN31 6QT).

Opening Times

Trains usually operate on Saturdays, Sundays and on a variety of weekdays between April and October.

Line Mileage and Journey Time

0.00	Tenterden Town
1.50	Rolvenden
4.75	Wittersham Road
6.50	Northiam
10.25	Bodiam

A return journey from Tenterden takes about 1 hour 50 minutes.

Stock List

Type	Number	Builder	Details
Steam	1	Dodman & Co	0-4-2WT
Steam	1638	British Railways	0-6-0PT
Steam	23 (3791)	Hunslet	0-6-0ST
Steam	25 (3797)	Hunslet	0-6-0ST

Steam	75008 SWIFTSURE	Hunslet	0-6-0ST
Steam	14 CHARWELTON (1955)	Manning Wardle	0-6-0ST
Steam	2670	LBSCR	0-6-0T
Steam	2678	LBSCR	0-6-0T
Steam	5753	SECR	0-6-0T
Steam	65	Vulcan Iron Works	0-6-0T
Steam	300	Vulcan Iron Works	0-6-0T
Steam	5668	GWR	0-6-2T
Steam	6619	GWR	0-6-2T
Steam	376	Norwegian State Railways	2-6-0
Steam	4253	GWR	2-8-0T
Diesel	423661	Ruston & Hornsby	0-4-0DE
Diesel	D2023	British Railways	Class 03
Diesel	D2024	British Railways	Class 03
Diesel	3174	British Railways	Class 08
Diesel	D4118	British Railways	Class 08
Diesel	D9504	British Railways	Class 14
Diesel	D9518	British Railways	Class 14
Diesel	D9526	British Railways	Class 14
Diesel	7594	British Railways	Class 25
DMU	50971 & 51571	British Railways	Class 108
DMU	20	GWR	Railcar
Electro-Diesel	40	British Thomson-Houston	Bo-Bo

Attractions

The Colonel Stephens Railway Museum is at the railway's Tenterden base; it opens on the days when trains operate and is free to enter. The railway is also the home of the Cavell Van, a luggage van that was used to carry the remains of The Unknown Soldier in 1920 and has been restored as such. Behind the scenes tours can be arranged at Tenterden, which include a visit inside the carriage and wagon workshop. There is a viewing gallery for the locomotive engineering workshop at Rolvenden. Various walks can be taken from the stations along the course of the railway. Other attractions in the area include Lashenden Air Warfare Museum, Bodiam Castle, Camber Sands, Rye Castle Museum and Rye Harbour Nature Reserve.

Special Events

Events that are planned for 2023 include:

4–13 April: The Great Railway Easter Hunt.
29 April–1 May: Real Ale Festival.
21 May: Festival of Transport.
23–25 June: Spring Gala.
1–2 July: The 1940s Experience.
15 July: Real Ale Train.
29 July: Summer Concert.
25–28 August: Island Steam Fair.
3 September: Morris Minor Rally.
9–10 September: Cider & Cheese Festival.
16–17 September: 1960s Weekend.
23–24 September: Autumn Gala.
December & early January: Santa Specials & Steam into the New Year.

The Lavender Line

Introduction and History

The railway between Uckfield and Lewes opened in 1858, providing an alternative route between London and Brighton. Closure of the line was suggested in Dr Beeching's 1963 report; however, due to considerable opposition, it did not close until 1969 and the track was lifted in 1970. Isfield station was purchased privately in 1983 after which the owner renovated the station and signal box, and rebuilt the waiting room (the original building had been moved to the Bluebell Railway's nearby Sheffield Park site). A stretch of track was laid and a steam locomotive subsequently arrived at Isfield. In 1991 ownership of the station and railway was transferred to the Lavender Line Preservation Society, the name being taken from Lavender & Sons, a local firm that was previously based at Isfield station. In recent years there has been a campaign for the Uckfield–Lewes line to reopen as a commercial railway, connecting to the main line network. The Lavender Line aims to extend; however, that would be subject to the main line project not proceeding.

Contact Details

Website: www.lavender-line.co.uk
Tel: 01825 750515
Email: Written enquiries can be made from the website.
Address: The Lavender Line, Isfield Station, Near Uckfield, East Sussex, TN22 5XB.

Transport Links

By Rail: The nearest stations are Uckfield (three miles) and Lewes to the south (six miles).
By Road: Free parking is available at Isfield (TN22 5XB).

Opening Times

The railway operates on selected Sundays and on some other dates for special events. Trains depart from Isfield approximately every half hour between 11.00 and 16.30.

Line Mileage and Journey Time

The railway is just over three quarters of a mile long and a return journey takes about 20 minutes.

Stock List

Type	Number	Builder	Details
Steam	2945	Cockerill	0-4-0VBT
Diesel	354	Andrew Barclay	0-4-0
Diesel	830	Drewry	0-4-0
Diesel	15	Hibberd	4wDM
Diesel	D4113	British Railways	Class 09
DMU	56408	Metropolitan Cammell	Class 101
DMU	56279	British Railways	Class 108
DMU	999507	Wickham	Railbus
DEMU	60117, 60122, 60151, 60820, 60828 & 60832	British Railways	Class 205
EMU	61928, 75965 & 75972	British Railways	Class 309
EMU	69333	BREL	Class 422

Attractions

Driver experiences can be arranged in advance, using the railway's Class 205 "Thumper" units. Isfield station has a restored Grade II listed signal box, a gift shop, station buffet, picnic area and children's play area. There is a 5-inch gauge miniature railway which operates on selected Sundays, the proceeds from which are given to St. Thomas Childrens' Hospital. The Bluebell Railway's southern terminus at Sheffield Park is eight miles from Isfield. Other attractions in the area include Wilderness Wood, the market town of Lewes and the South Coast.

▲ One of the Lavender Line's two Class 205 diesel-electric multiple units, 1133 (205033), is seen at Isfield station on 10 July 2022.   **Ian Beardsley**

▼ During the final months of its current boiler ticket, Schools Class 4-4-0 30925 "CHELTENHAM" arrives at the Mid Hants Railway's Medstead and Four Marks station with a matching rake of Southern Region green coaches on 2 June 2022.   **Martyn Tattam**

Mid Hants Railway

Introduction and History

The railway between Alton and Winchester via Alresford opened in 1865 and became known as the Watercress Line, due to the large volumes of the locally produced crop that it carried. The line from London to Alton was electrified in 1937, which brought an end to regular through trains to and from London, and when the London–Southampton line was electrified in 1967, the line between Alton and Winchester via Alresford became an isolated diesel section. The route survived the mass rural line closures of the 1960s, but only until 1973 when British Rail closed it between Alton and Winchester Junction. The Alresford–Alton section was purchased from BR in 1975 and the first heritage trains worked between Alresford and Ropley in 1977. The railway was extended to Medstead in 1983 and to Alton in 1985 where the line is now connected to the national network.

Contact Details

Website: www.watercressline.co.uk
Tel: 01962 733810
Email: info@watercressline.co.uk
Address: Mid Hants Railway Ltd, New Alresford, Hampshire, SO24 9JG.

Transport Links

By Rail: There is a rail connection at Alton; cross to the Mid Hants Railway platform.
By Road: Car parking is available at Alresford (SO24 9JG) and Alton (GU34 2PZ). It is chargeable at both locations and the rates are lower at Alresford.

Opening Times

Trains operate on most weekends and Bank Holidays through the year and on selected weekdays, including most weekdays between April and August.

Line Mileage and Journey Time

0.00	Alton
4.50	Medstead and Four Marks
7.25	Ropley
10.25	Alresford

A return journey takes about 1 hour 40 minutes.

Stock List

Type	Number	Builder	Details
Steam	KILMERSDEN (1788)	Peckett	0-4-0ST
Steam	1 (3781)	Hunslet	0-6-0T
Steam	41312	British Railways	2-6-2T
Steam	80150	British Railways	2-6-4T
Steam	53808	Robert Stephenson & Co	2-8-0
Steam	925	Southern Railway	4-4-0
Steam	73096	British Railways	4-6-0
Steam	75079	British Railways	4-6-0
Steam	30499	LSWR	4-6-0
Steam	30506	LSWR	4-6-0
Steam	30828	Southern Railway	4-6-0
Steam	850	Southern Railway	4-6-0
Steam	34105	British Railways	4-6-2
Steam	34007	Southern Railway	4-6-2
Steam	34058	Southern Railway	4-6-2
Steam	35005	Southern Railway	4-6-2
Diesel	08032	British Railways	Class 08
Diesel	08377	British Railways	Class 08
Diesel	D3358	British Railways	Class 08
Diesel	12082	British Railways	Class 11
Diesel	D8059	English Electric	Class 20
Diesel	D8188	English Electric	Class 20
Diesel	47579	Brush Traction	Class 47
Diesel	50027	English Electric	Class 50
DEMU	60124 & 60824	British Railways	Class 205

Attractions

Behind the scenes tours of the engineering hub are available on selected dates at Ropley, where there is also a miniature railway. There is a gift shop and model railway at Alton. The railway operates various food and drink themed services, including cream tea, evening dining and real ale trains. The Curtis Museum in Alton town centre is nearby and Jane Austen's house in Chawton village is a few miles away. There are several themed walks in the area, including the Jane Austen Trail linking Alton with her home in Chawton, the one-mile Alresford Millennium Trail exploring Alresford and the Watercress Way which continues along the route of the former railway west of Alresford.

Special Events

Events that usually take place on the railway include:

Day Out with Thomas.
War on the Line.
Steam and Diesel Galas.
Wizard Weekend during October
Steam Illuminations during November & December.

Spa Valley Railway

Introduction and History

The railway from East Grinstead to Groombridge and Tunbridge Wells West opened in 1866 and the Groombridge to Eridge, Uckfield and Lewes section opened in 1868. After declining use and with costly upgrade work being necessary, British Rail announced its intention to close the line between Tunbridge Wells and Eridge in 1983. Objections were overridden and the line was closed in 1985. In the same year, the Tunbridge Wells and Eridge Railway Preservation Society formed with the aim of reopening the line. The footprint of Tunbridge Wells West station was reduced after planning permission was given for a supermarket to be built on the rail yard; however, this was subject to the company covering the cost of a new heritage railway station platform. In 1996 the group acquired the railway line as far as Birchden Junction near Eridge and operated its first trains from Tunbridge Wells West for about half a mile. The operational section was extended to Groombridge in 1997, Birchden Junction in 2005 and to Eridge in 2011, where the railway now connects with main line trains.

Contact Details

Website: www.spavalleyrailway.co.uk
Tel: 01892 300141
Email: Written enquiries can be made from the website.
Address: Spa Valley Railway, West Station, Nevill Terrace, Royal Tunbridge Wells, TN2 5QY.

Transport Links

By Rail: The railway shares Eridge station with main line services which arrive from Uckfield and London; discounted fares are available if travelling by rail to Eridge, when SVR tickets are purchased with a main line ticket. Alternatively, Tunbridge Wells West is less than a mile from Tunbridge Wells main line station.
By Road: Free parking is available at High Rocks (TN3 9JJ) and and there is pay & display parking near to Eridge (TN3 9LE) and Tunbridge Wells West (TN2 5QY) stations.

Opening Times

The railway operates on selected Saturdays, Sundays and Bank Holidays, and on some weekdays.

Line Mileage and Journey Time

0.00	Tunbridge Wells West
1.25	High Rocks
3.00	Groombridge
5.00	Eridge

A return journey takes about 1 hour 10 minutes.

Stock List

Type	Number	Builder	Details
Steam	3 (2315)	Andrew Barclay	0-4-0ST
Steam	68077	Andrew Barclay	0-6-0ST
Steam	2193	Bagnall	0-6-0ST
Steam	1589	Hunslet	0-6-0ST
Steam	57 (7668)	Robert Stephenson & Hawthorns	0-6-0ST
Steam	62 (7673)	Robert Stephenson & Hawthorns	0-6-0ST
Steam	32650	LBSCR	0-6-0T
Steam	47493	Vulcan Foundry	0-6-0T
Steam	34072	British Railways	4-6-2
Diesel	SOUTHERHAM (2591)	Drewry	0-4-0
Diesel	09026	British Railways	Class 09
Diesel	D3489	British Railways	Class 10
Diesel	15224	British Railways	Class 12
Diesel	31430	Brush Traction	Class 31
Diesel	33063	BRCW	Class 33
Diesel	33065	BRCW	Class 33
Electro-Diesel	73140	English Electric	Class 73
DEMU	60142, 60616 & 60916	British Railways	Class 207
EMU	62402, 76764 & 76835	BREL	Class 421
EMU	69306	British Railways	Class 422
EMU	61277	British Railways	Class 489

Attractions

The Spa Valley line runs through High Weald, which is an Area of Outstanding Natural Beauty. At the railway's Tunbridge Wells West base, the 1886 engine shed can be seen and there is a buffet housed within a multiple unit. Steam and diesel locomotive driving experiences can be arranged. Nearby heritage railways include the Bluebell Railway (13 miles away), the Lavender Line (14 miles), the Rother Valley Railway (17 miles) and the Kent & East Sussex Railway (24 miles). Groombridge Place and Enchanted Forest are a 15–20 minute walk from Groombridge station. Other attractions in the area include Ashdown Forest, Dunorlan Park and Royal Tunbridge Wells, home of the Pantiles and the Chalybeate Spring.

Special Events

Events planned for 2023 include:

29–30 April: See Bluey.
4–6 August: Summer Diesel Gala.
23–24 September: Model Railway Weekend.
November & December: Polar Express Trains.

SOUTH-WEST

Swindon & Cricklade Railway

Avon Valley Railway

Somerset & Dorset Railway

East Somerset Railway

Yeovil Railway Centre

North Dorset Railway (Proposed)

Swanage Railway

Dean Forest Railway

Vale of Berkeley Railway (proposed)

Bristol Harbour Railway

West Somerset Railway

Bideford Railway Heritage Centre

South Devon Railway

Dartmouth Steam Railway

Tarka Valley Railway (proposed)

Tamar Belle Heritage Centre

Plym Valley Railway

Bodmin & Wenford Railway

Helston Railway

Alderney Railway

Pallot Steam, Motor & General Museum

Region 8 – South-West

Alderney Railway

Introduction and History
The Alderney Railway was built by the British Government to carry the stone quarried from the east of the island which was used to construct the breakwater and Victorian forts. The line opened in 1847 and the first official passengers to be carried were Queen Victoria and Prince Albert in 1854. Stone quarrying ceased for several years from 1940, when German forces occupied Alderney and replaced part of the railway with a 60 cm gauge system. After the war, the British Home Office took over the railway and the standard gauge line was reinstated. The Alderney Railway Society formed in 1978 and operated its first passenger trains on the line in March 1980. The railway continues to carry passengers today and follows a coastal route from Braye Road to Mannez Quarry and Lighthouse.

Contact Details
Website: www.alderneyrailway.gg
Tel: 07911 739572
Email: Written enquiries can be made from the website.
Address: PO Box 75, Alderney, Channel Islands, GY9 3DA.

Transport Links
By Rail: There are no other railways on Alderney.
By Road: Car parking is available at Braye Road station.
By Air: There are daily flights to Alderney from Southampton and Guernsey.
By Sea: A variety of providers offer ferries to Alderney from Guernsey, Sark and Cherbourg, France.

Opening Times
Trains operate on selected afternoons between April and September, and during December for Santa Specials.

Line Mileage and Journey Time
0.00   Braye Road
1.75   Mannez Quarry

A return journey takes about 45 minutes.

Stock List

Type	Number	Builder	Details
Diesel	D100	English Electric	0-4-0
Diesel	2	Ruston & Hornsby	0-4-0

Attractions
The trains consist of a diesel shunter which hauls two 1959 former London Underground coaches, providing a unique view of Alderney. At Mannez Quarry visitors can ride the quarter mile long 7¼-inch gauge railway, which usually operates at times that connect with the standard gauge train services. The rail shed at Mannez Quarry, which houses the Wickham cars and diesel locomotives, can also be visited. Mannez Quarry station is close to the coast, lighthouse and forts at the north-eastern end of the island. Braye Road station is adjacent to the beach, harbour and breakwater, and is a short walk from the centre of St Anne.

Special Events
Events that usually take place on the railway include:

Easter Bunny Express.
Santa Specials during December.
Trains can be chartered for weddings and private functions.

Avon Valley Railway

Introduction and History
The railway through Bitton was part of the Midland Railway's Mangotsfield and Bath branch line which opened in 1869 as a through route from the Midlands to the south coast and connected with the Somerset & Dorset Railway. After being earmarked for closure in Dr Beeching's Reshaping Britain's Railways report, the final trains ran in 1966. A preservation group then formed in 1972, initially leasing Bitton station and the first heritage trains operated on a short stretch of track in 1974. The line has since been extended to a length of nearly three miles and there is potential for the railway to extend further south towards Bath.

Contact Details
Website: www.avonvalleyrailway.org
Tel: 0117 932 5538
Email: info@avonvalleyrailway.org
Address: Bitton Station, Bath Road, Bristol, South Gloucestershire, BS30 6HD.

Transport Links
By Rail: Keynsham is the nearest railway station and is one and a half miles away.
By Road: There is free parking at Bitton station (BS30 6HD), which is on the A431 between Bristol and Bath.
By Bike: Bitton station has a cycle parking area and can be reached on the Bristol and Bath Railway Path (Route 4 of the National Cycling Network).

Opening Times
The station buffet at Bitton opens daily for breakfast, lunch and afternoon tea. Trains operate at weekends (predominantly diesel hauled on Saturdays and steam on Sundays) and on most Wednesdays during school holidays. Trains usually depart from Bitton at 10.45, 12.00, 13.15, 14.30 and 15.45.

Line Mileage and Journey Time
0.00	Oldland Common
1.00	Bitton
2.50	Avon Riverside

A round trip from Bitton to Oldland Common and Avon Riverside takes about one hour.

Stock List
Type	Number	Builder	Details
Steam	7492 Somerdale	Sentinel	0-4-0
Steam	44123	LMS	0-6-0
Steam	1798 EDWIN HULSE	Avonside	0-6-0ST
Steam	132 (3163)	Hunslet	0-6-0ST
Steam	5	Manning Wardle	0-6-0ST
Steam	4015	Fablok	0-6-0T
Steam	7151	Robert Stephenson & Hawthorns	0-6-0T
Diesel	235519	Robert Stephenson & Hawthorns	4wDM
Diesel	RH252823	Robert Stephenson & Hawthorns	4wDM
Diesel	70043 Grumpy	Ministry of Defence	0-4-0
Diesel	610 General Lord Robertson	Sentinel	0-8-0
Diesel	D2994	Ruston & Hornsby	Class 07
Diesel	08202	British Railways	Class 08
Diesel	08663	British Railways	Class 08
Diesel	09015	British Railways	Class 09
Diesel	31101	Brush Traction	Class 31
Diesel	31130	Brush Traction	Class 31

Attractions
The railway is based at the beautifully restored Bitton station. This is part way along the 13-mile Bristol and Bath Railway Path, which connects the two cities and runs alongside the heritage railway. There is a small museum and a buffet at Bitton. Driving Experiences are available, with the choice of a steam locomotive, diesel locomotive or diesel multiple unit. The Avon Valley

Adventure and Wildlife Park is very close and the nearby cities of Bath and Bristol have many attractions, including the Roman Baths and Bristol Zoo.

Special Events
Events that usually take place on the railway include:

Brick Express Trains.
Chocolate Sundays.
Teddy Bears' Picnic.
1940s Weekend.
Santa Specials & Mince Pie Trains during December.
In addition there are a variety of Dining Trains and Murder Mystery Services.

Bideford Railway Heritage Centre

Introduction and History
The broad gauge railway from Barnstaple first reached Instow and Bideford in 1855 and was extended south to Torrington in 1872. It was converted to a standard gauge line in 1877 and lost its passenger services in 1965. Milk traffic from Torrington continued until 1978 and ball clay from Petrockstow and Meeth used the route through Torrington until 1982. A final railtour visited Torrington in November 1982 and the line then closed. The track was lifted in 1985, which was when the first preservation group formed. Devon County Council purchased the trackbed from British Rail to create a coastal walkway and assisted the group's preservation efforts. These included redeveloping both the Bideford and Instow sites and laying a short stretch of railway track on part of the former route at Bideford, along which trains have operated since 2004. A museum, located within a former parcels van, was opened at Bideford in 2019.

Contact Details
Website: www.bidefordrailway.co.uk
Tel: 07854 590503
Email: enquiries@bidefordrailway.co.uk
Address: Bideford Railway Heritage Centre, 4 Station Hill, Bideford EX39 4BB.

Transport Links
By Rail: Instow is six miles from Barnstaple station and the Bideford site is nine miles from both Barnstaple and Chapelton stations.
By Road: There are car parks a short walk from both Bideford station (EX39 4BB) and Instow signal box (EX39 4HW).
By Bike: Both sites are conveniently located on the traffic-free Tarka Trail and bicycles can be hired from various outlets along the trail, including at Bideford.

Opening Times
The museum, signal box and refreshment carriage are now open daily, all year round (subject to staff being available and weather permitting). Trains operate on selected dates, please check the website for the latest information. Instow signal box opens on occasional Sunday afternoons; please telephone or check the website for the latest opening times. Both sites can be seen from the outside on dates when they are not open.

Line Mileage and Journey Time
The track at Bideford is nearly a quarter of a mile long and the journey time is relatively short.

Stock List

Type	Number	Builder	Details
Diesel	DS1170 (3832)	Hibberd	4wDM

Attractions
Diesel-hauled brake van rides are due to be introduced at Bideford in 2023; the site includes a museum, an interactive visitor centre, a model railway and a rebuilt signal box with a working lever frame. At Instow, the signal box is preserved as it was when train services ended; visitors can pull the levers and turn the level crossing gate wheel. Bideford is also home to the medieval Long Bridge, a museum, gallery and various other attractions. Bideford station and Instow signal box are on the Tarka Trail, which is one of the country's longest traffic-free walking and

cycling trails and forms part of the Devon Coast to Coast cycle route. The former Torrington Station, the base of the Tarka Valley Railway, is five miles to the south on the Tarka Trail (see the Proposed Railways section).

Bodmin & Wenford Railway

Introduction and History
The broad gauge railway between Plymouth and Truro opened in 1859, with a station at Bodmin Road, which is now known as Bodmin Parkway. The standard gauge branch from Bodmin Road to Bodmin General opened in 1887, extending to Boscarne in 1888 and making a connection with the existing Bodmin & Wadebridge Railway which had opened as early as 1834. Passenger services from Padstow to Bodmin ended in 1967, with freight continuing to Wadebridge until 1978 and china clay traffic to Wenfordbridge (via Bodmin General) surviving until 1983. The branch from Bodmin Parkway then closed. Shortly after closure, in 1984, the Bodmin Railway Preservation Society formed and the trackbed from Bodmin Parkway to Boscarne Junction was subsequently purchased from British Rail. The first shunting operations were carried out at Bodmin General station in 1986 and the first heritage passenger trains ran from Bodmin General to Bodmin Parkway in 1990, with services being extended to Boscarne Junction in 1996. A second platform has recently been built at Bodmin General to increase capacity. The railway plans to extend to the outskirts of Wadebride in stages, sharing the route of former line to Padstow with the Camel Trail.

Contact Details
Website: www.bodminrailway.co.uk
Tel: 01208 73555
Email: enquiries@bodminrailway.co.uk
Address: Bodmin & Wenford Railway, General Station, Bodmin, Cornwall, PL31 1AQ.

Transport Links
By Rail: There is a main line rail connection at Bodmin Parkway; simply cross to Platform 3.
By Road: Free parking is only available at Bodmin General station (PL31 1AG).
By Bike or on Foot: The traffic-free Camel Trail runs from Padstow and Wadebridge, directly to Boscarne Junction station. There are several locations along the route where bikes can be hired.

Opening Times
Trains operate on almost all days between late-March and the end of October, and for Santa Specials during December.

Line Mileage and Journey Time
0.00   Bodmin Parkway
1.25   Colesloggett Halt
3.50   Bodmin General
6.25   Boscarne Junction

A return journey takes around two hours, depending on the starting station.

Stock List

Type	Number	Builder	Details
Steam	2962	Bagnall	0-4-0ST
Steam	2572 JUDY	Bagnall	0-4-0ST
Steam	3058 ALFRED	Bagnall	0-4-0ST
Steam	75178	Bagnall	0-6-0ST
Steam	6435	GWR	0-6-0PT
Steam	5552	GWR	2-6-2T
Diesel	22928	Fowler	0-4-0
Diesel	443642	Ruston & Hornsby	0-4-0
Diesel	P403D	Sentinel	0-4-0
Diesel	08359 (D3429)	British Railways	Class 08
Diesel	08444	British Railways	Class 08
Diesel	D3452	British Railways	Class 10
Diesel	37142	English Electric	Class 37

▲ On 8 October 2022, 47306 makes its way along the Bodmin & Wenford Railway with a short demonstration goods train consisting of three hooded china clay wagons and a brake van.
Tony Christie

▼ BR Standard Class 4MT 75014 "BRAVEHEART" crosses Hookhills Viaduct on the Dartmouth Steam Railway with the 15.25 Paignton–Kingswear on 16 May 2022.
Glen Batten

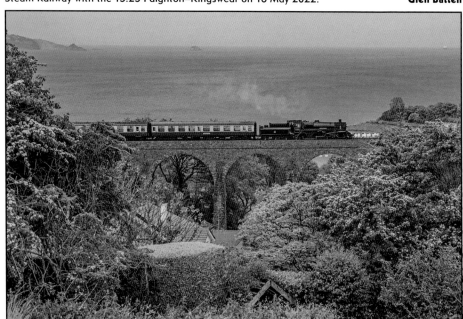

Diesel	47306	Brush Traction	Class 47
Diesel	50042	English Electric	Class 50
DMU	55020	Pressed Steel	Class 121

Attractions

The branch line from Bodmin travels through the scenery of rural Cornwall. Luxury dining trains and train driving experiences are available. The traffic-free Camel Trail to Wadebridge and Padstow follows the route of the current and former railway and the River Camel. There are many other attractions in the region, including Bodmin Moor and many Cornish coastal walks and beaches, which can be reached from the railway and the Camel Trail.

Special Events

Events that usually take place on the railway include:

Mother's Day Cream Tea Train.
Easter at the Railway.
Spring Steam Gala during May.
Autumn Diesel Gala.
China Clay & End of Season Galas during September and October.
Santa Specials during December.

Bristol Harbour Railway

Introduction and History

When it opened in 1872, the Bristol Harbour Railway was a commercial rail network operating within Bristol Harbour. The direct line from Bristol Temple Meads, which accessed the harbour from the east, closed in 1964, requiring all traffic to arrive via Ashton Junction, which was on the Portishead branch to the west. A heritage railway was established in 1978 as part of Bristol Museum (now known as M Shed) and this began using the line between the museum and the SS Great Britain. The last trains from the main line network ran in 1987, when trains to Wapping Wharf Coal Depot ceased running. After this, the connection from Ashton Junction was closed and lifted, and the museum railway expanded to include the section than runs between Cumberland Road and the northern bank of the River Avon. Unfortunately, in 2018 subsidence led to the suspension of trains on this western part of the heritage railway and trains currently only run between M Shed and the SS Great Britain. Repair work began during 2021, but it is not known when this will be completed, allowing trains to again travel beside the River Avon.

Contact Details

Website: www.bristolmuseums.org.uk/m-shed
Tel: 0117 352 6600
Email: Written enquiries can be made from the M Shed website.
Address: M Shed, Princes Wharf, Wapping Road, Bristol, BS1 4RN.

Transport Links

By Rail: Bristol Temple Meads station is just under one mile from M Shed.
By Road: Chargeable parking is available nearby at The Grove (BS1 4RB) and Wapping Wharf (BS1 4RH).
By Bike: There is a cycle path to the south of M Shed; bicycle stands are on Museum Street.
By Boat: Ferries from Temple Meads station and Hotwells run to Prince Street Bridge and these are operated by Bristol Ferry Boats.

Opening Times

M Shed is open 10.00–17.00 Tuesdays to Sundays (except Christmas Day). Train services operate at selected times, subject to availability.

Line Mileage and Journey Time

The operational section between M Shed and SS Great Britain runs for 0.4 miles and a return journey takes about 15 minutes. The southern spur, which runs for 0.7 miles from the site of M Shed, in not currently in use.

Stock List

Type	Number	Builder	Details
Steam	1764	Avonside	0-6-0ST
Steam	242	Fox Walker	0-6-0ST
Steam	1940 HENBURY	Peckett	0-6-0ST
Diesel	418792	Ruston & Hornsby	0-4-0

Attractions
As well as an operational railway, M Shed has a 1950s working dockside with electric cranes, boats, train transit and quayside operations. Behind the scenes tours are available and the site also has a café and shop. M Shed is located within Bristol Harbour, a short walk from SS Great Britain and it is close to the city centre, Bristol Museum & Art Gallery and Bristol Zoo.

Special Events
Until 29 May 2023: Wildlife Photographer of the Year Exhibition.
Until 1 October 2023: Disability Activism in Bristol Display.

Dartmouth Steam Railway

Introduction and History
The broad gauge branch line from Newton Abbot reached Torre in 1848, was extended to Paignton in 1859 and to Kingswear in 1864. The line was converted to a standard gauge railway in 1892. The Dart Valley Railway was a commercial venture established in 1962 to operate the line from Totnes to Buckfastleigh, after the route was closed by British Rail in 1962 (see South Devon Railway). The line from Paignton to Kingswear was first threatened with closure in 1968. In 1972 the Dart Valley Railway acquired the route and started operating trains on it from the start of 1973. In 2010 the Dart Valley Railway acquired two passenger carrying boats and its two heritage railways became separate organisations. The route from Paignton to Kingswear, with its connecting river cruises, is now known as the Dartmouth Steam Railway & River Boat Company.

Contact Details
Website: www.dartmouthrailriver.co.uk
Tel: 01803 555872
Email: Written enquiries can be made from the website.
Address: Dartmouth Steam Railway, Queens Park Station, Torbay Road, Paignton, TQ4 6AF.

Transport Links
By Rail: The railway connects with the main line network at Paignton.
By Road: Churston (TQ5 0LL) is the only station with free parking and this is very limited. There are chargeable car parks near to Paignton (TQ4 6AF), Goodrington (TQ4 6LN) and Kingswear stations (TQ6 0AA), which can be very busy during the peak season.
By Boat: River crossings from Dartmouth to Kingswear carry foot passengers. As the River Dart is tidal, the crossing times vary.

Opening Times
Trains operate daily from late March to late October and on selected days at other times.

Line Mileage and Journey Time
0.00	Paignton
0.75	Goodrington Sands
3.00	Churston
4.00	Greenway Halt
6.75	Kingswear

A return journey takes 1 hour 15 minutes.

Stock List

Type	Number	Builder	Details
Steam	2253	Baldwin Locomotive Works	2-8-0
Steam	2873	GWR	2-8-0
Steam	3803	GWR	2-8-0
Steam	4277	GWR	2-8-0T
Steam	5239	GWR	2-8-0T
Steam	7827	British Railways	4-6-0
Steam	75014	British Railways	4-6-0
Diesel	03371	British Railways	Class 03
Diesel	D2192	British Railways	Class 03
Diesel	D3014	British Railways	Class 08
Diesel	6975	English Electric	Class 37
DMU	59719	British Railways	Class 115
DMU	59003 & 59004	British Railways	Class 116
DMU	59488, 59494, 59503, 59507, 59513 & 59517	Pressed Steel	Class 117

Attractions

The railway offers a variety of round trips, with different combinations of rail, river cruise, paddle steamer and bus tours available. Trains offer views of the English Channel and River Dart and there are various walks which can be taken from or between the railway's stations. Steam locomotive footplate experiences can be arranged. Greenway House and Garden are a short walk (or shuttle bus ride) from Greenway Halt. The region, which includes the towns of Brixham, Torquay, Totnes and Dartmouth, is a popular holiday destination, with plenty of coastlines, beaches and attractions within reach from the railway.

Special Events

Events that usually take place on the railway include:

Dartmouth Regatta in August, during which additional trains operate.
Train of Lights from late November to late December.
Santa Express during December.

Dean Forest Railway

Introduction and History

A three foot six inch gauge horse-drawn plateway from Lydney to Parkend opened in 1810. This was used to carry minerals from the Dean Forest to the River Severn for onward transit and it became part of a larger tramway network. When the broad gauge main line from Gloucester to Chepstow opened in 1851, an interchange station was built at Lydney, allowing the minerals to be carried further by rail. The railway's owners purchased five three foot six inch gauge steam locomotives in the 1860s. However, the line was converted to Brunel's seven foot broad gauge in 1872 and then further converted to standard gauge within 20 years. Traffic on the route increased as passenger services from Lydney to Parkend and beyond commenced in 1875 and when the original Severn Bridge opened in 1879, it connected the railway with Sharpness Docks (see Vale of Berkeley Railway). Passenger services ended in 1929 and freight on the line declined through the 20th Century. Traffic across the Severn Bridge ended when it was damaged beyond repair in 1960 and by 1967 there was just one daily goods train from Lydney Junction to Parkend. A preservation group formed in 1970 and held its first event in 1971. The trackbed was purchased from British Rail in 1985 and the heritage railway has been extended in stages, reaching Norchard, then Lydney Junction in 1995 and Parkend in 2005. There are various plans to develop the railway; a new carriage shed and restoration works are planned for Lydney and a passing loop and second platform are to be built at Whitecroft. It is hoped that work can begin soon on a three-mile northern extension to a new station near Beechenhurst Lodge and there are long-term plans for the railway to be extended a further three miles north to Cinderford.

Contact Details

Website: www.deanforestrailway.co.uk
Tel: 01594 845840
Email: contact@deanforestrailway.co.uk
Address: Dean Forest Railway, Norchard Station, Forest Road, Lydney, Gloucestershire, GL15 4ET.

Transport Links

By Rail: The nearest station is Lydney, which is a five-minute walk to Lydney Junction.
By Road: Free parking is available at Norchard (GL15 4ET). There is no parking at the other stations.

Opening Times

The railway operates on most weekends, Wednesdays and Bank Holidays and on selected other dates.

Line Mileage and Journey Time

0.00	Lydney Junction
0.75	Lydney Town
1.50	Norchard Low Level & High Level
3.00	Whitecroft Halt
4.25	Parkend

A return journey takes about 1 hour 45 minutes, depending where the journey starts from.

Stock List

Type	Number	Builder	Details
Steam	2221	Andrew Barclay	0-4-0ST
Steam	ROCKET	Peckett	0-4-0ST
Steam	USKMOUTH 1 (2147)	Peckett	0-4-0ST
Steam	9681	British Railways	0-6-0PT
Steam	9682	British Railways	0-6-0PT
Steam	65 (3889)	Hunslet	0-6-0ST
Steam	2411	Hunslet	0-6-0ST

▲ Class 14 D9521 has just arrived at the Dean Forest Railway's northern terminus, Parkend, after working the 11.35 from Lydney Junction on 18 September 2022. **Andy Chard**

Steam	2413	Hunslet	0-6-0ST
Steam	WARRIOR (3823)	Hunslet	0-6-0ST
Steam	WILBERT (3806)	Hunslet	0-6-0ST
Steam	RENNES (WD152)	Robert Stephenson & Hawthorns	0-6-0ST
Steam	5541	GWR	2-6-2T
Diesel	4210127	Fowler	0-4-0
Diesel	6688	Hunslet	0-4-0
Diesel	DON CORBETT (5622)	Hunslet	0-4-0
Diesel	08238	British Railways	Class 08
Diesel	08473	British Railways	Class 08
Diesel	08769 (D3937)	British Railways	Class 08
Diesel	D9521	British Railways	Class 14
Diesel	D9555	British Railways	Class 14
Diesel	31210	Brush Traction	Class 31
Diesel	31235	Brush Traction	Class 31
DMU	50619, 50632, 51566, 51914, 52044, 56492 & 59387	British Railways	Class 108

Attractions

There is a railway museum at Norchard, which has a large number of exhibits. The site also has a locomotive restoration shed (guides are usually available to show visitors around), a railway bookshop and a café. Parkend Yard has recently been re-connected and signalling works completed, including the commissioning of the GWR signal box, formerly of Maesmawr; this project was recently shortlisted for a National Railway Heritage Award. There are various food themed trains and footplate experiences can be arranged. Many walks can be made, with routes from each of the railway's stations, including a one mile walk from Lydney Junction along the trackbed to Lydney Harbour, where there are views of the River Severn and Sharpness. Parkend station is less than half a mile from route 42 of the National Cycle Network, some of which continues along the railway trackbed. Other attractions in the area include Clearwell Caves and the Forest of Dean, with its sculpture trail.

Special Events

Events that usually take place on the railway include:

Brake Van Specials.
Diesel Galas.
Evening Steam Fish & Chip Trains.
Evening Steam & Beer Trains.
Murder Mystery on a Steam Train.
Trolleys & Trivia Event during June.
Royal Forest of Steam Gala during October.
Santa Specials during December.

East Somerset Railway

Introduction and History

The railway from Witham (between the extant Frome and Bruton stations) to Shepton Mallet opened in 1858 and was later extended to Wells where the railway continued to Yatton. The line carried locally quarried rock as well as passengers, originally as a broad gauge railway, until it was converted to a standard gauge line in 1874. Passenger traffic ended in 1963 and through freight to Wells ceased in 1969, after which the line beyond Cranmore was closed, reducing it to a freight branch that accessed Merehead Quarry and the bitumen terminal at Cranmore. In the early 1970s, when the late artist David Shepherd was looking for a home for two steam locomotives he had acquired, he purchased Cranmore station and began to develop the site. This became the base of the East Somerset Heritage Railway, which first opened in 1974 and now occupies a section of the former line towards Shepton Mallet. It remains connected to the main line network, as traffic to the nearby Torr Works Quarry also uses the branch. It is hoped that the railway will be extended, with the potential to do so in either direction, however there are no immediate plans to proceed with this.

Contact Details

Website: www.eastsomersetrailway.com
Tel: 01749 880417
Email: info@eastsomersetrailway.com
Address: Cranmore Railway Station, Cranmore, Shepton Mallet, Somerset, BA4 4QP.

Transport Links

By Rail: The nearest railway stations are Frome (nine miles) and Bruton (eight miles).
By Road: There is a large, free car park a short walk from Cranmore Station (BA4 4QP).

Opening Times

Trains operate on almost every Saturday & Sunday from March to December inclusive, every Wednesday from May to October and on selected other days.

Line Mileage and Journey Time

0.00	Cranmore
0.50	Cranmore West
1.00	Merryfield Lane
2.00	Mendip Vale

A return journey takes about 40 minutes.

Stock List

Type	Number	Builder	Details
Steam	1719	Andrew Barclay	0-4-0ST
Steam	1 (7609)	Robert Stephenson & Hawthorns	0-6-0T
Steam	46447	British Railways	2-6-0
Steam	4110	GWR	2-6-2T
Steam	4555	GWR	2-6-2T
Steam	4247	GWR	2-8-0T
Diesel	10165	Sentinel	0-4-0
Diesel	10175	Sentinel	0-4-0
Diesel	10199	Sentinel	0-4-0
Diesel	DH16	Sentinel	0-4-0
Diesel	10218	Sentinel	0-6-0
Diesel	10221	Sentinel	0-6-0
DMU	51909, 51947 & 56271	British Railways	Class 108
EMU	483009 (129 & 229)	Metropolitan Cammell	Class 483

Attractions

Cranmore station was refurbished in 2020 and now houses a museum. The Cranmore base is also home to the David Shepherd Discovery Centre which showcases the artist's life and the railway's history, a museum, signal box, miniature railway, children's play area and café. Visitors can explore the engine shed and workshop, where restoration projects are underway. The railway offers footplate and driving experiences, with a choice of a steam locomotive or a multiple unit. Nearby attractions include Nunney Castle, Shepton Mallet, Glastonbury and Wells. The Strawberry Line Trail is located to the west and this mainly traffic-free route between Yatton and Cheddar follows the course of the former railway.

Special Events

Events that usually take place on the railway include:

Steam Gala.
Easter Event.
Takeover Day (for 7–14 years olds).
Santa Specials & Visit Santa by Starlight during December.

▲ On 28 August 2021, GWR 2-6-2T 4555 climbs away from Mendip Vale with the 12.00 East Somerset Railway service to Cranmore. **Glen Batten**

▼ LMS Class 2MT 41312 hauls a short train along the Somerset & Dorset Railway near Midsomer Norton on 16 September 2022. **Glen Batten**

Helston Railway

Introduction and History

The branch line from Gwinear Road, between Hayle and Camborne, to Helston opened in 1887, creating the most southerly railway and station in mainland Britain. Despite much opposition to the threatened closure, the final passenger train left Helston behind Class 22, D6312 on 3 November 1962. Freight services continued until October 1964 and the track was lifted in 1965. The first preservation group formed 40 years later in 2005; a base was established at Trevarno Halt and vegetation clearance along the disused trackbed began. One mile of track was relaid and the first trains from Truthall Halt to Prospidnick ran in 2011. Two sections of trackbed have since been acquired; the line is in the process of being extended north to a new station at Prospidnick and there are plans to extend south to Nancegollan and Water-Ma-Trout on the outskirts of Helston, which would increase the length of the line to around three miles.

Contact Details

Website: www.helstonrailway.co.uk
Tel: 07901 977 597
Email: info@helstonrailway.co.uk
Address: Trevarno Farm, Prospidnick, Helston, Cornwall, TR13 0RY.

Transport Links

By Rail: The nearest railway station is Camborne, which is seven miles away.
By Road: Free car parking is available at Prospidnick Halt (TR13 0RY).

Opening Times

The railway operates on Sundays, Thursdays and Bank Holidays from late March until late October and on Wednesdays during July and August, with departures between 10.30 and 15.00.

Line Mileage and Journey Time

0.00   Truthall Halt
1.00   Prospidnick Halt

A return journey takes about 30 minutes from Prospidnick.

Stock List

Type	Number	Builder	Details
Steam	WILLIAM MURDOCH	Peckett	0-4-0ST
Steam	2000	Peckett	0-6-0ST
Diesel	446 Kingswood	Andrew Barclay	0-4-0
Diesel	97649	Ruston & Hornsby	0-4-0
Diesel	395305	Ruston & Hornsby	0-4-0
DMU	50413 & 56169	Park Royal	Class 103
DMU	59521	Pressed Steel	Class 117
DMU	51616	British Railways	Class 127

Attractions

Two of the three surviving Class 103 Park Royal multiple unit vehicles are based at the railway, although these are not currently operational and are used as a buffet. There is also a gift shop with railway books and souvenirs. Truthall Halt has been rebuilt as an exact replica of the original building and the quality of the rebuild was recognised with a Heritage Railway Association award in 2019. There are many other attractions in western Cornwall, including the Cornish Seal Sanctuary, Poldark Mine, Lizard Peninsula and the South West Coastal Path.

Special Events

Events that usually take place on the railway include:

Easter Family Event.
Back to the 1940s during May.
Heritage Transport Weekend during September.
October Spooky Specials.
Santa Specials during December.

Pallot Steam, Motor & General Museum, Jersey

Introduction and History
The museum is one of the few sites within this book which is not located on the site of a former railway. Don Pallot (1910–1996) was an engineer and inventor, who after collecting various mechanical items including steam engines, created a museum to house these and this opened in 1990. The collection includes locomotives from mainland Britain, Belgium and Alderney. In 1996 the engine shed, railway line and station were opened and the engine shed was extended in 2002. Train services were suspended during 2022, as major track repair works are required and the steam locomotive that is used to haul trains is in need of a boiler inspection, requiring a qualified inspector to visit from mainland Britain.

Contact Details
Website: www.pallotmuseum.co.uk
Tel: 01534 865307
Email: pallotmuseum@gmail.com
Address: The Pallot Steam, Motor & General Museum, Rue de Bechet, Trinity, Jersey, Channel Islands, JE3 5BE.

Transport Links
By Rail: There is no rail service on Jersey.
By Road: There is ample free car parking at the museum (JE3 5BE).

Opening Times
The museum usually opens Monday to Saturday from the start of April until the end of October, with the exception of some bank holidays. Steam trains usually depart on the hour between 11.00 and 16.00 on Thursdays and during occasional specials events; during 2023 this will be subject to the track upgrade works and the locomotive's boiler inspection being completed.

Line Mileage and Journey Time
Trains operate on an oval shaped circuit, which runs for just over a quarter of a mile and the journey time is relatively short.

Stock List

Type	Number	Builder	Details
Steam	J T DALY	Bagnall	0-4-0ST
Steam	2085	Peckett	0-4-0ST
Steam	2129 Kestrel	Peckett	0-4-0ST
Steam	LA MEUSE	Belgian	0-6-0T
Diesel	27734	North British	0-4-0

Attractions
The museum's exhibits include a 1912 steam roller, steam locomotives, tractors, classic and vintage motor vehicles, toys, a church pipe organ, a Compton theatre organ and details of Jersey's history. The museum is close to Jersey Zoo (two miles), St Helier (three and a half miles), the island's coast and various other attractions.

Special Events
Events that usually take place at the museum include:

Liberation Day Steam & Motor Fayre in May.
Steam Threshing & Motor Fayre in September.

Plym Valley Railway

Introduction and History

The original broad gauge railway from Devonport Junction (to the east of Plymouth) to Tavistock South and Lydford opened in 1859. This was extended to Launceston in 1865 and the line was converted to standard gauge in 1892. Passenger services ended in 1962 and it closed as a through route when freight ceased in 1964. A group formed in 1980 and began working towards creating a heritage railway. The first section of track was laid in 2001 and preserved train services began in 2008, travelling north along the original route from Marsh Mills. The line was extended to a new station at Plym Bridge in 2012, which opened exactly 50 years after the final passenger train ran in 1962. There are long-term aims to extend the railway further north towards Tavistock.

Contact Details

Website: www.plymrail.co.uk
Tel: 01752 345078
Email: plymvalleyrailway@gmail.com
Address: Plym Valley Railway, Marsh Mills Station, Coypool Road, Plympton, Plymouth, PL7 4NW.

Transport Links

By Rail: The nearest station is Plymouth, which is four miles from Marsh Mills.
By Road: There are car parks at Coypool Park and Ride (PL7 4TB) and Plymbridge Road (PL7 4SR), which are very close to Marsh Mills and Plym Bridge stations respectively.
By Bike: Route 27 of the National Cycle Network follows the course of the present and former railway.

Opening Times

The railway usually operates on Sundays from March to November and on selected other dates.

Line Mileage and Journey Time

0.00   Marsh Mills
1.25   Plym Bridge

A return journey takes about half an hour.

Stock List

Type	Number	Builder	Details
Steam	705	Andrew Barclay	0-4-0ST
Steam	ALBERT (2248)	Andrew Barclay	0-4-0ST
Steam	BYFIELD (2655)	Bagnall	0-6-0ST
Steam	TKH49 (5374)	Fablok	0-6-0T
Diesel	10077	Sentinel	0-4-0
Diesel	125V	Thomas Hill	0-4-0
Diesel	429	Ruston & Hornsby	0-6-0
Diesel	466618	Robert Stephenson & Hawthorns	0-6-0DH
Diesel	D2046	British Railways	Class 03
Diesel	13002	British Railways	Class 08
Diesel	31190	Brush Traction	Class 31
DMU	51365 & 51407	Pressed Steel	Class 117
DMU	142023 (55564 & 55614)	BREL/Leyland	Class 142
DMU	143618 (55659 & 55684)	Alexander/Barclay	Class 143

Attractions

The 7¼-inch gauge Plym Valley Miniature Railway can be found at the railway's Marsh Mills base, along with a museum, the locomotive shed, a shop and café. The Devon Coast to Coast walking and cycle route (Route 27 of the National Cycle Network) travels alongside the railway on its journey from Plymouth to Barnstaple. Saltram House is near to Marsh Mills and Plymbridge Woods is adjacent to Plym Bridge station (both National Trust). Further nearby attractions include Plymouth Snowsports Centre, Crownhill Fort, the National Marine Aquarium and Merchant's House Museum.

Special Events
Events that usually take place on the railway include:

New Year Mince Pie Specials.
Easter Egg Hunt.
Summer Family Fun Day.
Halloween Event during October.
The Christmas Express during December.
Evening dining and cream tea trains operate on selected dates.

Somerset & Dorset Railway, Midsomer Norton

Introduction and History
Midsomer Norton South station opened in 1874, when the single-track extension of the Somerset & Dorset Railway (S&D) to Bath was completed. The track was doubled in 1886, but after declining use, Midsomer Norton station and the S&D route were closed in 1966. The Somerset & Dorset Railway Heritage Trust acquired the Midsomer Norton site in 1995 and has since restored the station building, signal box and goods shed. A stretch of operational track was laid, running south from the station and this was extended towards Chilcompton Tunnel in 2019, increasing the railway's length to one mile. There is potential to extend the line in both directions, although before it can be extended further south, substantial quantities of landfill waste will need to be excavated.

Contact Details
Website: www.sdjr.co.uk
Tel: 01761 411 221
Email: general@sdjr.co.uk
Address: Somerset & Dorset Railway, Midsomer Norton Station, Silver Street, Midsomer Norton, BA3 2EY.

Transport Links
By Rail: The nearest stations are Frome (11 miles), Bath (11 miles) or Trowbridge (14 miles).
By Road: There is limited disabled parking at Midsomer Norton South station (BA3 2EY). Free parking is available at Norton Hill School (BA3 4AD) at weekends and during school holidays, or nearby in the town centre.
By Bike: The Five Arches Cycle & Walkway from Radstock to Midsomer Norton is a spur off the Colliers Way, which is route 24 of the National Cycle Network.

Opening Times
The station, shop and museum open on Sundays, subject to volunteer availability. Trains usually operate on Sundays and on selected other days.

Line Mileage and Journey Time
0.00   Midsomer Norton
1.00   Southern limit

A return journey takes about 25 minutes.

Stock List

Type	Number	Builder	Details
Steam	7109	Sentinel	4wVBT
Diesel	D1120	English Electric	0-6-0
Diesel	03901 (03128)	British Railways	Class 03
Diesel	D4095	British Railways	Class 08
DMU	52006 & 52025	British Railways	Class 107

Attractions
The Midsomer Norton base is home to the restored Victorian station buildings, a museum devoted to the S&D, a small pill box war museum, a gift and second-hand bookshop. The East Somerset Railway and Avon Valley Railway are 8 and 13 miles away respectively. Other nearby attractions include Radstock Museum, The Colliers Way cycle route, the city of Bath and the Mendip Hills.

Special Events
Events that usually take place include:

Fathers' Day Event during June.
Summer Mixed Traffic Gala.
End of Season Gala in autumn.
Santa Specials during December.
New Year's Day Steam & Mince Pie Specials.

South Devon Railway

Introduction and History
The broad gauge branch line from Totnes to Ashburton opened in 1872 and was converted to standard gauge over a single weekend in 1892. After usage declined, it was closed to passengers in 1958 and to freight in 1962. The Dart Valley Light Railway formed in 1962 to operate the route as a commercial tourist railway. In 1965 the DVLR acquired the line and the first locomotives arrived. The railway was formally opened by Dr Richard Beeching in 1969 but the Light Railway Order did not allow passenger services to run between Buckfastleigh and Ashburton. This northern section was then lost in 1971, when the A38 was redeveloped. The independent railway later became uneconomical and was threatened with closure in 1989. It survived when an existing charity based at the railway took it over and this was renamed the South Devon Railway Association. The first trains to officially operate in preservation ran in 1991 and in the years since, the railway has continued to grow in popularity and success. Ashburton station building survives; plans to redevelop the site have been successfully fought off, with the hope that it might be reconnected to the South Devon Railway in future.

Contact Details
Website: www.southdevonrailway.co.uk
Tel: 01364 644370
Email: trains@southdevonrailway.org
Address: South Devon Railway, Dartbridge Road, Buckfastleigh, Devon, TQ11 0DZ.

Transport Links
By Rail: Totnes railway station is less than half a mile away and the journey to Totnes Riverside involves crossing a footbridge over the River Dart.
By Road: Ample car parking is available at Buckfastleigh (TQ11 0DZ). There are a number of car parks near Totnes Riverside station, the nearest of which is about half a mile away.

Opening Times
The railway usually operates during most weekends through the year, with regular weekday running from mid-March until early November and during December for Santa and Mince Pie Specials.

Line Mileage and Journey Time
0.00   Buckfastleigh
3.00   Staverton
6.75   Totnes Riverside

A return journey takes about 1 hour 15 minutes.

Stock List

Type	Number	Builder	Details
Steam	151 TINY	Sara & Co	0-4-0 Broad Gauge
Steam	1690	Peckett	0-4-0T
Steam	2031	Peckett	0-4-0T
Steam	1420	GWR	0-4-2T
Steam	3205	GWR	0-6-0
Steam	GLENDOWER	Hunslet	0-6-0ST
Steam	L92 (5786)	GWR	0-6-0PT
Steam	6430	GWR	0-6-0PT

Steam	4160	GWR	2-6-2PT
Steam	5526	GWR	2-6-2T
Steam	5542	GWR	2-6-2T
Diesel	MFP4	Fowler	0-4-0
Diesel	2745	Yorkshire Engine Co.	0-6-0
Diesel	D2246	Robert Stephenson & Hawthorns	Class 04
Diesel	D2271	Robert Stephenson & Hawthorns	Class 04
Diesel	D3721	British Railways	Class 09
Diesel	D7535	British Railways	Class 25
Diesel	D7541	British Railways	Class 25
Diesel	D7612	British Railways	Class 25
Diesel	D6501	BRCW	Class 33
Diesel	6737	English Electric	Class 37
Diesel	D402	English Electric	Class 50
DMU	59740	British Railways	Class 115
DMU	51352, 51376 & 59493	Pressed Steel	Class 117
DMU	55000	GRCW	Class 122

Attractions

The railway travels along a secluded and scenic route that follows the River Dart. There is a museum at Buckfastleigh which tells the story of the line and houses the UK's only surviving original broad gauge locomotive. There is a large gift and model shop at Buckfastleigh and footplate driving experiences can be arranged. Nearby attractions include Totnes Rare Breeds Farm, Buckfast Butterfly Farm & Dartmoor Otter Sanctuary, Buckfast Abbey and Totnes with its historic market.

Special Events

Events that usually take place on the railway include:

Kids for a Quid.
Days Out with Thomas.
Diesel Gala.
South Devon 1940s Festival.
The Polar Express and Mince Pie Specials during December.

Swanage Railway

Introduction and History

The branch from Wareham to Swanage opened in 1885 and remained in use until early 1972 when British Rail (BR) withdrew the line's passenger services. BR then promptly lifted the track on the southern part of the line and the northern section was retained for liquid petroleum gas (LPG) traffic to the BP terminal at Furzebrook Sidings. The Swanage Railway Society formed in 1972 and successfully thwarted several attempts to demolish Swanage station which became its base. Trains first worked on a short section of track there in 1979 and this was lengthened in several stages, reaching Norden in 1995. Once LPG traffic came to an end in 2005, a reconnection could be made between the heritage railway and the main line network, although it wasn't until 2017 that the first heritage trains ran through to Wareham. During 2018 and 2019, the main line operator South Western Railway ran summer Saturday trains from Salisbury to Corfe Castle, returning through services to Swanage for the first time in many years. It is hoped that the Swanage Railway will be able to run a regular shuttle service to Wareham from 2023.

Contact Details

Website: www.swanagerailway.co.uk
Tel: 01929 425800
Email: info@swanagerailway.co.uk
Address: Swanage Railway, Station House, Swanage, Dorset, BH19 1HB.

Transport Links

By Rail: There is a main line rail connection at Wareham. However, the railway only operates through trains to Wareham seasonally.
By Road: Norden station has a 350-space car and coach park just off the A351 and charges apply (BH20 5DW). There is no car parking at Corfe Castle station or Herston Halt. Harmans Cross has a small car park where charges apply (BH19 3EB) and there is limited paid parking near Swanage station (BH20 1PW).
By Boat: From April to October www.citycruises.com operate between Poole Quay and Swanage; the journey takes one hour each way.

Opening Times

Trains usually operate throughout the year, with daily services from late March until mid-October.

Line Mileage and Journey Time

0.00	Swanage
0.50	Herston Halt
3.00	Harmans Cross
5.00	Corfe Castle
5.50	Norden
11.00	Wareham

A return journey takes about one hour.

Stock List

Type	Number	Builder	Details
Steam	30053	LSWR	0-4-4T
Steam	31625	Southern Railway	2-6-0
Steam	31806	Southern Railway	2-6-0
Steam	31874	Southern Railway	2-6-0
Steam	30120	LSWR	4-4-0
Steam	34070	Southern Railway	4-6-2
Steam	34028	Southern Railway	4-6-2
Diesel	4210132	Fowler	0-4-0
Diesel	Beryl	Hibberd	0-4-0
Diesel	08436	British Railways	Class 08
Diesel	D3591	British Railways	Class 08
Diesel	33111	BRCW	Class 33
Diesel	D6515	BRCW	Class 33
DMU	51356, 51388, 51392 & 59486	Pressed Steel	Class 117
DMU	55028	Pressed Steel	Class 121
EMU	69332	British Railways	Class 421
EMU	70855, 76275 & 76298	British Railways	Class 491
EMU	70824 & 76322	Metropolitan Cammell	Class 491

Attractions

In 2021, the Swanage Railway became the first heritage railway to feature on the website Realtime Trains, which provides useful live information on the trains that are operating. The railway has a variety of main line locomotives, which are often joined by visiting examples for special events. There is a small railway museum at Corfe Castle station and Purbeck Mining Museum can be found at Norden station. Corfe Castle is visible from the railway and can be reached by way of an uphill walk from its namesake station. There is plenty to see in the busy town of Swanage, the surrounding Isle of Purbeck and other well-known sites nearby, including Lulworth Cove, Durdle Door, Poole and the Jurassic Coast.

Special Events

Events that usually take place on the railway include:

Diesel Gala during May.
Classic Transport Rally.
Driving Experiences.
A variety of dining trains.
Seasonal Steam & Lights trains during December.

Swindon & Cricklade Railway

Introduction and History

The railway from Swindon Town to Cirencester Watermoor opened in 1883. Cricklade and Blunsdon were intermediate stations on the route and opened in 1883 and 1895 respectively. Blunsdon closed to passengers in 1924 and all passenger services were withdrawn in 1961. After this trains occasionally ran to Moredon Power Station, which was near the site of the present-day Taw Valley Halt, until 1969. The Swindon & Cricklade Railway Preservation Society formed in 1978 and took over the empty trackbed. Track laying began in 1980 and the first heritage steam trains used the route in 1984. In 2000 the railway reached Hayes Knoll and there are plans to further extend the line in both directions. A 1.25-mile northern extension to a new station near the village of Cricklade is under construction, with track having recently been laid as far as Farfield Lane cutting. There are also plans to build a new larger station at Moulsdon Country Park at the southern end of the line.

Contact Details

Website: www.swindon-cricklade-railway.org
Tel: 01793 771615
Email: Written enquiries can be made from the website.
Address: Swindon & Cricklade Railway, Blunsdon Station, Tadpole Lane, Swindon, SN25 2DA.

Transport Links

By Rail: Swindon railway station is five miles from Blunsdon.
By Road: Free car parking is available at Blunsdon station (SN25 2DA). At Mouldon Hill car park, which is a short walk from Taw Valley Halt (SN25 1WH), parking is provided by Swindon Borough Council. There is no road access at Hayes Knoll station.

Opening Times

The railway usually operates on Sundays for the majority of the year, on Saturdays from April to September and on selected weekdays.

Line Mileage and Journey Time

0.00   Taw Valley Halt
1.25   Blunsdon
1.75   Hayes Knoll

A return journey takes about one hour.

Stock List

Type	Number	Builder	Details
Steam	2354	Andrew Barclay	0-4-0ST
Steam	3135	Fablok	0-6-0T
Steam	1464	Hudswell Clarke	0-6-0T
Steam	6695	Armstrong Whitworth	0-6-2T
Steam	5637	GWR	0-6-2T
Steam	35011	Southern Railway	4-6-2
Diesel	4210137	Fowler	0-4-0DM
Diesel	4220031	Fowler	0-4-0DM
Diesel	21442 WOODBINE	Fowler	0-4-0
Diesel	D2022	British Railways	Class 03
Diesel	D2152	British Railways	Class 03
Diesel	D3261	British Railways	Class 08
Diesel	97651	Ruston & Hornsby	Class 97
Electro-Diesel	E6003	British Railways	Class 73
DMU	79978	AC Cars	Railbus
DMU	59514	Pressed Steel	Class 117
DMU	51074 & 51104	GRCW	Class 119
DEMU	60669 & 60822	British Railways	Class 205
DEMU	60127	British Railways	Class 207

Attractions

There are two museums at Blunsdon; one showcases the area's railway history and the other is a wartime museum which is adjacent to the Whistlestop Café. The railway's restoration and maintenance centre and a restored signal box are at Hayes Knoll. Train driver experience days are available. The nearby Cotswold Water Park consists of the largest amount of redundant gravel pits in the country, which have been converted for social uses including an inland beach resort, power boating and sailing.

Special Events

Events that usually take place on the railway include:

Mother's Day Event.
Easter Eggs-spress.
Days out with Thomas.
Kids for a Quid.
Father's Day Event.
Past & Present Family Festival.
Steam, Diesel and Mixed Traffic Galas.
Military Weekend.
Santa Specials from late November.

▲ On 3 July 2022, Class 73 electro-diesel E6003 (73003) stands at the Swindon and Cricklade Railway's Blunsdon station.   **Tony Christie**

Tamar Belle Heritage Centre

Introduction and History

Bere Ferrers station opened in 1890, on the new railway between Devonport and Lydford, which completed the line across central Devon linking Exeter and Plymouth via Okehampton. During its first seven years the station was known as Beer Ferris, until it was given the spelling that it retains today, which was thought to be more sophisticated as it did not contain the word "beer"! Through services west of Okehampton were withdrawn in 1968, after which the line through Bere Ferrers continued to what became its terminus at Gunnislake. Bere Ferrers' station building then moved into private ownership and was first opened to the public when it celebrated its centenary in 1990. A section of standard gauge railway was laid and Bagnall 0-4-0ST "ALFRED" and a brake van were borrowed from the Bodmin & Wenford Railway, so that passenger rides could be provided to mark the occasion. Since then, the site has been developed into a heritage centre with a collection of railway exhibits, including on-site bed & breakfast accommodation within two ex-LNER teak corridor carriages.

Contact Details

Website: www.tamarbelle.co.uk
Tel: 07813 360066
Email: enquiries@tamarbelle.co.uk
Address: The Tamar Belle Heritage Centre, Bere Ferrers Station, Yelverton, Devon, PL20 7LT

Transport Links

By Rail: The Heritage Centre is on the site of Bere Ferrers station, which is approximately half way along the branch line between Plymouth and Gunnislake.
By Road: Free parking is available at the centre (PL20 7LT).

Opening Times

The railway operates on-demand and visitors should contact the owner in advance to make arrangements to travel on it. Open days are occasionally held and these are advertised in advance.

Line Mileage and Journey Time

The demonstration line is approximately 200 metres long and the journey time is relatively short.

Stock List

Type	Number	Builder	Details
Steam	HILDA	Peckett	0-4-0ST
Diesel	A.S. HARRIS	Hunslet	0-4-0DM
Diesel	EARL OF MOUNT EDGECUMBE	Hunslet	0-4-0DM
Diesel	LORD ST. LEVAN	Hunslet	0-4-0DM

Attractions

The Heritage Centre at Bere Ferrers has an exhibition coach and a visitor centre situated within a former sleeping coach. The original station building and various railway exhibits can be seen, including a restored L&SWR signal box, a second signal box within a converted cattle wagon, a wagon turntable, a yard crane and a collection of carriages. Signalling demonstrations which use an interactive computer are available and these should be arranged in advance. In addition to carrying passengers, the railway can also operate demonstration freight and mixed traffic trains. Ex-LNER teak coaches 3132 & 1459 have been converted to bed and breakfast accommodation and the Tamar Belle dining coach is adjacent to these. The saloon car can be booked for meetings and social functions. There are several nearby heritage railways including the Plym Valley, the South Devon and the Dartmouth Steam Railway. Other nearby attractions include Dartmoor National Park, Dartmoor Prison Museum, the market town of Tavistock and the coastal city of Plymouth.

West Somerset Railway

Introduction and History

The broad gauge branch line from Taunton to Watchet opened in 1862; this was extended to Minehead in 1874 and converted to a standard gauge line in 1882. By the 1960s it was only profitable during the summer months, when it carried large volumes of seasonal passengers. British Rail closed the line in 1971, but unlike many other closed lines, the track was left in place. A society formed in 1971 to preserve the railway and the first stage of this aim was realised in 1973, when Somerset County Council purchased the line from BR and leased it back to the group. In 1975 vegetation was cleared to allow Class 25 25059 to make a trip to Minehead to collect LMS 6229 "Duchess of Hamilton" from the Butlins holiday camp. The first heritage passenger services operated between Minehead and Blue Anchor in 1976 and these were extended to Bishops Lydeard in 1979. When BR upgraded the signalling in the Taunton area in 1981, the rail connection to Bishops Lydeard was removed. The structure of the railway changed during the 1980s, utilising more volunteers which, along with support from Somerset County Council, triggered a growth in passenger revenues and infrastructure investment. The main line connection at Taunton was reinstated in the late 1980s and continues to be used by occasional through charter trains. There have been long-held plans to return regular through passenger services to Taunton and in 2022 a working group with a variety of stakeholders was set up to consider how this can move forward.

Contact Details

Website: www.west-somerset-railway.co.uk
Tel: 01643 704996
Email: info@wsrail.net
Address: West Somerset Railway, The Railway Station, Minehead, Somerset, TA24 5BG.

Transport Links

By Rail: The nearest station is Taunton, which is five miles from Bishops Lydeard.
By Road: There is a large free car park at Bishops Lydeard with a 2.1 metre height limit (TA4 3RU) and pay & display parking at Watchet (TA23 0AQ) and Minehead (TA24 5BG).

Opening Times

The railway usually operates at weekends and on the majority of weekdays from April to October, plus for Santa Expresses during December.

Line Mileage and Journey Time

0.00	Bishops Lydeard	0.00	Bishops Lydeard
4.00	Crowcombe Heathfield	2.25	Norton Fitzwarren
6.50	Stogumber	5.00	Taunton
9.75	Williton		
10.75	Doniford		
11.50	Watchet		
14.00	Washford		
16.25	Blue Anchor		
18.00	Dunster		
19.50	Minehead		

A return journey takes about 3 hours.

Stock List

Type	Number	Builder	Details
Steam	1984	Andrew Barclay	0-4-0F
Steam	2201	Andrew Barclay	0-4-0ST
Steam	9466	Robert Stephenson & Hawthorns	0-6-0PT
Steam	1 (2074)	Andrew Barclay	0-6-0ST
Steam	9351	GWR	2-6-0
Steam	4561	GWR	2-6-2T
Steam	5199	GWR	2-6-2T
Steam	7822	British Railways	4-6-0
Steam	7828	British Railways	4-6-0
Steam	6024	GWR	4-6-0

Diesel	200793	Ruston & Hornsby	4wDM
Diesel	1 (578)	Andrew Barclay	0-4-0
Diesel	2 (579)	Andrew Barclay	0-4-0
Diesel	D2133	British Railways	Class 03
Diesel	D4107	British Railways	Class 09
Diesel	D6566	BRCW	Class 33
Diesel	D6575	BRCW	Class 33
Diesel	D7017	Beyer Peacock	Class 35
Diesel	D7018	Beyer Peacock	Class 35
Diesel	D1010	British Railways	Class 52
DMU	51859, 51880, 51887 & 59678	British Railways	Class 115
DMU	51354	Pressed Steel	Class 117

Attractions
The WSR is one of the longest heritage railways in Britain and one of the most popular attractions in the South-West. There are two museums on the railway; the Gauge Museum at Bishops Lydeard, which benefited from significant investment in 2022, and the Great Western Railway Museum at Blue Anchor, which opens on Sundays & Bank Holidays from Easter to September and during special events. The Diesel & Electric Preservation Group's depot at Williton is often open at weekends. There is a bookshop and café at Minehead. Driving courses can be arranged, using either a steam or diesel locomotive. Dunster Castle (National Trust) is a 20-minute walk from Dunster station. Bishops Lydeard is situated at the foot of the Quantock Hills, Watchet station is located next to the picturesque harbour and Minehead station is adjacent to the beach and town centre.

Special Events
Events that usually take place on the railway include:

Steam Gala.
Diesel Gala (usually in June).
1940s event.
Santa Express and Winterlights Trains during December.

Yeovil Railway Centre

Introduction and History
The Railway Centre is located within the sidings of the yard immediately south of Yeovil Junction station. The station opened in 1860 and the site which the centre occupies included a transfer shed, where goods were transferred between broad gauge and standard gauge railway wagons. Closure of Yeovil Junction station was proposed in 1964 and whilst local opposition prevented this, much of the freight traffic was lost and the railway was downgraded to a single track line during the 1960s. The first heritage railway group formed in 1994 and a lease for the site was agreed. A new engine shed was constructed, opening in 1999 and since then various steam and diesel locomotives have visited or been renovated at the centre.

Contact Details
Website: www.yeovilrailway.freeservers.com
Tel: 01935 410420
Email: yeovilrailway@hotmail.com
Address: Yeovil Railway Centre, Yeovil Junction Station, Stoford, Yeovil, BA22 9UU.

Transport Links
By Rail: The Railway Centre is adjacent to Yeovil Junction station.
By Road: There is free parking on-site, turn right under the railway bridge when approaching Yeovil Junction (BA22 9UU).

Opening Times
The shop opens 10.00–12.00 on Sundays (except Christmas & New Year) and the railway operates 10.30–16.00 on alternate Sundays from March to October and on selected other dates (see Special Events below).

Line Mileage and Journey Time
The railway line runs for one third of a mile and the journey time is relatively short.

Stock List

Type	Number	Builder	Details
Steam	1398 LORD FISHER	Andrew Barclay	0-4-0ST
Steam	1579 PECTIN	Peckett	0-4-0ST
Diesel	44	Fowler	0-4-0DM
Diesel	22898	Fowler	0-4-0DM
Diesel	22900 SAM	Fowler	0-4-0DM
Diesel	DS1174	Ruston & Hornsby	4wDM
DMU	59515	Pressed Steel	Class 117

Attractions
The Centre has a 70-foot operational turntable which is used when main line steam locomotives are serviced, as well as the signalling display panel from Chard Junction and a model railway which is in use when the standard gauge railway operates. Steam locomotive driver experience courses can be arranged. The visitor centre has various railway themed exhibits, a railway bookshop and it serves light refreshments. Nearby attractions include Yeovil Country Park, several National Trust sites and various rural locations across Somerset and nearby Dorset.

Special Events
Trains will operate on the following dates during 2023. They will be steam hauled except on the dates marked in bold when they will be diesel hauled.

9–10 & 23 April, 6–7 May during the Model Railways weekend, 21 May, **30 May**, 4 & 18 June, 2 July, **25 July**, 29–30 July during the Tractor weekend, **1 August**, 6 August, **8 & 15 August**, 20 August, **22 & 29 August**, 3 & 17 September, 28 & 31 October, 3, 10, 16–17, 21 & 23 December for Santa Specials.

▲ The sole surviving Class 17, D8568, approaches Leigh Woods Crossing on the West Somerset Railway with the 15.35 Norton Fitzwarren–Minehead on 10 June 2022.   **Glen Batten**

Proposed Heritage Railways

New heritage railways have opened almost every year since 1960 and as the chart in the introduction shows, the years in which the sites in this book opened are spread over six decades, although this has slowed in recent years. It usually takes many years from the formation of a preservation group to the time when passenger services first begin, as the histories for the nearly 100 railways in the listings above summarise. This section showcases standard gauge projects that are well-established and are advancing towards their aim of operating passenger trains. It is by no means an exhaustive list, as there are plenty of other prospective heritage railways, where the preservation efforts are at an earlier stage. The uphill struggle that operational heritage railways currently face, as summarised in the introduction, is even steeper for those that are at an earlier stage, as they don't benefit from the regular income that visitors bring to the lines that are running trains. As these modern preservation pioneers progress, it is hoped that the railways they restore and create will move into the regional chapters in future editions of this book.

The criteria for inclusion in this section is most or all of the following:

- The organisation has been granted access to the railway line or trackbed. In most cases, this consists of an agreement with Network Rail or the land owner to lease or access the railway line.
- They are in possession of rolling stock for operating passenger carrying trains. This could be minimal, such as a brake van and a small shunting locomotive, or a DMU that requires renovation.
- The group have an online presence, with details of their activities, aims and any events which are open to the public.

The proposed heritage railway listings follow a similar format to their established relatives. Any readers considering visiting or volunteering with these organisations are encouraged to do so, making advance arrangements as necessary.

Invergarry & Fort Augustus Railway Museum, Scotland Region

Background
The original Invergarry & Fort Augustus Railway was a 23-mile branch line which ran from Spean Bridge, along the banks of Loch Lochy and Loch Oich, terminating at Fort Augustus at the southern end of Loch Ness. The railway opened in 1903 and was used by King George VII in 1905, when he took the royal train to Invergarry to visit Lord and Lady Burton at Glenquoich Lodge. As the line ran through a sparsely populated area, passenger numbers were low. Consequently, it was a short-lived venture and passenger services were withdrawn as early as 1933. Infrequent freight trains carrying coal and timber continued until 1946, when the line was closed. Part of the trackbed has since been converted to the Great Glen Way, which is a well-used footpath between Fort William and Inverness.

Heritage Railway Progress and Future Plans
In 2012 a group formed with the intention of preserving the remains of Invergarry station and establishing a museum there. Invergarry was one of four intermediate stations on the line and is approximately half way between Spean Bridge and Fort Augustus. A 150-metre section of standard gauge track was laid in 2015, running north-east from the station, enabling the first train movements to take place that year. The line has since been extended to a length of approaching half a mile. A signal cabin has been built on the station platform. During 2022 a level crossing that complies with Network Rail's specifications was completed, work to restore an underpass bridge began and progress was made on installing a goods siding that will connect to a maintenance shed for which planning permission has been applied. There is a visitor centre with displays on the station and the railway's history. A Saxby & Farmer lever frame from Tyndrum Upper was donated by Network Rail and this will be installed and used on the site. Other plans include the construction of a replica 1930s station building and when the required license has been issued, passengers rides can begin, using the Ruston & Hornsby shunter and a restored brake van.

Contact Details
Website: www.invergarrystation.org.uk
Email: info@invergarrystation.org.uk
Address: Station Approach Road, South Laggan, PH34 4EA.

Opening Times & Transport Links

Regular volunteer working days usually take place on most Tuesdays and the site opens on selected Sundays between May and September. Note however, that Route 78 of the National Cycling Network, which passes through the site of the station, is due to close for up to two years. Volunteers will still be able to access the site, but the closure will restrict access for visitors. Please check the website for the latest information.

By Rail: Spean Bridge is the nearest railway station and this is 13 miles away.
By Road: Parking for up to 12 cars is available at Invergarry (PH34 4EA).
By Bike: Invergarry station is on Route 78 of the National Cycling Network.
By Water: From the Caledonian Canal and Loch Oich; alight at the Great Glen Water Park landing stage.

Local Attractions

Invergarry station is located on the banks of Loch Oich, on the route of the Great Glen Way and on Route 78 of the National Cycling Network. Many walks through the rugged Scottish landscape can be made within the area and Invergarry Castle is two miles away.

Poulton & Wyre Railway, Northern England Region

Background

The railway from Poulton-le-Fylde to Fleetwood opened in 1840 and was one of the first railways in the world to regularly carry holidaymakers. It also served the busy port at Fleetwood and was part of the fastest route between London and Glasgow until 1848, when a direct rail connection between Preston and Glasgow opened. Before then, trains ran from London to Fleetwood, where passengers continued north by steam ship to Ardrossan. In 1966 Fleetwood station closed and the line was cut back to a new terminus at Fleetwood Wyre Dock. Passenger services to Fleetwood ended in 1970 and the line was singled in 1973. Freight trains continued to use the route until 1999, when the final train to the chemical plant at Burn Naze ran. The track from Poulton-le-Fylde to Fleetwood remains in place; however, the main line connection at Poulton was removed in 2018, when the line between Preston and Blackpool North was electrified and resignalled. In November 2019, Prime Minister Boris Johnson visited Thornton-Cleveleys station, where he announced the £500 Restoring Your Railway Fund for reopening disused lines and indicated that the line to Fleetwood would be restored.

Heritage Railway Progress and Future Plans

The Poulton & Wyre Railway Society (PWRS) formed in 2006 and Network Rail provided the group with a license to access the track, Thornton-Cleveleys and Burn Naze stations. The Society then began clearing vegetation, restoring the railway and the two stations. In 2010 a Fowler shunter was acquired, followed by a Class 108 DMU in 2016 which is being restored at Thornton-Cleveleys. It was initially hoped that the heritage railway would connect with the national network at Poulton-le-Fylde, but this became less likely when Network Rail removed Poulton Junction in 2018. There are plans to open a museum and heritage centre, and to operate trains on a section of track; the long-term aim is for regular services between Poulton and a newly constructed Fleetwood South station.

Contact Details

Website: www.pwrs.org
Email: Written enquiries can be made from the railway's website.
Address: Poulton & Wyre Railway Society, The Print Room, Hillhouse Business Park, Thornton, Lancashire, FY5 4QD.

Opening Times & Transport Links

Volunteer working sessions usually take place on most Saturdays and Wednesdays at Thornton or Burn Naze. Membership of the PWRS is required to participate in these.

By Rail: Poulton-le-Fylde station is approximately two miles from Thornton.
By Road: Free parking is available near to Thornton station. There is no parking at Burn Naze station.

Local Attractions

The Wyre Way is a walking route which begins at Fleetwood, where it crosses the railway and continues along the Wyre estuary and to the Forest of Bowland in north-east Lancashire. Nearby attractions include Farmer Parr's Animal World and the coastal resorts of Fleetwood and Blackpool, which are home to many museums, theme parks and attractions.

Anglesey Central Railway, Wales Region

Background

The 17.5-mile branch line from Gaerwen, on the North Wales Coast main line, to Amlwch opened in stages between 1864 and 1867. In 1951 a one-mile extension was laid from a junction outside Amlwch station to the bromine works on the coast, beyond the town centre. Passenger services to Amlwch were withdrawn in 1964, after which the line was used to carry chemicals to and from the works site until 1993, when they were transferred to road haulage. Instead of being formally closed, the line was then mothballed and it has remained dormant since. The track remains in place, although the railway was severed in 2018, when a bridge in Llangefni was removed after being struck by a lorry.

Heritage Railway Progress and Future Plans

A preservation group formed in 1991, with the aim of restoring passenger services on the Amlwch branch. When freight traffic ended in 1993, there were calls for seasonal steam-hauled trains to operate on the line, but these didn't materialise. in 2011 Network Rail issued the group with a license to access the track and vegetation clearance began. The license also permits members to push a non-powered trolley on the railway. Members of the public are not currently permitted to access the line. A Fowler diesel 0-4-0 shunter is based at Llanerchymedd station, although this is not currently used. In 2011 the Welsh government commissioned a feasibility study on reintroducing main line passenger trains to Llangefni, using the first 4.5 miles of the branch and in 2020 a successful bid was made for funding from the Restoring Your Railways fund, for a study on reopening the line. During 2021 the Anglesey Central Railway was issued a 99 year lease on the entire 17.5-mile line from Gaerwen to Amlwch and since then vegetation clearance works have continued.

Contact Details

Website: www.leinamlwch.co.uk or "Lein Amlwch of Anglesey Central Railway" on Facebook. **Email:** leinamlwch@gmail.com Written enquiries can be made from the website and Facebook page.

Opening Times & Transport Links

The railway across Anglesey is currently only accessible to members of the Anglesey Central Railway and therefore not currently open to the public.

Local Attractions

Anglesey has many visitor attractions, including Amlwch Copper Centre, Oriel Mon museum & arts centre in Llangefni, South Stack Lighthouse, Pili Palas Nature World, Plas Newedd House & Gardens and Holyhead Maritime Museum.

Garw Valley Railway, Wales Region

Background

The railway from Tondu to Nantymoel opened in 1865 and the steeply graded branch from Brynmenyn Junction near Tondu to Blaengarw opened in 1876. The area's small population grew substantially after the railway opened, enabling the Garw Valley's rich coal resources to be exported via the ports of South Wales. Blaengarw lost its passenger services in 1953, although coal trains continued using the route until 1986, ending shortly after Ocean Colliery closed. The nearby line to Tondu and Maesteg was reopened to passenger trains in 1992 and trains briefly returned to Pontycymer during the 1990s to remove spoil tips. The northern-most section of the line between Pontycymer and Blaengarw was demolished in the 1990s, but the majority of the route from Tondu to Pontycymer has remained in situ since.

Heritage Railway Progress and Future Plans

The first preservation group formed in 1988, with the aim of creating a museum and heritage railway centre. Since then, a base and locomotive shed has been established at Pontycymer, where the heritage centre is to be built and the 4.75-mile line to Brynmenyn has been leased from Network Rail. In 2016, the first section of a new station at Pontycymer was built and a 200-metre section of track was laid. The line has since been extended to a length of 600 metres and it is hoped that trains can operate on this in the near future. The next phase will be to extend the operational line to a length of approximately 1.25 miles and the long-term aim is for it to continue south to Tondu, where it would meet the Bridgend to Maesteg line.

Contact Details

Website: www.garwvalleyrailway.co.uk or www.facebook.com/garwvalleyrailway
Email: enquiries@garwvalleyrailway.co.uk
Address: Garw Valley Railway, Pontycymer Locomotive Works, Old Station Yard, Pontycymer, Bridgend, CF32 8AZ.

Opening Times & Transport Links

The locomotive shed at Pontycymer is open on Wednesdays and Saturdays; visitors are welcome and there is no admission charge (donations are welcome though!) In addition, three open days are usually held each year, taking place on the May and August Bank Holiday weekends and during the Christmas period.

By Rail: The nearest railway station is Tondu, which is six miles away.
By Road: There is free parking at Pontycymer, which is shared with the leisure centre (CF32 8AZ).

Local Attractions

The 10¼-inch Garw Valley Miniature Railway, which is 104 yards long, was repositioned in 2019 and this runs next to the standard gauge shed. There is a walking path that follows the route of the railway between Pontycymer and Bryngarw Country Park in the south. Attractions in the area include South Wales Miners Museum, Parc Slip Nature Reserve and Bridgend Miniature Railway.

Leiston Works Railway, Eastern Region

Background

Richard Garrett & Sons was established in 1778 and manufactured steam engines, traction engines and a variety of agricultural machinery across two sites in Leiston, Suffolk, which were known as The Works. Initially horse-drawn transport was used and when the railway from Saxmundham to Leiston opened in 1859 it connected to The Works, allowing products to be transported within and away from the two sites. In 1860 the railway was extended to Aldeburgh. By the early 20th Century, there was a comprehensive track network within Leiston linking the two sites and at its height the company employed over 3500 people. By the 1950s the industry was in decline, as road transport and motor vehicles were increasingly replacing steam traction. Passenger services on the railway from Saxmundham to Aldeburgh were withdrawn in 1966 and the line to The Works closed in 1968. After further decline, both sites of The Works closed in 1981. Much of the two sites were demolished and used for property development; however, some parts have been preserved and these can be seen in The Long Shop Museum. The railway track between Aldeburgh and Sizewell was lifted after passenger services ended, leaving a single line for nuclear fuel traffic from Saxmundham to Sizewell. This remains in the possession of Network Rail and currently only sees intermittent trains. That will soon change though, as the plans for the new Sizewell C Power Station include a new 2.75-mile line that will begin at a junction to the west of Leiston and be used by up to four construction trains per day for up to twelve years. As the new line won't pass through Leiston, it will not affect the heritage railway.

Heritage Railway Progress and Future Plans

In 2011 a group of railway enthusiasts formed the Leiston Works Railway Trust with the aim of reopening a section of The Works railway. They purchased and cleared some of the trackbed and laid a 100-metre section of track to the north of the Long Shop Museum, using track panels from the former Ipswich Docks line. To celebrate the 160th anniversary of the railway reaching Leiston Works, in June 2019 the first preserved train ran. This consisted of a Ruston shunter making a series of light engine movements on the newly laid track. The next phase is to extend the line north to Buller Road, which is less than 100 metres from the Network Rail line to Sizewell Power Station, giving around 200 metres of operational track. Longer-term aims include reconnecting the railway to the former Garrett Works site at the Long Shop Museum and it is hoped that it may be possible to reconnect to the Sizewell branch. The group are also restoring vintage carriages and a brake van which will be used to carry passengers. The steam locomotive "Sirapite", which worked on the site until 1962, has been restored to operational condition and can be seen at the Long Shop Museum.

Contact Details
Website: www.lwr.org.uk
Tel: 07774 640708
Email: theleistonworksrailway@gmail.com
Address: Access is by prior arrangement. Please contact the railway.

Opening Times & Transport Links
Working parties for members usually meet weekly at the workshop. There is a £10 annual charge for membership and please contact the railway if you are interested in joining.

By Rail: Saxmundham is the nearest railway station and is four miles away.
By Road: Free car parking is available for Long Shop Museum visitors (IP16 4ES).

Local Attractions
The Long Shop Museum is housed within the former works site at Leiston and showcases the town's industrial history. Other nearby attractions include RSPB Minsmere, Orford Ness National Nature Reserve and various coastal and rural sites across Suffolk.

Rother Valley Railway, South East Region

Background
The railway between Robertsbridge on the Tonbridge–Hastings main line and Rolvenden opened in 1900. Details of the background and history of this route are given in the listing for the Kent & East Sussex Railway (K&ESR).

Heritage Railway Progress and Future Plans
The Rother Valley Railway (RVR) formed in 1991, with the intention of acquiring the trackbed and reinstating the disused railway between Robertsbridge and Bodiam, which is the western terminus of the K&ESR. Sections of trackbed at each end of the 2.5-mile Rother Valley route were acquired and, starting in 2009, the railway relaid approximately three quarters of a mile of track near Bodiam. The first heritage trains operated in 2011. A further half mile of track was subsequently relaid at Robertsbridge and trains first used this in 2013. The RVR is in the process of acquiring the remainder of the route, which has been met with some local opposition. In 2017 Rother District Council issued planning permission for the line to be reinstated and the Transport & Works Act Order was applied for in April 2018. Nearly five years later, this has still not been approved, but when it has, the remaining track can be relaid. Once the two sections have been joined, it is planned for the RVR to be absorbed into the K&ESR, which could then operate through trains from Tenterden to Robertsbridge.

Contact Details
Website: www.rvr.org.uk
Tel: 01580 881833
Email: reception@rvr.org.uk
Address: Rother Valley Railway, Robertsbridge Junction Station, Station Road, Robertsbridge, East Sussex, TN32 5DG.

Opening Times & Transport Links
There is a small shop and visitor centre at Robertsbridge, which opens 10.00–16.00 on Sundays.

By Rail: The railway has a main line connection at Robertsbridge.
By Road: There is a pay & display car park at Robertsbridge station.

Local Attractions
As well as the visitor centre at Robertsbridge, there is also a small collection of railway vehicles. The Kent & East Sussex Railway is nearby and details of other attractions in the area are given in the K&ESR listing.

North Dorset Railway, Shillingstone, South West Region

Background
The railway through Shillingstone opened in 1863, when the Templecombe to Blandford section of the recently formed Somerset & Dorset Railway was completed, creating a railway linking the Bristol Channel and the South Coast. Shillingstone station was closed when British Rail withdrew all traffic from the route in 1966 and the track was lifted the following year. Dorset County Council then purchased the trackbed through Shillingstone, with the intention of building a bypass on it, but the project was later abandoned. The station site was then used by a number of commercial occupiers in the years that followed.

Heritage Railway Progress and Future Plans
A group of enthusiasts formed the North Dorset Railway Trust in 2001 and began negotiations with Dorset County Council. A 99-year lease on Shillingstone station and part of the trackbed was granted in 2005. Restoration of the station commenced in 2006 and since then the down platform and signal box have been rebuilt. The site opened to the public in 2008 and a section of almost a quarter mile of track has been laid through the station. In 2021, the railway's plans to extend the line north by a further quarter mile, running along the existing trackbed to Bere Marsh, were approved by Dorset Council. Clearance work began in late 2021, so that the cycle path can be re-sited to allow the railway line to be extended north. There are long term aspirations to further extend the railway to Sturminster Newton, with the track running alongside the North Dorset Trailway.

Contact Details
Website: www.northdorsetrailway.co.uk
Tel: 01258 860696
Email: info@northdorsetrailway.co.uk
Address: North Dorset Railway, Shillingstone Station, Station Road, Shillingstone, Blandford Forum, Dorset, DT11 0SA.

▲ This scene gives an idea of the infrastructure that a heritage railway needs to acquire and restore before it can begin operating trains. The North Dorset Railway's Hudswell Clarke diesel-mechanical 0-6-0 D1186 stands at the platform of Shillingstone station during the early months of 2022.
Courtesy the North Dorset Railway

Opening Times & Transport Links

Shillingstone station opens on Wednesdays, Saturdays and Sundays from 10.00 to 16.00. Events planned for 2023 include an Easter Egg Hunt (9 April), Classic Car & Vintage Vehicle Rally (26–28 August) when the 160th anniversary of Shillingstone station will be celebrated and Flight Refuelling On-Air in the signal box during September, with the Flight Refuelling Amateur Radio Society, which broadcast to many other railway stations. The NDR will also be at the Three Okefords Steam-Up in Shillingstone (20–21 May) and the Hey-Day Spring Fair at Child Okeford (21 July).

By Rail: The nearest railway stations are Gillingham (12 miles) and Templecombe (13 miles).
By Road: There is limited parking at Shillingstone station.
By Bike: Shillingstone station is on the North Dorset Trailway, a 14-mile walking and cycling route between Sturminster Newton and Spetisbury, which predominantly follows the course of the former railway.

Local Attractions

Shillingstone station has a museum, signal box, model railway and a collection of standard gauge rolling stock. The site also has a garden, shop and café. Nearby attractions include Shillingstone Hill, Sturminster Newton Mill, Hambledon Hill, Hod Hill and the traffic free North Dorset Trailway.

Tarka Valley Railway, South West Region

Background

The broad gauge railway from Barnstaple reached Bideford in 1855 and was extended to Torrington in 1872, where it initially terminated. The line was converted to standard gauge in 1877. In 1880 the three foot gauge Torrington & Marland Railway opened, travelling south from Torrington. This was converted to standard gauge in 1925 and extended south to Halwill, where it connected with the railway to Bude, creating a through route from Barnstaple to Bude. This closed to passenger traffic in 1965; however, milk traffic continued until 1978 and ball clay and occasional charter trains from Barnstaple to Torrington ran until 1982. The track was lifted in 1985 and Devon County Council purchased the trackbed from British Rail in order to create a traffic free walkway.

Heritage Railway Progress and Future Plans

The Tarka Valley Railway Group formed in 2008 to preserve the remaining traces of the railway at Torrington station and investigate the possibility of reinstating a railway line towards Bideford. A short length of track was laid alongside the platform of the former Torrington station in 2008 and in 2013 the group gained planning approval to extend this north by almost 300 metres to the first overbridge. In 2018 the Tarka Trail was realigned slightly, to create space for the railway to run beside the path and a dividing fence was erected. Track laying then commenced, including an additional 100 metre section which created two sidings alongside the old coal loading bay. This first stage of work is now complete, with the re-laid line reaching the overbridge. In November 2022, the railway acquired a Class 143 Pacer and it is hoped that passenger rides can begin soon, either using the Pacer or brake vans hauled by one of the diesel shunters. Negotiations with the council are currently taking place regarding extending the railway by a further 400 metres, which would double the length of the line. The long-term aim is to create an operational railway between Torrington and Bideford, which is five miles to the north (see the listing for the Bideford Railway Heritage Centre). There are three small river bridges, a tunnel and a viaduct between Torrington and Bideford, all of which require engineering works before the railway beside the Tarka Trail can be reinstated.

Contact Details

Website: www.tarkavalleyrailway.org or "Tarka Valley Railway CIO" on Facebook.
Tel : 07454 673809
Email: tarkavalleyrailway@gmail.com
Address: TVR Membership Secretary, Puffing Billy, Torrington Station, Station Hill, Great Torrington, Devon, EX38 8JD.

Opening Times & Transport Links

The visitor's centre and shop open 09.30–1600 on Thursdays and regular working parties take place on Saturdays. There are also occasional open days and these are advertised on the TVR website.

By Rail: The nearest railway station is Barnstaple, which is 11 miles away.
By Road: Car parking is available at the Torrington site (EX38 8JD).
By Bike: By way of the traffic-free Tarka Trail.

Local Attractions

The Puffing Billy is a public house within the former Torrington station building, located directly on the Tarka Trail and this opens daily. Bicycle hire is available nearby, allowing visitors to explore the traffic-free Tarka Trail; this connects Torrington station with the Bideford Railway Heritage Centre.

Vale of Berkeley Railway, South West Region

Background

The four mile branch line from Berkeley Road (between Bristol and Cheltenham) to Sharpness opened to freight in 1875 and to passengers in 1876. In 1879 it became a through route when the Severn Railway Bridge opened, connecting Sharpness to Lydney Town, which is now part of the Dean Forest Railway. The bridge was damaged beyond repair in 1960 and Sharpness was then relegated back to terminus status until passenger services ended in 1964. Shortly after this Sharpness and Berkeley station buildings were demolished. Network Rail owns the line from Berkeley Road Junction to Sharpness Docks and the branch is used by Direct Rail Services' nuclear waste trains which begin in the sidings on the site of the former Berkeley station. This is half way between Berkeley Road Junction and Sharpness, but as there are no run-round facilities there, the trains have to proceed to Oldminster Sidings, near Sharpness Docks, in order for the locomotives to run round.

Heritage Railway Progress and Future Plans

The preservation group formed in 2013 and since 2015 it has leased the old engine shed at Sharpness Docks as a base. This is being used to restore various locomotives and other rolling stock. Discussions are in progress with the various stakeholders regarding the creation of a run-round loop at the Berkeley loading site, which would alleviate the need for main line trains to travel further along the branch to the run-round loop at Oldminster Sidings, Sharpness. The western half of the branch could then be freed-up for heritage use, with stations rebuilt at Berkeley and on the site of the original Sharpness station at Oldminster. After receiving a licence from Network Rail in 2018, the group cleared the vegetation on the former Oldminster Exchange Sidings, which occupy a four-acre site adjacent to Sharpness Docks. Discussions with Direct Rail Services have begun to ascertain whether and when heritage trains could run on the line beyond Sharpness. The VoBR's Oldminster section was separated by fencing in Oct 2022, providing the railway with exclusive access to the upper reaches of the branch. The long-term aim is to create a heritage railway from Berkeley to Sharpness, using the main-line connection at Berkeley Road when the nuclear traffic has come to an end.

Contact Details

Website: www.vobr.org.uk
Email: valeofberkeleyrailway@gmail.com
Address: Vale of Berkeley Railway, The Old Engine House, The Docks, Sharpness, Gloucestershire, GL13 9UD.

Opening Times & Transport Links

The Engine Shed opens 10.00–16.30 on Wednesdays and Saturdays. During these times visitors can look around, meet volunteers and guided tours may be available subject to staff availability.

By Rail: The nearest railway station is Cam and Dursley which is nine miles away.
By Road: Parking is available at The Old Engine House site (GL13 9UD).

Local Attractions

There are a number of locomotives, items of rolling stock, signalling and railway equipment which can be seen at the Old Engine House site in Sharpness. Attractions in the area include Wildfowl & Wetlands Trust Slimbridge Wetland Centre, Cattle Country Adventure Park, Dr Jenner's House and Berkeley Castle.

Appendix I: Locomotive and Multiple Unit Builders

Builder name used in listings	Builder's Full Name
82045 Steam Locomotive Trust	82045 Steam Locomotive Trust
ABB	ASEA Brown Boveri
AC Cars	AC Cars Ltd
AEG, Berlin	Allgemeine Elektricitäts-Gesellschaft, Berlin
Alan Keef	Alan Kccf Ltd
Alexander	Walter Alexander Coachbuilders
American Locomotive Co.	American Locomotive Company
Andrew Barclay	Andrew Barclay Sons & Co.
Armstrong Whitworth	Armstrong Whitworth & Co
Aveling & Porter	Aveling & Porter
Avonside	Avonside Engine Company
B17 SLT	B17 Steam Locomotive Trust
Baby Deltic Project	Baby Deltic Project
Bagnall	W. G. Bagnall
Baguley	E. E. Baguley Ltd
Baldwin Locomotive Works	Baldwin Locomotive Works, USA
Beyer Peacock	Beyer, Peacock & Company
Black Hawthorn	Black, Hawthorn & Co.
Bluebell Railway SC2P	Bluebell Railway Standard Class 2 Project
Borrows	E Borrows & Sons
BRCW	Birmingham Railway Carriage & Wagon Co.
BREL	British Rail Engineering Limited
British Rail	British Rail
British Railways	British Railways
British Thompson Houston	British Thomson Houston
Brown Boveri	Brown, Boveri & Cie, Switzerland
Brush Traction	Brush Traction
Bury Curtis & Kennedy	Bury, Curtis & Kennedy
Caledonian Railway	Caledonian Railway
Clayton	Clayton Equipment Company
Cockerill	John Cockerill Company
Consett	Consett Iron Company
Cravens	Cravens
Danske Statsbaner	Danske Statsbaner, Denmark
DB, Germany	Deutsche Bahn, Germany
Dodman & Co	Dodman & Co.
Drewry	Drewry Car Co.
Dübs & Company	Dübs & Company
Duro Dakovic	Duro Dakovic, Yugoslavia
Electroputere	Electroputere S.A., Romania
English Electric	English Electric
Fablok	Fablok, Poland
Fairfield Shipbuilding & Engine Co.	Fairfield Shipbuilding & Engine Co.
Fire Fly Trust	The Fire Fly Trust
Fletcher Jennings	Fletcher, Jennings & Co.
Foster Rastrick	Foster Rastrick & Co
Fowler	John Fowler & Co.
Fox Walker	Fox, Walker & Company
Friends of MOSI	Friends of the Museum of Science and Industry
GEC Traction Ltd	GEC Traction Ltd
George England	George England & Co.
George Stephenson	George Stephenson
GER	Great Eastern Railway
Gmeinder & Co.	Gmeinder & Co., Germany
GNR	Great Northern Railway
Grafton	Grafton & Sons of Bedford
Grant Richie	Grant Richie & Company
GRCW	Gloucester Railway Carriage & Wagon Co. Ltd
Great Central Railway	Great Central Railway
Great Western Society	The Great Western Society

Greenwood & Batley	Greenwood & Batley Ltd
GWR	Great Western Railway
Hagglund and Soner	Hagglund and Soner, Sweden
Hartmann	Richard Hartmann, Germany
Hawthorne Leslie	Hawthorn Leslie & Company
Haydock	Haydock Foundry
Head Wrightson	Head Wrightson
Hibberd	F. C. Hibberd & Co.
Hitachi	Hitachi Ltd
Howard	J & F Howard
Hudswell Clarke	Hudswell Clarke
Hunslet	Hunslet Engine Company
ICI South Central Workshops	Imperial Chemical Industries, South Central Workshops
Kerr Stuart	Kerr, Stuart and Company
Kitson	Kitson and Company
L&NWR	London and North Western Railway
Lancashire & Yorkshire	Lancashire and Yorkshire Railway
LBSCR	London, Brighton and South Coast Railway
Leyland	Leyland Bus
Lima Locomotive Co	Lima Locomotive Corporation
Lister Blackstone	Lister Blackstone
Liverpool & Manchester	Liverpool and Manchester Railway
LMS	London, Midland and Scottish Railway
LMS-Patriot Project	LMS-Patriot Project
LNER	London and North Eastern Railway
LNWR	London and North Western Railway
Locomotion Enterprises	Locomotion Enterprises
LSWR	London and South Western Railway
LT&SR	London, Tilbury and Southend Railway
Manning Wardle	Manning Wardle
Markham & Co	Markham & Co Ltd
Metropolitan Cammell	Metropolitan Cammell
Metropolitan Railway	Metropolitan Railway
Metropolitan Vickers	Metropolitan Vickers
Midland Railway	Midland Railway
Ministry of Defence	Mininstry of Defence
Motala Verkstad	Motala Verkstad, Sweden
Nasmyth Wilson	Nasmyth, Wilson & Co.
Neilson & Co.	Neilson & Co.
Neilson Reid	Neilson, Reid & Co.
NER	North Eastern Railway
North British	North British Locomotive Company
North London Railway	North London Railway
North Staffordshire Railway	North Staffordshire Railway
Norwegian State Railways	Norwegian State Railways (NSB)
Park Royal	Park Royal Vehicles Limited
Peckett	Peckett and Sons
Port Talbot Railway	Port Talbot Railway & Docks Company
Pressed Steel	Pressed Steel Company
R & W Hawthorn	R & W Hawthorn
Resco Railways	Resco (Railways) Ltd
Robert Heath	Robert Heath and Sons Ltd
Robert Stephenson & Co	Robert Stephenson & Company
Robert Stephenson & Hawthorns	Robert Stephenson & Hawthorns
Rolls Royce Sentinel	Rolls Royce Sentinel
Ruston & Hornsby	Ruston & Hornsby
Sara & Co	Sara & Co
SECR	South Eastern and Chatham Railway
Sentinel	Sentinel Waggon Works
Sharp Stewart	Sharp Stewart and Company
Siemans Harton	Siemans Harton
Simplex	Simplex (Motor Rail)
South Durham Steel & Iron	South Durham Steel & Iron Co
Southern Railway	Southern Railway

Stephen Lewin	Stephen Lewin
The Fire Fly Trust	The Fire Fly Trust
Thomas Hill	Thomas Hill (Rotherham) Ltd
Timothy Hackworth	Timothy Hackworth
Trevithick 200	Trevithick 200
USATC	United States Army Transportation Corps
Vulcan Foundry	Vulcan Foundry
Vulcan Iron Works	Vulcan Iron Works, USA
Waggon & Maschinenbau	Waggon & Maschinenbau, Germany
Wickham	D. Wickham and Company
Yorkshire Engine Co.	Yorkshire Engine Company

Appendix II: Abbreviations

Steam Locomotive Suffixes

T	Side Tank.
CT	Crane Tank.
PT	Pannier Tank.
ST	Saddle Tank.
WT	Well Tank.
VBT	Vertical Boiler Tank.
VBGT	Vertical Boiler Geared Tank.
F	Fireless.
G	Geared.

Diesel Locomotive Suffixes

DE	Diesel Electric.
DH	Diesel Hydraulic.
DM	Diesel Mechanical.

Other Abbreviations Used

DMU	Diesel Multiple Unit.
EMU	Electric Multiple Unit.
DEMU	Diesel-Electric Multiple Unit.
BR	British Railways; later British Rail.

Appendix III: Index of Heritage Railways

Name	Region	Page
Alderney Railway	South West	154
Aln Valley Railway	Northern England	32
Angelsey Central Railway	Proposed	181
Appleby Frodingham Railway - Scunthorpe	East Midlands	92
Avon Valley Railway	South West	155
Barrow Hill Roundhouse Railway Centre	East Midlands	94
Barry Railway	Wales	67
The Battlefield Line	East Midlands	96
Beamish: The Living Museum of the North	Northern England	33
Bideford Railway Heritage Centre	South West	156
Bluebell Railway	South East	133
Bodmin & Wenford Railway	South West	157
Bo'ness & Kinneil Railway	Scotland	17
Border Union Railway	Scotland	19
Bowes Railway	Northern England	34
Bressingham Steam and Gardens	Eastern	117
Bristol Harbour Railway	South West	159
Buckinghamshire Railway Centre	South East	134
Caledonian Railway	Scotland	20
Cambrian Heritage Railways	West Midlands	77
Chasewater Railway	West Midlands	78
Chatham Dockyard Railway	South East	136
Chinnor & Princes Risborough Railway	South East	137
Cholsey & Wallingford Railway	South East	138
Churnet Valley Railway	West Midlands	80
Colne Valley Railway	Eastern	118
Crewe Heritage Centre	Northern England	36
Dartmouth Steam Railway	South West	160
Dean Forest Railway	South West	161
Derwent Valley Light Railway	Northern England	37
Didcot Railway Centre	South East	140
Doon Valley Railway	Scotland	22

▲ On a glorious 17 July 2021, D7018 rounds the curve at Bicknoller on the West Somerset Railway with the 13.25 Dunster–Bishops Lydeard, which ran via Norton Fitzwarren.   **Aubrey Evans**